T0370200

AI FIRST, HUMAN ALWAYS

AI FIRST, HUMAN ALWAYS

EMBRACING A NEW MINDSET FOR THE ERA OF SUPERINTELLIGENCE

SANDY CARTER

WILEY

Published by John Wiley & Sons, Inc., Hoboken, New Jersey.

Published simultaneously in Canada.

For general information on our other products and services or for technical support, please contact our Customer Care Department within the United States at (800) 762-2974, outside the United States at (317) 572-3993 or fax (317) 572-4002.

Wiley also publishes its books in a variety of electronic formats. Some content that appears in print may not be available in electronic formats. For more information about Wiley products, visit our web site at www.wiley.com.

Library of Congress Cataloging-in-Publication Data

Names: Carter, Sandy, 1963- author.
Title: The mind-machine merge : embracing an AI-first mindset for a
  limitless future / Sandy Carter.
Description: Hoboken, New Jersey : Wiley, [2025] | Includes index.
Identifiers: LCCN 2024045075 (print) | LCCN 2024045076 (ebook) | ISBN
  9781394189823 (hardback) | ISBN 9781394189816 (adobe pdf) | ISBN
  9781394189809 (epub)
Subjects: LCSH: Artificial intelligence—Industrial applications. |
  Artificial intelligence.
Classification: LCC HD45 .C373 2025 (print) | LCC HD45 (ebook) | DDC
  658/.0563—dc23/eng/20241118
LC record available at https://lccn.loc.gov/2024045075
LC ebook record available at https://lccn.loc.gov/2024045076

Cover Design: Wiley
Author Photo: © Unstoppable Domains

SKY10096414_011625

To my loving family, Todd, Kassie, Maria, and my mom and dad, who bought me that robot! They inspire me every day!

and

To all the amazing women in AI, thanks for your untiring impact!

and

To all of you who are exploring the future as an AI-first business leader!

Contents

Foreword

A few years ago, I had the honor of interviewing Walter Isaacson, the great American historian and author of books on geniuses such as Albert Einstein, Benjamin Franklin, and Steve Jobs. When I spoke to him, he had just finished a triumphant 800-page book on Leonardo da Vinci, perhaps the most creative man who ever lived.

The obvious question for a man who has spent much of his life studying geniuses was, "What common characteristics make a person a genius?"

He had a ready answer: "Insatiable curiosity and an ability to connect the dots in a new way."

These are also the traits that come to mind when considering Sandy Carter.

If you look at the history of digital technology, Sandy's curiosity has always kept her on the cutting edge, from the earliest websites to the pioneering days of AI with IBM's Watson, from e-commerce to Web3. Naturally, she has immersed herself in the world of artificial intelligence (AI). Where else would she be?

Sandy's incredible career and global connections help her uniquely connect the dots, as you'll see in the inspiring case studies in this book, which teach us to consider AI as our new home base.

However, there is also something that sets Sandy apart from other contemporary thought leaders. She exudes a caring humanity that makes her as accessible, kind, and patient as your favorite third-grade teacher. That is exactly who we need to help us navigate this hurricane-force world of AI in a way that we can trust and understand.

In short, she is the perfect person to write a book on an AI-first approach to leadership, and we are lucky to have this gift. Her work is not merely theoretical; it is grounded in real-world applications and hard-won insights from the frontlines of technological innovation.

The concept of an AI-first philosophy that Sandy champions isn't just a catchy phrase—it represents a fundamental reimagining of how businesses operate, innovate, and compete. This philosophy recognizes that AI is not just another technological tool to be adopted piecemeal, but a transformative force that should inform every aspect of an organization's strategy and operations.

Sandy's human touch shines through as she tackles the multifaceted challenges of AI integration. From the technical aspects of implementation to the equally crucial dimensions of change management, ethical considerations, and fostering an AI-ready culture, this book provides a comprehensive road map for organizations of all sizes and across all sectors.

This is not a book of AI-prompt magic tricks. Sandy has delivered a blueprint for success in the age of AI. I encourage you to approach it with an open mind and a willingness to embrace her bold thinking. Through Sandy's lens, we don't merely glimpse the potential of an AI-driven world—we gain the tools and mindset to actively create it, responsibly and brilliantly.

Mark Schaefer
Marketing futurist and author

CHAPTER

1

Embracing the AI-First Era

In today's rapidly evolving technological landscape, we've seen buzzwords like *cloud first* and *mobile first* dominate the conversation over the past decade. These first focuses were all about the technology.

But today, let me introduce you to the new mantra that's transforming the way we think about business: *AI-first*. Why is this shift so crucial? Artificial intelligence (AI) isn't just about technology; it's a transformative force that's changing our lives at an incredible pace, redefining how we connect, work, and experience the world around us. I've seen firsthand how AI can improve lives, from simplifying daily tasks to providing insights that were once unimaginable. For instance, using AI to analyze health data has given my family critical insights that helped manage a chronic illness more effectively. It's personal because I've experienced the positive impacts and believe in its potential to create a better future for everyone.

The AI-First Mindset: A New Paradigm

Think about a future where AI is deeply embedded in our daily lives. Imagine a humanoid robot arriving at your doorstep to deliver a pizza. But this is not just any delivery service—it's an AI-driven experience. The robot doesn't just hand you the pizza and leave. It walks into your home, sets the table, pours the drinks, and serves the pizza. When the meal is over, it even cleans up, selecting the right dish soap and doing the dishes for you.

This might sound like science fiction, but it's a near-future reality. The implications for brands are profound. If a robot is serving your drinks, do you need to market to the company that makes the robot? Does the AI decide which product to use based on pre-programmed preferences? How do companies like Coca-Cola or Pepsi adjust their strategies when the point of consumer interaction shifts from human to robot? These are the questions that AI-first leaders must ponder.

Just yesterday, I was at the dentist, and instead of the usual manual examination, they used an AI-powered tool for tooth recognition. This device scanned my teeth and identified potential issues with pinpoint accuracy. Interestingly, it wasn't the dentist who operated the AI tool but the dental hygienist. When I asked her how she felt about it, she said, "I was so intrigued that I took two classes on AI to understand how to use it better." This shows how AI is not just replacing roles but transforming them, requiring new skills and training.

Consider another innovation—mood jackets. Remember mood rings from the past? These jackets work on a similar principle but are far more advanced. They sense your emotions and physical states, such as when you're hot, cold, or sad. In factories in Asia, they are being tested to determine the best break schedules for workers based on their physiological data. This raises important questions for managers: How do you manage change when implementing such personal data-driven technology? How do you explain to employees that their jackets are monitoring their moods and breaks?

These scenarios aren't some distant future—they're happening now. AI is already making breakthroughs, like in the mining industry, where an AI system discovered a significant copper deposit in Kenya.

A forward-thinking exploration company used AI to analyze massive geological datasets. Traditionally, mineral exploration is labor-intensive and slow, but AI changed the game. The system processed satellite images, geological surveys, and historical mining data, identifying a high-potential region in Kenya. When the company verified the findings on the ground, they uncovered a major copper deposit. This breakthrough is set to boost Kenya's economy and create jobs, proving AI's transformative power in resource exploration.

This isn't just about technology; it's about revolutionizing industries. AI enhances precision, accelerates discoveries, and minimizes environmental impact. The discovery in Kenya showcases AI's potential to solve complex problems and open new opportunities.

The message is clear: we can't resist AI. It's time to learn and adapt. AI-first isn't just a strategy—it's a fundamental shift in business and technology thinking.

What It Means to Put AI-First

So, what does it mean to put AI-first at the heart of your business strategy?

Adopting an AI-first approach means deeply integrating AI into the fabric of your organization's decision-making processes, operations, and customer interactions. It's about leveraging AI as a fundamental driver of innovation, efficiency, and competitive differentiation. "Innovation in the future means applying a layer of AI to everything you do," commented Kevin Kelly, cofounder and senior maverick at *Wired* magazine.[1] He discusses this topic in his Ted Talk about the pervasive impact of AI across various aspects of our lives and industries.

But how do you go about doing this?

When you adopt an AI-first strategy, AI becomes the engine of innovation within your organization. This could mean using AI to develop new products or services that were previously unimaginable. For instance, consider Netflix. They use AI to personalize content recommendations, thereby enhancing user experience and keeping customers engaged. Their AI algorithms analyze vast amounts of viewing data to predict what you might want to watch next, ensuring a personalized and satisfying user experience. This level of innovation was made possible by embedding AI into their core business strategy.

This means that one principle is that AI, combined with humans, should be a driver of innovation.

AI-first also means using AI to streamline and optimize your operations. Take Amazon as an example. They use AI-driven robots in their fulfillment centers to automate the sorting and packing of products. This integration of AI not only speeds up the delivery process but also reduces operational costs, allowing Amazon to maintain its competitive edge in the e-commerce market. By leveraging AI, Amazon continuously improves its operational efficiency, setting a high bar for logistics and supply chain management.

Customer service is another area where an AI-first approach can transform business operations. Traditional chatbots often provide scripted responses that can frustrate customers more than they help. However, AI-powered systems, such as those used by Apple's Siri or Google Assistant, engage in more sophisticated interactions. They learn from each interaction to provide more accurate and personalized responses. This capability goes beyond mere automation, creating new opportunities for meaningful and engaging customer experiences.

Embracing an AI-first strategy means more than just adopting new technologies; it's about fundamentally rethinking how your organization operates and competes. It involves a strategic shift toward leveraging AI as a driver of innovation, efficiency, and customer engagement.

But not the only driver. Humans are critically important. We will still want handcrafted items from the farmer's market. The goal is to ensure that AI becomes a key component of your business strategy with your teams. Humans bring unique characteristics that will always be part of the narrative of a company's success.

As we navigate the AI-first era, the most successful organizations will be those that can integrate AI into the crucial facets of their operations while balancing it with the invaluable contributions of human insight and creativity. By doing so, they will not only stay competitive but also lead the way into the future of business and technology.

Examples of AI-First Success

Organizations that excel with AI-first strategies tend to share common traits: they will integrate AI deeply into their operations, enabling it to drive innovation and efficiency across multiple facets of their business. (I say *will* as most companies today have not matured enough to integrate AI deeply into operations.) They will prioritize AI as a key component of their decision-making processes, enabling them to anticipate and respond to market demands more swiftly and accurately. (See Appendix A for a simple AI marketecture.)

Moreover, these organizations see AI not merely as a set of tools but as a transformative force that fundamentally reshapes how they deliver value to their customers. By fostering a culture that embraces continuous learning and experimentation with AI, these leaders position themselves to not only keep pace with technological advancements but to also set the pace in their respective industries.

- **Healthcare:** In the healthcare sector, SimBioSys developed TumorScope, a simulation engine that uses diagnostic data to create virtual replicas of individual tumors. It predicts responses to therapy, assisting physicians in personalized treatment planning.
- **Retail:** Retailers like Zara use AI to optimize their inventory management and predict fashion trends. Their AI systems analyze customer behavior, social media trends, and sales data to forecast demand for different products, ensuring that they stock the right items at the right time. This AI-driven approach helps Zara stay ahead in the fast-paced world of fashion retail.
- **Financial services:** In financial services, companies like JP Morgan Chase use AI for fraud detection and risk management. Their AI systems analyze transaction data in real-time to identify unusual patterns that might indicate fraudulent activity. By leveraging AI, JP Morgan enhances its ability to protect customer assets and maintain trust.

These examples illustrate the transformative potential of AI when it is placed at the heart of a company's strategy. (Note: We will go deeper into these examples as well later in the book - these were to get your interested in the stories too!) Whether in health care, retail, or financial services, AI-first organizations are redefining their industries and setting new standards for innovation and customer engagement.

What AI-First Does Not Look Like

As we venture into the AI-first world, it's just as crucial to understand what this strategy is not. Missteps in adopting AI can be as instructive as success stories, providing a clear picture of pitfalls to avoid.

Being AI-first is more than just integrating AI tools or launching AI projects; it's about embedding AI into the fabric of your organization to drive meaningful change. Meaningful change occurs over time. The best AI projects start small and then grow with success! It's not merely about keeping up with trends or experimenting with AI in isolated pockets. Instead, it's about making AI a core component of your operational and strategic vision, ensuring it complements and enhances human capabilities rather than sidelining them.

Let's explore a few examples of what AI-first does not look like and how these common pitfalls can hinder the true potential of an AI-driven approach.

- **Superficial AI adoption:** Simply adopting AI for the sake of following a trend does not constitute an AI-first strategy. For instance, installing chatbots on your website without a clear plan for how they will enhance customer experience or integrate with other systems is a superficial approach. AI-first is not about having AI for the sake of AI; it's about making it a central part of how your business operates and delivers value.
- **Isolated AI projects:** AI should not be limited to isolated projects within your organization. If AI initiatives are confined to one department or a single-use case, your organization is missing out on the broader benefits of an AI-first strategy. AI should permeate various aspects of the business,

from supply chain and logistics to customer service and product development. Companies that keep AI confined to the lab rather than integrating it across business units will struggle to see the full transformative potential of AI.

- **Ignoring the human element:** An AI-first strategy that overlooks the importance of human intuition, creativity, and empathy is incomplete. AI is a powerful tool, but it works best when combined with human insight. Organizations must focus on how AI can augment human capabilities rather than replace them. For instance, in health care, AI can analyze medical images faster than humans, but the final diagnosis and treatment plan should still involve human judgment and patient interaction.

- **Lack of Trust:** AI First does not move forward without the trust of those using the tool. In the latest Stanford University study, ChatGPT demonstrated an impressive 92% accuracy in medical diagnoses, yet integrating it into doctors' workflows didn't significantly improve diagnostic accuracy. The issue wasn't AI's capability but rather a trust gap, as many physicians hesitated to fully rely on the tool. Additionally, the study highlighted that insufficient training in AI collaboration left this powerful tool underutilized, limiting its potential impact. For AI to truly transform industries, we must focus on building trust, providing comprehensive training, and fostering seamless integration between humans and machines to unlock its full potential.

These points illustrate common missteps that can derail an AI-first strategy. Avoiding these pitfalls is essential for leveraging AI's full potential and driving significant, sustained value in your organization.

Timing: Navigating the AI Adoption Curve

In today's fast-paced digital landscape, timing is everything when it comes to adopting new technologies, especially AI. According to recent data from McKinsey, 65% of respondents report that their organizations are regularly using generative AI in their business operations.[2]

In the IBM Global AI Adoption Index by IBM, 42% of companies are actively exploring how to integrate AI into their processes, and over 50% plan to incorporate AI technologies. This means that a staggering 77% of companies are either using or considering the use of AI.[3] And different industries are progressing at different rates. Per IBM research, 63% of Energy CEOs surveyed expect to realize value from generative AI and automation.[4]

The takeaway? You and your company need to figure out the first project to take in the AI world. Make that small project successful, and then move forward. Move at the right pace for your business to stay competitive. The top barriers preventing deployment include limited AI skills and expertise (33%), too much data complexity (25%), and ethical concerns (23%).[5]

Given this momentum, businesses should not hesitate to begin their AI journey with the right project. The rapid acceleration of AI adoption signals that those who delay might find themselves playing catch-up in a landscape that is increasingly driven by data and machine learning. However, this does not mean rushing in blindly.

Instead, organizations should adopt a strategic approach, starting with small, manageable AI projects that align with their core business goals. These early initiatives can serve as proof of concepts, helping to build internal support and demonstrate the tangible benefits of AI. As these projects gain traction, businesses can scale their AI efforts more broadly across the organization.

Speed is important, but so is prudence. Moving too quickly without a solid strategy can lead to wasted resources and failed projects. It's essential to strike a balance between urgency and thoughtful planning. Leaders should prioritize building a strong foundation, which includes investing in AI education and training for their workforce, establishing robust data management practices, and creating a flexible technology infrastructure that can support future AI initiatives.

AI-first leaders also need to think through causal AI. It's not just a buzzword. Causal AI is about evolving your AI strategy beyond predictive models to systems that truly understand cause and effect. Start by educating yourself and your team on the principles of causal inference. This isn't just about upgrading your tech stack—it's about shifting your entire approach to problem-solving. Causal AI enables you to ask why questions and explore interventions in ways traditional AI can't. It's the difference between knowing a correlation exists and understanding how to influence outcomes.

To implement this shift, begin by identifying key business challenges where understanding causal relationships could drive significant value. This might be in areas like customer behavior, operational efficiency, or product development. Start experimenting with causal models alongside your existing AI systems, looking for opportunities to enhance decision-making by incorporating causal insights.

Foster a culture of causal thinking across your organization, encouraging teams to move beyond what questions to why and how questions when analyzing data and making decisions. Invest in tools and talent that can bridge the gap between data science and domain expertise because causal AI requires a deep understanding of both the technical aspects and the business context. Be patient and iterative—implementing causal AI is a journey, not a quick fix. Start with small, high-impact projects and scale as you learn.

For example, in marketing, causal AI can help determine the optimal mix of tactics, spending, and offers to maximize return on investment. For customer retention, it can pinpoint the root causes of churn in specific markets, allowing for targeted interventions. In manufacturing, causal AI can uncover the complex relationships between inventory management and product failures, leading to more efficient processes. Financial institutions can use it to model how various Federal Reserve rate cut strategies might affect market indices. Even in human resources, causal AI can reveal how different staffing models affect revenue across retail locations. These examples showcase the versatility and power of causal thinking in driving strategic decision-making across diverse business functions.

By taking these steps, organizations can accelerate their AI adoption while minimizing risks, ensuring they are well positioned to harness the transformative power of AI in the years ahead.

Do You Need a Chief AI Officer?

The question of whether you need a chief AI officer (CAIO) depends largely on your organization's size, complexity, and AI maturity. In many leading companies, a CAIO or equivalent role is crucial for orchestrating AI initiatives across the enterprise. This role focuses on ensuring that AI is aligned with the company's strategic objectives, overseeing AI talent development, and fostering a culture that embraces AI-driven innovation.

However, having a CAIO is not the only way to achieve an AI-first strategy. Smaller organizations or those in the early stages of AI adoption might find it more practical to embed AI responsibilities within existing leadership roles or create cross-functional AI teams. The key is to ensure that AI is not siloed but integrated across all business functions.

Despite all the buzz about AI transforming the world, its influence in the boardroom has been limited until recently. Not long ago, the idea of appointing a chief metaverse officer or CAIO would have seemed absurd, yet the CAIO role is now rapidly becoming one of the most sought-after positions in the C-suite.

Did you see that Genius Group Limited "appointed" an avatar as their CAIO? This intriguing move raises an interesting question: what is the role of AI in corporate leadership? This decision by Genius Group blurs the traditional lines between human and machine roles in an organization, raising questions about decision-making processes, ethics, and the human touch in leadership.

Although some might view the appointment of a virtual AI officer as a publicity stunt, it underscores a deeper integration of AI into strategic roles. Companies need to discern between leveraging AI for genuine operational enhancement versus using it as a marketing gimmick. As AI takes on more responsible positions, companies must navigate regulatory requirements and ethical considerations. There is a need for clear guidelines on accountability, especially when AI-made decisions could have significant consequences.

This move by Genius Group highlights the necessity for organizations to balance the innovative potential of AI with practical and ethical implications. Whether this step proves to be a pioneering success or a cautionary tale, it certainly sets the stage for a broader discussion on the evolving role of AI in leadership.

These new C-level roles, which didn't exist just a few years ago, are being filled not only by cutting-edge start-ups but also by more established enterprises. According to Foundry's AI

Priorities Study 2023, 11% of midsize to large organizations have already appointed a CAIO, and an additional 21% are actively looking to fill this position (see Figure 1.1).[6]

Merely appointing a new C-suite member doesn't guarantee that you'll address the challenges or seize the opportunities presented by AI. The tougher (but ultimately more rewarding) task is to understand how these roles fit into your organization's core strategy, what their work involves, and how new technologies transform the dynamics and responsibilities within the boardroom. This might require a new, dedicated C*x*O (chief *x* officer), or it could be more effective to adapt an existing role. Instead of hastily filling a new boardroom position, companies should pause and carefully determine their objectives and the best person to achieve them.

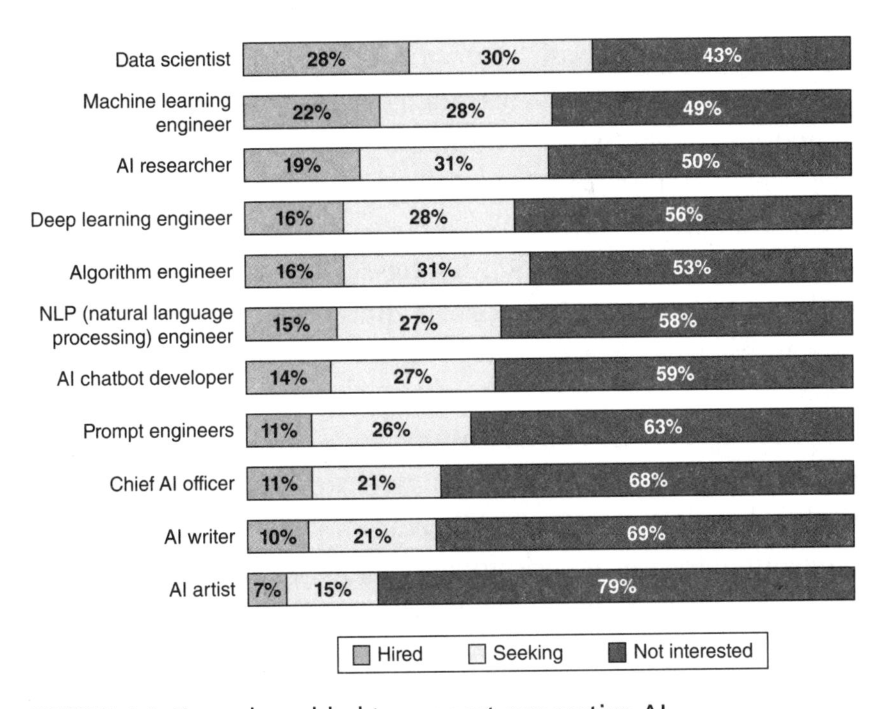

FIGURE 1.1 Key roles added to support generative AI.

Source: Foundry.

At first glance, creating new "chief" positions seems logical. Who better to lead and oversee AI transformations than someone with a dedicated place at the top?

But consider this: if your organization is an insurance firm, deeply affected by AI, what value is there in appointing a data scientist to the C-suite if they don't understand the difference between an underwriter and a broker?

The key takeaway is don't be blinded by those who only understand AI. Remember, you know your business best, and that's what matters most.

There's a strong case that the best person to manage AI initiatives might already be in the boardroom. For instance, it could be the chief marketing officer (CMO) if AI is expected to have a significant, transformative impact there. Similarly, it might be the chief technology officer (CTO), given their comprehensive understanding of both tech and business priorities. It could even be the CEO.

Recent history shows us that new job titles are often integrated into other, more traditional C-suite roles. Consider the chief cloud officer role, essential during the transition to cloud computing but eventually becoming part of the CTO's or chief information officer's responsibilities. The same could happen with the CAIO and CMO, despite efforts like the CAIO Summit to make them indispensable.

However, having a dedicated C*x*O might still be the best option. Lan Guan, CAIO at Accenture, a leading multinational IT company with over 730,000 employees, supports this. She believes every business should have a CAIO. "I believe this is a technology for everyone," she said. "But 90% of the clients out there are still grappling with this technology."[7] Internally, Guan said she's helping Accenture's workforce develop AI skills and attract talent that is already well versed in the technology.

No matter how advanced, technology is always a tool best applied to clearly defined and well-understood problems. It serves wider organizational goals rather than becoming the master. That's why the best individuals to oversee AI and initiatives might already be in charge.

The New C-Suite

I know from personal experience just how impactful an effective CAIO can be in transforming a business. When Accenture recently introduced its new CAIO, it brought a wave of innovation and efficiency that reshaped their strategies and operations. The integration of AI at such a high level in the organization demonstrated the profound potential of AI to drive growth and adapt to rapidly changing environments.

However, true success hinges not just on the role itself, but on how well enterprises grasp the shifts in traditional boardroom dynamics that these roles bring about. Because new technologies have an almost limitless range of applications affecting numerous business operations, the person leading AI initiatives needs to be a true Renaissance individual. They must build teams with diverse technical and vertical skills and adeptly navigate the intricate organizational politics that come with a broad scope of responsibilities. For instance, will this individual oversee both internal investments and external partnerships? How much authority will they have over budget allocation and expenditures? Who will report to them, and to whom will they report? How will this alter the existing chain of command?

These are just some of the critical questions to ponder when integrating new technology into existing corporate structures. They are also vital considerations when deciding who should be in charge.

In the wake of executive order on AI, federal agencies are now required to appoint CAIOs to promote AI and manage its risks and rewards.[8] This trend is likely to spread to the corporate world, but the role's responsibilities in business will be far more diverse and challenging than in government.

Cathy Hackl, often referred to as the "godmother of the spatial computing," vividly illustrates the complexity of these emerging roles. "Every day is different, and you never know what challenges are going to land in your inbox," she explains. "The only thing that never really changes is that my role requires me to be an evangelist and educator. I spend a lot of my time traveling, presenting, and speaking—both at industry events and internally at my company."[9]

She further elaborates on the breadth of the role: "I work across practically every line of business, so it's a big challenge to be thoroughly on top of the detail about each department. I need to ensure I understand what their goals are, and they need to know how new technology can help accomplish them. But there's also a lot of roll-your-sleeves-up, down-and-dirty work with the technology itself, whether it's designing virtual components or shepherding implementation projects."[10]

However, the challenges extend beyond technical expertise. Ethical considerations are paramount, particularly in ensuring AI integration is transparent, honest, and free from unintended biases. As the recipient of the Women Leaders in Data and AI's Executive Champion Award, I'm acutely aware of the importance of ethics in this field.[11]

The role must balance driving innovation with predicting and mitigating unforeseen risks, managing change, and safeguarding against discrimination. This complexity suggests that organizations might need to consider roles like chief ethics officers alongside their AI leadership.

As we navigate this technological revolution, it's crucial not to rush into creating new positions without careful consideration. The key is to focus on what you want to achieve rather than hastily naming roles. Take the time to think strategically about how AI and related technologies can best serve your organization's goals and values.

Preparing for Disruption

The rapid advancement of AI means that disruption is not a question of if, but when. Businesses must be agile and forward thinking to navigate these changes. Change management becomes essential, not just in adopting new technologies but in helping people adapt to them.

A new report from YouGov and the Reuters Institute for the Study of Journalism reveals that only 7% of people in the United States use generative AI daily.[12] Interestingly, most people have only used AI once or twice. This finding sparked some thoughts and questions for me. Although AI's potential is vast, its current use highlights the gap between early adopters and the general population.

This gap is why I've started a project called AI for Everyone to ensure all have access to AI's power. I recently ran workshops for Vets, Dry Cleaners, and Dentists to educate them on AI's value. More is needed in this space.

As AI continues to evolve, it's crucial to recognize and address the concerns of those who fear that their jobs might be at risk. The goal is to balance the incredible potential of AI with the irreplaceable value of human creativity and empathy. In the AI-first era, leaders need to be both visionaries and pragmatists. They must create environments where AI can thrive and where teams are empowered to leverage its capabilities. This means fostering a culture of continuous learning and innovation, where experimentation is encouraged, and failure is seen as a stepping stone to success.

The Human Element: Balancing AI with Empathy

Although AI offers remarkable capabilities, it's crucial to balance these with the irreplaceable value of human intuition and creativity. AI can process and analyze data at scales and speeds beyond human capability, but it lacks the understanding and emotional intelligence that humans bring to the table.

In an AI-first world, the role of humans is to interpret AI-driven insights, make complex decisions, and build relationships. For example, in customer service, AI can handle routine inquiries and provide recommendations, but human agents are needed to resolve complex issues and empathize with customers.

Leaders must recognize that AI is a complement to human abilities, not a replacement. They should focus on fostering a collaborative environment where AI and human expertise work together to achieve greater outcomes. This involves training employees to understand and effectively use AI tools while emphasizing the importance of their unique skills and judgment.

Embracing the AI-First Future

Embracing an AI-first philosophy is about more than just adopting new technologies—it's about transforming your mindset and approach to business. It involves prioritizing AI in your strategy, integrating it into your operations, and preparing for the disruptions it will bring. By doing so, businesses can not only stay competitive in an AI-driven world but also unlock new opportunities for growth and innovation.

Success in the AI-First era demands more than adopting technology—it requires visionary leadership, strategic integration, and a balance between innovation and human creativity. To begin this journey, focus on three core principles:

- **Start Small, Scale Strategically:** Launch pilot projects that showcase AI's potential while embedding ethical practices and leveraging high-quality data. Use these successes to integrate AI across departments for greater impact.
- **Empower Teams with Skills and Collaboration:** Train your workforce to partner with AI, fostering a culture of creativity, continuous learning, and ethical innovation. Human intuition combined with AI's capabilities will define success.
- **Innovate and Adapt Continuously:** Regularly refine your AI initiatives, staying curious and proactive. Balance automation with empathy to ensure AI aligns with your organization's values and drives meaningful change.

As we move forward, the key to success will be balancing the power of AI with the irreplaceable value of human intuition and creativity. Organizations that can effectively harness the potential of AI while maintaining their human touch will be best positioned to thrive in the future. Whether you are a leader, employee, or entrepreneur, now is the time to embrace AI-first thinking and prepare for the exciting changes ahead.

What will your AI-First move be? Start small, think big, and lead boldly.

CHAPTER

2

Exponential Baby!

The term *exponential* is frequently used in the tech world, but it truly captures the essence of our times: a period of relentless, accelerating change. This exponential growth isn't confined to a few select areas but permeates nearly every industry and aspect of our lives. As we enter what I call the *exponential baby* era, understanding and adapting to these rapid changes becomes crucial for businesses and individuals alike.

My favorite quote comes from *Alice in Wonderland* where Alice comments that she has to run twice as fast just to stay in place. Talking to leaders all over the world, and hosting roundtables with teams, Alice's feeling is mild compared to the change that everyone is feeling today.

What's driving this change?

This era is defined by the convergence of multiple groundbreaking technologies—artificial intelligence (AI), quantum computing, blockchain, the Internet of Things (IoT), spatial computing, and more—reshaping our world. These technologies don't evolve in isolation; they are interlinked, creating a powerful synergy that accelerates innovation and transformation.

But technological advancement isn't the only exponential shift we face. Our workforce is also evolving at an unprecedented pace, becoming a complex tapestry of diverse ages, cultures, and work preferences. As baby boomers extend their careers alongside millennials, gen X, and gen Z, organizations must adapt to varying expectations and work styles. This generational mix brings a wealth of perspectives and experiences, driving innovation but also challenging traditional management approaches.

Moreover, the COVID-19 pandemic has accelerated the adoption of hybrid work models, blending in-office and remote work. The future of work is now more flexible, with a significant portion of the workforce preferring the option to work from home. This shift requires businesses to rethink how they operate, communicate, and maintain culture across dispersed teams.

In this exponential baby era, it's not just about keeping up with the pace of technological change; it is also about embracing the dynamic nature of our workforce and work environments. We must prepare to navigate an ever-changing landscape where adaptability, continuous learning, and an open mindset are key to staying ahead.

As we move forward, recognizing these intertwined trends will be essential. By embracing both technological and workforce evolution, we can harness the full potential of the exponential baby era, creating opportunities for growth and innovation in ways we have yet to imagine.

Getting Started with Some Definitions

It's valuable to understand a little about these new technologies, even if we don't need to become experts. Learning about their basics can help us see how they might benefit us. Let's take it one step at a time. I know this might feel like a lot to take in, and that's okay. Even a small amount of knowledge can be useful.

Let's start with some definitions.

Quantum Computing

Quantum computing is a revolutionary technology that uses the principles of quantum mechanics to process information in ways that classical computers cannot. Unlike traditional computers, which use bits as the smallest unit of data, quantum computers use quantum bits, or qubits. Qubits can represent both 0 and 1 simultaneously, thanks to a property called *superposition*. This allows quantum computers to perform many calculations at once, making them exponentially more powerful for certain tasks.

Quantum computing matters especially for AI because it can dramatically speed up data processing and enhance machine learning capabilities. AI relies on analyzing large datasets and solving complex algorithms, tasks that can be time-consuming for classical computers. Quantum computers, with their ability to handle vast amounts of data simultaneously, can optimize these processes, leading to faster and more accurate AI models.

For example, NVIDIA is at the forefront of this convergence, developing quantum hardware and software solutions, and collaborating with companies to use AI and quantum simulations for advancements in drug discovery and battery design. This integration positions quantum computing as a game changer in the AI landscape, promising significant improvements in efficiency and innovation.

Blockchain

Blockchain is a digital ledger technology that securely records transactions across many computers so that the records cannot be altered retroactively. It's like a decentralized database where information is shared across a network of computers, ensuring transparency and security. Each transaction is grouped into a block and added to a chain of previous transactions, hence the name *blockchain*. You've been hearing a lot about blockchain recently as crypto is one of the first use cases of this technology.

Blockchain matters especially for AI because it enhances data security, integrity, and transparency. AI systems rely heavily on vast amounts of data to learn and make decisions. By using blockchain, the data fed into AI models can be verified and tamperproof, ensuring that the AI operates on accurate and reliable information. This is crucial for maintaining trust in AI systems, particularly in sensitive applications like finance, health care, and supply chain management. For example, integrating blockchain with AI can prevent data tampering, secure patient records, and facilitate transparent supply chain tracking, thus significantly boosting the reliability and effectiveness of AI technologies.

Internet of Things (IoT)

IoT refers to the network of physical objects—things—embedded with sensors, software, and other technologies for the purpose of connecting and exchanging data with other devices and systems over the internet. It's like a vast digital nervous system where everyday objects, from smart home devices to industrial machines, can collect and transmit data. Each connected device becomes a data point, contributing to a massive, continually growing pool of information. Examples of IoT include the following:

- Smart home devices
  - Smart thermostats like Nest that learn your preferences and adjust the temperature automatically
  - Voice-activated assistants like Amazon Echo or Google Home that control lights, play music, and set reminders

    - Smart refrigerators that can track groceries and suggest recipes
- Wearable technology
    - Fitness trackers like Fitbit or Apple Watch that monitor your health metrics and activity levels
    - Smart clothing that can measure biometrics or adjust temperature
- Connected cars
    - Vehicles that provide real-time navigation, and traffic updates, and can even park themselves
    - Cars that can communicate with your smart home to adjust your house temperature as you approach
- Smart cities
    - Traffic lights that adjust timing based on real-time traffic flow
    - Waste management systems with sensors in trash bins to optimize collection routes

IoT matters especially for AI because it generates an enormous volume and variety of real-world data, fueling the data flywheel and enhancing multimodal AI capabilities. AI systems thrive on diverse, real-time data to learn and make decisions. By tapping into IoT-generated data streams, multimodal AI can process and analyze information from various sources simultaneously—visual data from cameras, audio from microphones, temperature from sensors, and more.

This creates a more comprehensive understanding of the environment. For example, in a smart city, IoT sensors can provide real-time data on traffic patterns, air quality, and energy use, which multimodal AI can then analyze to optimize city operations.

As AI systems improve their decision-making based on this IoT data, they can in turn enhance IoT devices' functionality, creating a positive feedback loop. This synergy between IoT and AI accelerates the data flywheel, continuously improving AI models and delivering more value from connected devices, thus significantly boosting the capabilities and applications of both technologies across industries like manufacturing, health care, agriculture, and smart home systems.

Spatial Computing

Spatial computing is the technology that enables computers to interact and understand the physical world in three dimensions. It encompasses a range of technologies, including augmented reality (AR), virtual reality (VR), and mixed reality (MR). These technologies enable users to interact with digital content in a way that feels natural and immersive, blending the digital and physical worlds. For example, AR can overlay digital information on the real world through a smartphone or AR glasses, and VR provides a completely virtual environment for users to explore and interact with.

The significance of spatial computing, particularly in relation to AI, lies in its ability to enhance how we interact with and use AI technologies. AI can process and analyze vast amounts of data, but spatial computing provides a more intuitive and immersive way to visualize and interact with this data. For instance, in education, spatial computing can create interactive 3D models that AI can manipulate and analyze, providing students with a deeper understanding of complex concepts. In health care, AI-powered spatial computing can assist surgeons with precise 3D visualizations during operations, improving accuracy and outcomes.

One of the practical applications of spatial computing is in the field of remote collaboration. AI can analyze and interpret spatial data to provide real-time feedback and suggestions, making virtual meetings and collaborative projects more efficient and effective.

For example, architects and engineers can use AI and spatial computing to collaboratively design buildings in a virtual space, making real-time adjustments and improvements. This not only saves time and resources but also enhances creativity and innovation.

Moreover, spatial computing can significantly affect industries like retail, where AI can analyze consumer behavior in a 3D environment to provide personalized shopping experiences. Customers can use AR to virtually try on clothes or see how furniture fits in their home, whereas AI provides recommendations based on their preferences and interactions. This convergence of AI and spatial computing creates a seamless and engaging user experience, driving customer satisfaction and business growth.

The Exponential Rise of AI

AI exemplifies the essence of exponential growth. A recent McKinsey Global Survey reveals that employees are far ahead of their organizations in using generative AI.[1]

This isn't a gradual increase; it's a significant leap in adoption and application. Companies like NVIDIA have become pivotal players in this movement, their valuation soaring as it powers AI operations across industries. Their advancements in computing platforms and AI capabilities drive a second wave of AI, more integrated and culturally nuanced. NVIDIA's CEO, Jensen Huang, points out that computing power is growing incredibly fast. He expects it to become 1,000 times more powerful in just a few years.[2]

This growth isn't just in AI but also in related areas like inference computing. *Inference computing* is simply the process of using a trained AI model to make predictions or decisions. It's like when your phone recognizes your face to unlock it—that's inference in action. This type of computing is becoming so powerful that it's now faster than all cloud-based regular computers combined. Huang's observations show how different technologies are advancing together, leading to big improvements in AI capabilities and uses around the world.

AI's contribution to productivity is also transformative. Although initial fears centered on AI displacing blue-collar jobs, the reality is different. Automation driven by AI is reshaping various sectors, significantly affecting roles traditionally thought safe from automation. For instance, 46% of office legal work is now automated, and the advent of tools like ChatGPT shows how quickly AI can become indispensable in everyday tasks.[3]

Convergence and Transformation

The convergence of AI with other technologies, such as spatial computing, drives profound changes in how we interact with data and each other. Spatial computing, encompassing AR, VR, and other technologies that blend digital and physical experiences, is advancing rapidly. In fact, it's so important that we have a whole chapter on Convergence later in the book.

This convergence transforms user interactions, making digital experiences as natural and intuitive as physical ones. Innovations in hardware and software enhance how we engage with data, entertainment, and social interactions.

To get immersive experiences, AI with spatial computing will be used. Spatial computing is a technology that blends digital information with the physical world around us. As it becomes more common and works together with AI, it will create deeply immersive experiences. This will change many areas of our lives. For example, imagine you're furnishing your home. With spatial computing, you could use your smartphone or special glasses to see virtual furniture in your real room. You could walk around a 3D sofa that isn't really there, change its color with a gesture, and see how it fits with your existing decor. This technology could transform not just home design but also areas like gaming, education, and remote work.

A couple of years ago, I worked with a retail company as a client, helping them optimize their operations and enhance the customer experience. Despite their success, they faced challenges like crowded aisles, long checkout lines, and underused shelf space. That's when I suggested diving into the world of spatial data and AI. We started by installing sensors and cameras throughout the store to collect data on customer movement patterns, the time spent in various sections, and peak shopping hours. The data was then integrated into an AI platform designed to analyze spatial information and provide actionable insights.

The results were eye-opening. The AI platform generated heat maps showing the most and least visited areas in the store. We discovered that certain high-demand products were placed in low-traffic zones, and less popular items occupied prime shelf space. Armed with this knowledge, we rearranged the layout to make the most sought-after products more accessible, boosting their sales significantly.

Another critical insight involved the checkout lines. The spatial data revealed that congestion was often caused by bottlenecks near the entrance, where customers would gather and chat. We redesigned the entrance area to include a small waiting lounge and moved the checkout counters further inside the store. This change not only reduced congestion but also created a more welcoming environment.

One of the most impactful changes was in the staffing strategy. By analyzing the data, we identified peak shopping times and adjusted staffing schedules accordingly. During busy periods, more staff members were available to assist customers and manage checkouts, improving the overall shopping experience. Conversely, during slower times, staff hours were reduced to optimize labor costs.

The spatial data also helped enhance marketing efforts. We noticed that certain promotional displays were in areas with low foot traffic. By repositioning these displays to high-traffic zones identified by the AI platform, their visibility and effectiveness increased. Sales for promoted items saw a significant uptick as a result.

The most rewarding part of this journey was the feedback from customers. Many commented on the improved layout and the ease of finding products. The changes we implemented, driven by spatial data and AI, not only boosted sales but also enhanced customer satisfaction and loyalty.

Reflecting on this experience, I realized the immense power of convergence in retail. It provided us with a granular understanding of customer behavior and store dynamics, enabling us to make informed decisions that positively affected operations.

This story highlights how integrating technologies can revolutionize retail management. From optimizing store layouts and staffing to enhancing marketing strategies and improving customer experiences, the possibilities are vast. For any retail manager looking to stay ahead in a competitive market, embracing spatial data and AI is not just an option—it's a necessity.

For businesses, this convergence means rethinking user interfaces and exploring new ways to collaborate and interact in digitally enhanced environments. The blending of AI and spatial computing will accelerate remote work capabilities, transform training procedures, and redefine social interactions. Organizations that understand and leverage these trends will lead the next wave of digital transformation.

Data Explosion: The Lifeblood of the AI Revolution

The most staggering aspect of exponential growth is the sheer volume of data we generate. Over the next decade, data is expected to increase by approximately 660 zettabytes. To put that in perspective, it's equivalent to adding 610 more 128GB iPhones for every person on the planet. This data deluge presents a challenge and an opportunity for businesses and leaders who must navigate this convergence and leverage data effectively to stay competitive.

This unprecedented surge in data, often termed the *data deluge*, presents both a challenge and an opportunity for businesses and leaders. Successfully navigating this convergence means leveraging data effectively to stay competitive and drive innovation.

Why Data Matters to AI

In the realm of AI, data is the lifeblood that fuels its capabilities. AI systems, whether for machine learning or deep learning, rely on vast amounts of data to learn, adapt, and evolve. Every decision an AI makes, from recommending a product to diagnosing a medical condition, is based on the patterns it finds within data. The more data these systems have access to, the more accurately they can learn and predict outcomes.

Ray Wang, the CEO and founder of Constellation Research, emphasized the critical importance of having a robust data strategy at the foundation of AI projects. In a survey conducted by Wang, it was revealed that the AI initiatives that achieve success are invariably those that begin with a well-defined and solid data strategy.[4]

This approach ensures that the AI models are built on reliable, high-quality data, which in turn drives more accurate and effective outcomes. Wang's findings suggest that without this foundational strategy, even the most ambitious AI projects are at risk of falling short of their potential. The survey underscores that a strong data strategy is not just a component of AI success but the very bedrock on which these projects should be built.

Data serves as the foundation on which AI algorithms build their understanding of the world. In supervised learning, for instance, labeled datasets enable AI to recognize patterns and make decisions with humanlike accuracy. In unsupervised learning, AI explores unstructured data to find hidden patterns and insights. This ability to process and analyze massive datasets at unprecedented speeds enables AI to drive significant advancements across various fields, including health care, finance, retail, and more.

Types of Data: Variety Is Key

The types of data that feed into AI systems are incredibly diverse, and this variety is crucial for developing robust and versatile AI models. As we delve into the exponential growth of data, it's crucial to understand that not all data is created equal. The sheer variety of data types that AI systems can process is as vast as the volume of data itself. Each type plays a critical role in the AI ecosystem, contributing to more accurate models, better decision-making, and innovative solutions. The rapid increase in data across all types underscores the need for businesses to develop strategies for managing and leveraging this information effectively.

Let's begin with structured data, the highly organized type you typically find in databases and spreadsheets. Think of customer records or transaction logs. This data is growing exponentially as businesses continue to digitize their operations and transactions. Structured data remains the backbone of many business intelligence applications because it's easy for AI to process and analyze. However, as companies increasingly adopt AI, they generate more structured data from these interactions, further accelerating its growth.

Then there's unstructured data, often referred to as the Wild West of data types. This includes everything from text documents and emails to social media posts and videos. The growth of unstructured data is exploding, driven by the proliferation of digital communication, social media, and multimedia content. Despite its complexity, unstructured data is a goldmine of insights.

Technologies like natural language processing and computer vision are designed to sift through this data to find patterns and make sense of it all. It's like trying to find a needle in a haystack, but the needle could be invaluable information for your business. The challenge and opportunity lie in developing AI systems capable of extracting valuable insights from this chaotic but rich data source.

Semi-structured data falls somewhere in between. It doesn't fit as neatly into traditional databases as structured data but still has some organizational properties, like XML files or JSON documents. The exponential growth of semi-structured data is driven by its flexibility and widespread use in various applications, such as APIs and log files. AI systems can parse and analyze semi-structured data to extract meaningful patterns, offering a middle ground between the order of structured data and the chaos of unstructured data. As businesses generate more semi-structured data through digital transformation and IoT deployments, its importance continues to rise.

Time series data, collected over intervals, is crucial for trend analysis and forecasting. Examples include stock prices, weather data, and sensor readings from IoT devices. The volume of time series data is skyrocketing, particularly with the expansion of IoT and real-time analytics. AI models use this data to predict future events and optimize operations, making it indispensable for businesses looking to stay ahead of the curve. The ability to analyze time series data accurately and swiftly is becoming a competitive differentiator in many industries.

Last, geospatial data provides information about geographic locations and spatial relationships. Think satellite images, GPS data, and maps. The exponential growth of geospatial data is fueled by the increasing use of location-based services, autonomous vehicles, and smart city initiatives. This data is indispensable for applications in logistics, urban planning, and autonomous driving. Understanding not just where things are but how they relate spatially enables businesses to optimize their operations and make more informed decisions.

Understanding these types of data and their exponential growth is more than an academic exercise; it's about recognizing how each can be leveraged to fuel the AI systems that will drive the next wave of innovation.

In the exponential baby era, businesses must not only keep up with the volume of data but also develop strategies to make it usable and valuable for AI learning models. This involves investing in data management and integration tools, ensuring data quality and diversity, and fostering a culture that values data-driven decision-making.

To make sense of the data and enhance its value for AI applications, companies should focus on a few key areas:

- **Data integration and management:** Implement robust data management practices that ensure data from various sources is clean, consistent, and integrated. This includes using advanced data lakes or warehouses that can handle diverse data types and volumes.
- **Data quality and governance:** Establish clear data governance policies to maintain data accuracy, reliability, and security. High-quality data is essential for training effective AI models and making sound business decisions.
- **Advanced analytics and AI tools:** Leverage AI and machine learning tools that can process and analyze vast amounts of data efficiently. These tools should be capable of handling both structured and unstructured data, providing insights that drive innovation.

- **Human expertise and creativity:** Encourage a culture of continuous learning and upskilling to ensure your team can effectively leverage AI technologies. Although AI can process and analyze data at scale, human expertise is crucial for interpreting these insights and making strategic decisions.
- **Ethical considerations and bias mitigation:** Be aware of the ethical implications of data use and AI applications. Implement frameworks to detect and mitigate biases in your data and AI models to ensure fair and unbiased outcomes.

By focusing on these areas, businesses can turn the data deluge into a strategic asset.

For example, I am on the Altair board. They have so many examples of the power of data. The collaboration between NYYC American Magic and Altair has brought AI + People + Data together to power the America's Cup. This high-tech partnership has led to the development of an advanced AC75 yacht capable of reaching speeds over 55 mph. With just 9–12 mph of wind, these hydrofoiling yachts can take off and reach speeds three to four times the wind velocity, showcasing groundbreaking advancements in sailing technology.

Altair's AI plays a crucial role by processing large data sets and using self-learning algorithms to optimize sailing routes and maneuvers. This AI optimization, combined with the expertise of experienced sailing crews, maximizes the yacht's performance. However, even with these technological advancements, weather remains an unpredictable element, adding an exciting challenge to the mix. This story is a perfect example of how data matters—integrating advanced data processing, real-time learning, and human expertise—and can revolutionize traditional industries and push the boundaries of what's possible.

Navigating the Impact on the Workforce

Adopting new technology doesn't happen overnight. It takes time for people to change their behaviors and recognize the value of new technology compared to their established ways of doing things. According to Statista, in 1995, just 14% of US adults used the internet, by 2005 two-thirds did. In 2014, 87% of US adults at least occasionally surf the web.[5] This shows that significant technological shifts require time and gradual acceptance. We are likely at a similar juncture with AI.

Debra Williamson, chief analyst with Sonata Insights, once shared in a LinkedIn post: "Whenever a new technology comes along, the optimists always think it is going to change behavior quicker than it does. I do think change will eventually happen, but it's important to provide a reality check."[6]

As AI continues to permeate various sectors, a common sentiment I've noticed is the preference for AI to handle mundane tasks rather than creative ones. Joanna Maciejewska, a science fiction author, captured this perfectly when she said she was interested in AI that does the laundry, not her creativity. People want AI to take over the drudgery of repetitive tasks, freeing them to focus on what they love and what makes them human.

However, the reality is that AI is already transforming job roles and industries, often leading to significant shifts in employment. According to Authority Hacker, more than four in five digital marketers believe content writers will lose jobs because of AI.[7] A number of my friends in the marketing and content writing sectors have been hit hard by layoffs, particularly in start-ups and tech firms. Roles that once required a team of 20 are now being managed by just a handful of employees, with AI dramatically enhancing speed and efficiency. This shift is also affecting areas like graphic design and programming.

Small and medium-sized businesses can now accomplish tasks that previously required large teams or significant resources. With AI tools, these businesses can create professional-quality content, design work, and even develop software more efficiently and cost-effectively. This levels the playing field, enabling smaller companies to compete with larger corporations in terms of output and quality. Although the job market is changing, new opportunities are emerging for those who can adapt and leverage these AI technologies effectively.

Timnit Gebru, cofounder of the Distributed AI Research Institute (DAIR), confirms: "The benefits of AI are undeniable, but we must be cautious about the potential for job displacement and the erosion of human creativity. It's essential that we focus on developing ethical AI frameworks that prioritize human well-being."[8]

Balancing Automation and Human Creativity

So, what does this mean for us as we move forward in the exponential baby era?

First, we need to ask some searching questions about what tasks we want our AIs to do for us. AI should be developed to handle the repetitive, tedious tasks that bog us down, enabling us to focus on our creative and strategic strengths. It begins by asking better questions and exploring how generative AI can be a creative multiplier.

Recent data suggests the impact of AI on job displacement might be less severe than initially feared. A survey by SEO.AI found that by May 2023, only 3,900 US job losses were directly attributed to AI, with 14% of workers reporting job displacement due to AI technologies.[9]

Rather than posing a threat to livelihoods, many view AI as a tool to enhance productivity and creativity. For creative professionals, AI offers unique opportunities to augment their work. We are still exploring how generative AI can amplify human creativity. Instead of viewing AI as a replacement, it's more beneficial to consider it a collaborator that can handle repetitive tasks, enabling humans to focus on the core creative process.

The development and adoption of AI in creative industries presents both opportunities and challenges. On the one hand, there's a vision of AI complementing human creativity: we could develop AI systems that handle repetitive aspects of creative work, such as generating initial drafts or designs. This would free up humans to focus on refining and perfecting ideas, potentially leading to a new era of creativity when humans and AI collaborate to produce innovative, high-quality work.

However, a more pragmatic view suggests a different trajectory: the economic incentives might drive AI development toward replacing human workers entirely. Companies might pursue AI solutions that can handle entire creative processes due to obvious cost savings, and customers might quickly adopt these cheaper, AI-driven services. This pattern has been observed in other industries undergoing technological transformation.

A balanced perspective acknowledges both possibilities:

Initially, we might see a push toward full AI automation in creative fields, driven by cost-saving potential. However, this could lead to a realization that human input remains valuable for certain aspects of creative work. The industry might then settle into a middle ground, where AI handles much of the production, but human oversight and creativity are reintegrated to maintain quality and innovation.

This cycle of overenthusiastic automation followed by a measured step back is not uncommon in technological advancement. The key will be finding the right balance that leverages

AI's efficiency while preserving the unique value of human creativity.

The goal should be to develop AI systems that complement human creativity rather than replace it. By handling routine aspects of creative work, such as generating initial drafts or designs, AI can free up humans to concentrate on refining and perfecting ideas. This collaborative approach could usher in a new era of creativity, with humans and AI working in tandem to produce innovative, high-quality work.

The AI revolution is reshaping our workforce, sparking intense debate about the future of employment. Optimists see a world of opportunity, where humans and AI collaborate symbiotically. They point to historical precedents: just as the industrial revolution created new jobs like machine operators and engineers, the AI era might spawn roles we can't yet imagine.

Consider the rise of social media managers or UX designers—jobs that didn't exist two decades ago. These enthusiasts advocate for reskilling programs focused on uniquely human traits: critical thinking, emotional intelligence, and creativity. They envision data analysts becoming AI ethicists, or customer service representatives evolving into AI–human interaction specialists.

But skeptics paint a starker picture. They argue that this time is different. AI's rapid advancement into cognitive tasks sets it apart from previous technological shifts. The question "reskill to what?" looms large, especially in industries facing widespread automation. Take autonomous vehicles, for instance. What becomes of the millions of truck drivers if their jobs disappear virtually overnight?

Critics worry that the pace of change might outstrip our ability to adapt. They call for more than just reskilling—they demand a fundamental rethinking of our economic structures. Universal basic income, shorter workweeks, and lifelong learning initiatives are just a few proposed solutions. As AI continues to evolve, so must our approach to work and education. The truth, as often happens, might lie somewhere in the middle: a future where some jobs disappear, others transform, and entirely new ones emerge. Our challenge is to navigate this transition thoughtfully, ensuring that the benefits of AI are broadly shared.

In this rapidly changing landscape, leaders and organizations must adopt an AI-first approach that balances the capabilities of AI with the irreplaceable value of human creativity and empathy. Only then can we truly harness the potential of this exponential era.

We will need a leader willing to lead through this incredible time of change.

Leading Through Exponential Change

Navigating the exponential growth of technology requires a proactive and adaptable approach to leadership. Here's how leaders can guide their teams through the transformative exponential baby era:

- **Change management:** Navigate through the innovation influx.

  In the face of rapid technological change, effective change management is crucial. It's not just about implementing new technologies but also about helping teams adapt to these changes smoothly. Leaders must provide clear communication about what changes are happening and why they are necessary. They should also create a structured plan for transitioning to new processes and technologies, ensuring that all team members are on board and understand their roles in the new landscape.

  For example, as AI and automation become more integrated into workflows, roles within organizations will evolve.

Employees might need to shift from routine tasks to more strategic roles, leveraging AI to enhance their productivity. Leaders must guide their teams through these transitions, providing the necessary training and support to help them adapt.

- **Empathy:** Understand and address human concerns.

  Empathy is a critical component of effective leadership, especially in times of significant change. Leaders must understand that although machines don't experience job insecurity, humans do. The rapid adoption of AI and other technologies can create uncertainty and fear among employees about their future roles. Addressing these concerns with empathy is essential.

  Leaders should engage with their teams, listen to their concerns, and provide reassurance and support. This could involve open forums for discussion, regular updates on the impact of new technologies, and highlighting opportunities for growth and development within the organization. By fostering an environment where employees feel valued and understood, leaders can build a more resilient and adaptable workforce.

- **Education:** Enable continuous learning and growth.

  Education is the cornerstone of navigating exponential change. As technologies evolve, so must our skills and knowledge. Leaders should encourage a culture of continuous learning within their organizations, providing opportunities for employees to upskill and reskill as needed.

  This includes formal training programs, workshops, and access to resources that enable employees to learn about new technologies and their applications. Encouraging a mindset of curiosity and lifelong learning will help teams stay ahead of the curve and be more prepared to embrace new challenges and opportunities.

- **Technical understanding:** Grasp the basics of emerging technologies.

  Although leaders don't need to become experts in every new technology, they should have a foundational understanding of how these technologies work and their potential impact on the organization. This knowledge enables them to make informed decisions about adopting and integrating new technologies.

  For instance, understanding the basics of AI, blockchain, or spatial computing can help leaders identify opportunities for innovation and growth within their organizations. It also enables them to communicate more effectively with technical teams and stakeholders, fostering a collaborative environment for driving technological advancement.

  I keep up with what's happening in AI through a few dedicated methods. First, I attend at least one AI hackathon and one startup pitch competition each month, which gives me firsthand insight into how people are using new technologies and evolving their thought processes. Additionally, I frequently speak at conferences and find immense value in the questions posed by attendees—echoing the Amazon principle that questions are a powerful learning tool.

  I also belong to several Slack and Discord groups where I stay updated on the latest developments, ask questions, and share my learnings. Finally, I am a member of the CEO AI Alliance, run by Paul Witkay, and participate in smaller roundtables where we share lessons learned each week. These combined activities ensure I remain at the forefront of AI advancements.

- **Experimentation:** Foster a culture of innovation.

  Creating a culture where innovation is anticipated and embraced is key to thriving in the exponential baby era.

Leaders should encourage experimentation and exploration, enabling teams to test new ideas and technologies in a low-risk environment. This could involve setting up innovation labs, running pilot projects, or simply fostering an open mindset toward new approaches and solutions.

By promoting a culture of innovation, leaders can harness the creative potential of their teams and drive continuous improvement and growth. This proactive approach ensures that organizations are not just reacting to change but actively shaping their future in the face of exponential growth.

The Inevitability of Exponential Growth

The pace of technological change is not slowing down; it is set to accelerate further. This trend is not confined to AI but extends to blockchain, machine learning, IoT, and more. Each converging technology brings new possibilities and challenges, reinforcing the need for businesses and leaders to stay agile and forward-thinking.

One aspect that often goes unaddressed is the psychological impact of this relentless pace of change. How do we, as humans, mentally cope with the sheer velocity at which our world is transforming? This question is rarely discussed but is of paramount importance. Humans, by nature, are not wired to adapt rapidly to such profound and continuous changes. The cognitive load required to keep up with these advancements can lead to stress, anxiety, and a sense of overwhelm.

This could probably fill an entire book (maybe my next book!), but it's crucial to start considering strategies to manage this mental burden. Leaders might need to invest in mental health resources, promote resilience training, and encourage practices like mindfulness and continuous learning as essential components of the modern workplace. By acknowledging and addressing these human factors, we can better equip ourselves to thrive in this era of unprecedented technological evolution.

Navigating these trends requires a leadership style that is dynamic, inclusive, and anticipatory. Change management, empathy, and continuous education are the pillars of effective leadership in the exponential age. The goal is to create a culture where innovation is not merely reacted to but is anticipated and embraced as an integral part of the organizational strategy.

Embracing the Exponential Baby Era

We stand on the cusp of an era of immense potential and profound change. As leaders, educators, and individuals, our task is to embrace this potential, ride the wave of change, and prepare for the world of tomorrow. The exponential baby era is not just about surviving the rapid pace of technological advancements; it's about thriving in it and shaping the future through innovation and strategic foresight.

As we navigate the exponential baby era, it's crucial to understand that the pace of change will only continue to accelerate. Embracing this reality, while preparing for the convergence of technologies such as AI, spatial computing, and blockchain, will be key to thriving in this new landscape. AI First Leaders must foster a culture of continuous learning, empathy, and proactive adaptation to harness the opportunities and navigate the challenges that lie ahead. By doing so, we can ensure that we are not only ready for the future but are also active participants in shaping it.

CHAPTER

3

The Rise of Multimodal Learning Models

When you hear the term *artificial intelligence* (AI), what springs to mind? For many, it's probably a chatbot like ChatGPT—type in a question and get a humanlike response. But that's just the tip of the AI iceberg. To truly revolutionize our world, AI needs to evolve beyond text-based interactions.

Enter *multimodal learning*, or what some call the *Internet of Senses*. This approach aims to make AI more humanlike by integrating multiple types of data—text, images, video, and sound—into a single, cohesive learning model. Although we've had lifelong training in these nuanced communication codes, AI hasn't. By embracing a multimodal approach, we're not just improving AI's ability to understand us; we're opening doors to a wide array of practical applications that could transform how we interact with technology.

Why is multimodal learning crucial? Because human communication is complex. We don't just rely on words; we interpret facial expressions, tone of voice, and contextual cues. As any *Star Trek* fan knows, even logical Spock found humans puzzlingly "illogical" at times.

Multimodal learning brings AI closer to humanlike perception and cognition. By combining different data types, these models can generate richer, more subtle insights vs nuanced insights by understanding not just our words, but our *meaning*. Similarly, recognizing an object might involve both its visual appearance and the sound it makes. This comprehensive data integration enables AI to make more informed decisions and provides a deeper understanding of complex scenarios. More human than human!

The journey from narrow, text-based AI to truly sensory-rich, context-aware AI is the next frontier in this field. It's a step that could bridge the gap between novelty chatbots and genuinely transformative AI technologies. Multimodal is not just a technological feat but a significant step toward making AI more intuitive and effective in real-world applications.

Revolutionary Impact

To appreciate the revolutionary impact of multimodal learning, let's look at some examples. Multimodal learning models are designed to process and integrate multiple types of data inputs simultaneously, much like how humans use their senses to gather information. Just as we rely on sight, sound, and touch to navigate our environment and make decisions, multimodal AI leverages text, images, audio, and even video data to build a comprehensive understanding of the world.

Consider a scenario where AI needs to interpret a conversation. It's not enough to analyze the words spoken; the system must also consider the speaker's tone of voice, facial expressions, and body language to fully grasp the context and intent. This is where multimodal learning shines because it combines these diverse inputs into a unified model, enabling the AI to understand and respond more naturally and effectively.

For example, imagine an AI agent tasked with diagnosing a mechanical issue in a car. A multimodal system would analyze not just the textual description of the problem but also listen to the sounds of the engine, examine images of the car's components, and review video footage of the vehicle in motion. This holistic approach provides a deeper, more accurate diagnosis than any single data type could offer.

The Game-Changing Nature of Multimodal Learning

The rise of multimodal learning represents not just an incremental enhancement in AI but a profound leap forward in how machines process and understand information. This evolution signifies a shift toward a more holistic and humanlike approach to learning, transforming AI from a text-based tool into a multisensory powerhouse. Yes, many of you might have heard about multimodal AI, but some of you might not have experienced its full potential. Let me share an example that truly illustrates the power of multimodal capabilities.

Recently, I was sipping on my favorite Chick-fil-A tea and decided to take a picture of the cup using a multimodal AI tool called ChatGPT. To my surprise, the AI came back with a detailed description: "This is a Styrofoam cup. It has a chicken logo on it, which looks like it's from Chick-fil-A." It was fascinating to see how the AI could analyze the image and provide relevant information about a simple teacup.

Intrigued, I decided to try the same with a bottle of Hint Water. I snapped a picture and waited for the AI's response. It identified the bottle and provided key marketing details: "This is a bottle of Hint Water. It has zero calories. Here are the ingredients." The AI even highlighted the health benefits and marketing points of Hint Water, which was incredibly insightful from a marketing perspective.

This experience got me thinking. As a marketer, it's crucial to understand how your products are perceived through the lens of multimodal learning models. If customers are taking pictures of your products and receiving descriptions from AI, what does it say about your brand? How accurately does the AI describe your product's features and benefits?

In today's digital age, when visual content is king, ensuring your product is presented accurately and appealingly by AI can significantly affect consumer perception. This small experiment with a teacup and a water bottle showcased the immense potential of multimodal AI in enhancing product descriptions and marketing strategies. It's a powerful reminder for marketers to consider the implications of AI-generated content on their brand image.

By seamlessly integrating various types of data—text, images, audio, and more—multimodal AI systems are revolutionizing how businesses operate, make decisions, and engage with their customers. This integration allows for richer, insights and creates a holistic view that single-mode systems simply cannot achieve. Imagine a customer service chatbot that can analyze not just the text of a complaint but also the tone of voice and relevant images, providing a response that is more empathetic and accurate. This ability to process and synthesize data from multiple sources in real time is redefining the standards for customer interactions, operational efficiency, and strategic decision-making.

Multimodal learning is not confined to corporate applications; its influence extends into our daily lives, making technology more accessible and intuitive. Think about how smart home devices now understand and respond to a combination of voice commands, visual inputs, and environmental data. This convergence of capabilities not only simplifies our interactions with technology but also makes it more adaptive to our needs.

We've talked about the capabilities of multimodal AI, but let me share another fascinating example that showcases its true power. Enter the world of robotic lawnmowers. Now, you might think, "I can buy a robotic lawnmower on Amazon today." However, the ones available online require a metal wire to define their boundaries. Imagine a lawnmower that's more like a Tesla than your average robotic gadget. This innovative machine creates a virtual map of your lawn using an array of sensors and AI technology. It employs cameras to visualize the surroundings, touch sensors to detect obstacles, and neural networks to learn and adapt to the environment. It can navigate around pets, avoid garden furniture, and mow your lawn with precision.

I recently got a demo of this next-generation lawnmower called Verdie.[1] Unlike traditional models, Verdie doesn't rely on physical boundaries. Instead, it uses advanced AI to understand and navigate the terrain autonomously. This isn't just a gadget; it's a smart machine that continually learns and improves. Interestingly, the company behind Verdie, Electric Sheep Robotics, isn't focused on selling these lawnmowers directly to consumers. Instead, they've adopted a "lawnmower as a service" business model. This means they offer a complete lawn care service, leveraging their cutting-edge robotic mowers as their competitive advantage.

This example highlights the transformative power of multimodal AI. By combining visual, tactile, and neural network data, Verdie represents a significant leap in technology, offering a glimpse into the future of smart, autonomous devices. As we continue to integrate these advanced technologies into everyday tools, the potential for innovation and improved quality of life is boundless.

As we continue to generate diverse types of data at an unprecedented rate, the ability to harness and integrate this information through multimodal learning is becoming crucial. This is why I believe multimodal AI represents the next significant leap in technology, promising to drive innovation, enhance user experiences, and create new competitive advantages across all sectors of society.

Multimodal learning empowers industries and individuals by offering a more comprehensive understanding of the world through data. For businesses, this means the ability to derive deeper insights, personalize customer experiences, and streamline operations in ways previously unimaginable. It enables companies to move beyond surface-level data analysis, diving into the complex interplay of various data types to uncover hidden patterns and opportunities.

For individuals, multimodal AI can make everyday interactions with technology more seamless and effective, from personalized health care recommendations to intelligent personal assistants that can anticipate and meet our needs. As we stand on the cusp of this new era, it's clear that embracing multimodal learning is essential for anyone looking to thrive in an increasingly complex and data-driven world.

The Five Superpowers of Multimodal Learning Models

Multimodal learning is a groundbreaking evolution in AI, enabling systems to learn and process information in a manner that mirrors human cognition. Unlike traditional AI models that rely predominantly on text or numerical data, multimodal learning combines inputs from text, images, videos, and audio. This fusion grants AI several superpowers that transform its capabilities and applications.

- **Enhanced cognitive understanding:** Multimodal learning systems possess the superpower of enhanced cognitive understanding. By integrating various types of data, AI can interpret and analyze information with a depth and breadth akin to human sensory perception. Imagine an AI that simultaneously understands spoken words, interprets facial expressions, and analyzes the surrounding environment. This multisensory approach provides AI with a richer and deeper understanding of the world.

  It enables the system to grasp complex scenarios and subtle nuances that single-mode data cannot capture. For instance, an AI that considers not only the words but also the tone of voice and body language in a conversation can better comprehend the emotions and intentions of the speakers, leading to more effective and interactions. This capability is vital in applications where understanding the full context is crucial, such as in customer service, therapeutic settings, and interactive technologies.
- **Deeper insights and patterns:** The ability to uncover deeper insights and more patterns is another superpower of multimodal AI. By simultaneously analyzing video, audio, and text, AI can reveal contexts and correlations that might remain hidden when each data type is considered in isolation. For example, in the retail industry, analyzing customer behavior through video footage alongside transaction records and social media interactions provides a more comprehensive view of shopping habits and preferences.

  This multidimensional analysis is invaluable for applications requiring a deep understanding of real-world complexities. Whether diagnosing medical conditions from a combination of patient records, imaging scans, and doctors' notes, or assessing environmental impacts through a fusion of satellite imagery, sensor data, and textual reports, multimodal AI delivers insights that are not only more accurate but also richer in context and detail. This profound understanding drives better decision-making and fosters innovative solutions across various sectors.

- **Enhanced accessibility and inclusivity:** One of the most significant superpowers of multimodal learning is its potential to enhance accessibility and inclusivity. By leveraging multiple data types, AI can create more inclusive and effective solutions for individuals with disabilities. A compelling example of this potential is seen in Google's Super Bowl ad, showcasing how AI assists visually impaired individuals by converting visual information into detailed audio descriptions.

  This capability goes beyond simple translations; it involves interpreting and conveying the subtlety of visual scenes, enabling users to navigate their surroundings with greater confidence and independence. Moreover, multimodal AI can adapt educational content to different learning styles by combining text, audio, and interactive elements, making education more accessible and engaging for everyone. In health care, integrating medical images, textual notes, and patient histories enables AI to provide comprehensive support tailored to both doctors and patients, ensuring that care is inclusive and personalized.

- **Real-time, context-aware responses:** Multimodal AI excels at providing real-time, context-aware responses that are both accurate and relevant. This superpower is particularly crucial in dynamic environments where context is constantly evolving, such as autonomous driving or interactive customer service. An autonomous vehicle equipped with multimodal AI can process inputs from cameras, light detection and ranging, Global Positioning System, and environmental sensors to navigate complex road conditions safely and efficiently.

Similarly, a customer service AI that integrates voice recognition, facial analysis, and contextual data can offer more personalized and timely assistance. It can adapt its responses based on the customer's emotional state and the specific details of their inquiry, enhancing the overall user experience. This ability to deliver contextually appropriate responses in real time not only makes interactions more efficient and satisfying but also expands the practical applications of AI across various industries.

- **Synergistic data integration:** The final superpower of multimodal learning is its ability to synergistically integrate diverse data types, enhancing the overall learning capabilities of AI systems. Traditional models are often limited by their reliance on a single type of data, which restricts their ability to fully understand and interact with the world. Multimodal AI overcomes this limitation by combining different forms of data—be it voice, sound, touch, or sight—into a cohesive understanding. This integration boosts the AI's learning capacity and enables it to perform complex tasks that were previously unattainable.

For example, an AI in a smart home system can use voice commands, visual recognition, and environmental sensors to create a seamless and intuitive user experience. By leveraging the synergy of various data inputs, multimodal AI systems generate a flywheel effect: increased data types lead to better models, which in turn provide superior analytics and drive more use. This virtuous cycle accelerates the adoption and effectiveness of AI technologies, paving the way for future advancements.

Multimodal learning represents a quantum leap in AI capabilities, unlocking these five superpowers that collectively transform how AI systems learn, interpret, and interact with the world. As this technology continues to evolve, its applications will expand, offering unprecedented opportunities for innovation and improvement across all facets of life and industry.

Impact of Multimodal Learning Superpowers on Brands

The superpowers of multimodal learning models are set to profoundly reshape how brands operate, interact with consumers, and position themselves in the market.

First, enhanced consumer insights become a game changer. Multimodal AI's ability to analyze diverse data types means brands can gain a deeper understanding of customer behavior, preferences, and emotions. By integrating text, video, audio, and image data, brands can uncover previously undiscovered consumer insights, allowing for more precise targeting and personalized marketing strategies. Imagine a retail brand that can analyze not just purchase history but also social media interactions, video reviews, and visual content engagement to tailor its product recommendations and promotional campaigns more effectively.

Second, improved customer engagement emerges as a key advantage. Multimodal AI systems offer real-time, context-aware responses that elevate customer service experiences. Brands can deploy AI-powered virtual assistants that understand voice commands, analyze user-submitted images or videos, and interpret textual queries to provide comprehensive and personalized support. This capability not only enhances the user experience but also fosters stronger, more interactive relationships between brands and their customers. For instance, a beauty brand could use multimodal AI to offer virtual try-ons, personalized skincare advice based on photos, and real-time support via voice and chat.

Last, increased brand accessibility and inclusivity are pivotal impacts. Multimodal learning enhances accessibility by providing solutions that cater to diverse needs, including those of people with disabilities. Brands that integrate these AI capabilities into their products and services can appeal to a broader audience, demonstrating a commitment to inclusivity. For example, a tech company could use multimodal AI to create devices that convert visual content into audio descriptions for the visually impaired or offer real-time sign language interpretation for the hearing impaired. This inclusivity not only expands market reach but also builds brand loyalty among consumers who value accessibility and diversity.

The integration of multimodal learning models empowers brands to deepen consumer insights, enhance customer engagement, and increase accessibility, positioning them to thrive in a rapidly evolving digital landscape.

Already Moving Forward: Real-World Examples of Multimodal Learning

Expanding on the transformative potential of multimodal learning, we can observe its profound impact across various industries. By seamlessly integrating different types of data, multimodal AI systems are revolutionizing the way businesses operate and interact with their customers. But it can also significantly enhance personal experiences and day-to-day life scenarios.

Health Care: Integrating Diverse Data for Holistic Patient Care

In the health care sector, multimodal learning is redefining how we approach diagnostics and patient care. Traditionally, medical professionals rely on individual data sources such as X-rays, lab results, or patient histories. However, multimodal AI systems can integrate these diverse data types, leading to more comprehensive and accurate diagnoses.

For example, Mayo Clinic is combining different types of medical imaging and AI to get a clearer picture of what's happening inside the body. When treating complex blood vessel problems in the brain, Mayo Clinic physicians use 3D models made from special magnetic resonance imaging scans. These models show doctors exactly how blood is flowing, which helps them plan the best treatment. They even use augmented reality during surgery to see 3D views of blood vessels and blood flow in real time.[2]

But Mayo Clinic isn't stopping there. They're working on a new AI system that can look at a patient's genetic information, medical history, and the latest medical research all at once. This multimodal approach—which means using many different types of information together—could help doctors predict how well a treatment might work for each patient. They're starting with rheumatoid arthritis, but this method could potentially be used for many other diseases in the future. By bringing together all these different pieces of information, Mayo Clinic hopes to make health care more personalized and effective for everyone.

Customer Service: Enhancing Interaction with Multisensory Inputs

Customer service is another area where multimodal learning is making a significant impact. Traditional customer service systems, often limited to text-based interactions, can be frustrating and inefficient. Multimodal AI transforms these interactions by allowing systems to understand and respond using multiple forms of data—text, voice, and images.

Take the case of Autodesk, a company that provides software for design and creation. Autodesk uses a multimodal AI system named AVA (Autodesk Virtual Agent), which handles customer support queries.[3] AVA can process customer inquiries through text, voice, and even images. If a customer has trouble with the software, they can upload a screenshot, and AVA analyzes the image, cross-references it with textual descriptions, and provides a solution. This integration of multiple data types enables AVA to offer more accurate and efficient support, reducing downtime and enhancing the customer experience.

Retail and E-Commerce: Personalizing Shopping Experiences

In retail, multimodal AI is revolutionizing how companies manage inventory and personalize the shopping experience. The retail industry leads in AI implementation, with 72% of retailers using AI.[4] Retailers can now analyze a combination of product images, customer reviews, and sales data to make more informed decisions.

For instance, Amazon is a pioneer in using multimodal learning to enhance its e-commerce platform, creating a more intuitive and personalized shopping experience. Amazon's AI systems look at product images, read through customer reviews, and study shopping behaviors all at once. This enables Amazon to make smarter product recommendations and improve search results, making it easier for customers to find what they're looking for. They've even taken this a step further with devices like the Echo Look, which can take full-body photos and videos of customers.[5] By combining this visual data with information about shopping preferences, Amazon can offer personalized fashion advice and product suggestions. This multimodal approach doesn't just make shopping more enjoyable for customers; it also helps

Amazon manage its vast inventory more efficiently and predict future demand more accurately. Just like in health care, this use of multimodal AI in retail shows how combining different types of information can lead to better, more personalized experiences.

Banking: Enhancing Security and Personal Financial Services

The banking sector is leveraging multimodal learning to enhance security and personalize services. Banks deal with vast amounts of data, from transaction logs to customer interactions, and multimodal AI can integrate these data types to improve both security and customer service.

Consider HSBC, which uses multimodal AI for fraud detection and personalized banking services. HSBC uses AI to help check about 1.35 billion transactions for signs of financial crime each month across 40 million customer accounts.[6] HSBC's AI systems analyze voice patterns during customer calls to detect stress or unusual behavior that might indicate fraud.

Simultaneously, it reviews transaction data and historical account use to identify anomalies. For personal banking, HSBC uses multimodal data to offer tailored financial advice. For instance, by analyzing spending habits and financial goals communicated through text or voice, the bank can provide personalized budgeting tips and investment recommendations. This comprehensive use of multimodal data ensures both enhanced security and a more customized banking experience for its customers.

Entertainment and Media: Crafting Tailored Content

In the entertainment industry, multimodal AI is transforming content creation and delivery. AI systems can analyze scripts, visual scenes, and audience reactions to create engaging and personalized content.

Disney is using multimodal AI to revolutionize how they produce and recommend content specifically through its participation in the 2024 Disney Accelerator program, which includes start-ups focusing on various AI technologies. One notable participant, PrometheanAI, offers tools for virtual world creation and digital asset management using natural language prompts, integrating different modes of data.[7]

Additionally, Disney is working with these start-ups to explore how AI can enhance storytelling and media experiences by combining text, audio, and visual data to create more immersive and interactive content. For example, these AI systems analyze scripts and storyboard elements alongside audience data to create compelling trailers and promotional material. These systems understand visual scenes, character emotions, and narrative arcs, enabling them to generate highlights that resonate with viewers. Moreover, Disney's streaming services use multimodal data to personalize content recommendations, combining viewer preferences with analysis of visual and thematic content to suggest shows and movies that align closely with user tastes. This results in a more engaging and tailored viewing experience.

Education: Tailoring Learning to Individual Needs

Educational platforms are embracing multimodal AI to enhance learning by catering to diverse styles and needs. These platforms combine text, images, videos, and interactive elements to create richer and more engaging educational experiences.

Khan Academy, an online educational platform, uses multimodal AI to provide a personalized learning experience. By integrating video lectures, interactive quizzes, and textual explanations, Khan Academy caters to various learning styles. The AI system tracks student progress and adapts the content to individual learning paces. For example, if a student struggles with a particular math concept, the AI can recommend supplementary video tutorials, interactive exercises, or alternative explanations to reinforce understanding.[8] This multimodal approach not only supports diverse learning preferences but also helps students achieve better educational outcomes through tailored support.

Personal Life: Simplifying Daily Routines

Multimodal learning is not confined to professional or commercial use; it's also enhancing our personal lives. Smart home devices equipped with multimodal AI can integrate data from voice commands, visual inputs, and environmental sensors to create a seamless and intuitive user experience.

Consider the use of Google Nest Hub, a smart display that uses multimodal AI to manage home automation.[9] Nest Hub can integrate voice commands, video inputs, and environmental data to provide a cohesive smart home experience. For example, you can use voice commands to control your home's lighting and temperature, while the device's camera can recognize who is in the room and adjust settings accordingly. It can also display recipes or news updates based on visual cues or spoken preferences. This integration of multiple data types simplifies daily routines and enhances convenience, making home life more comfortable and efficient.

Why Multimodal Learning Is the Next Big Movement

Multimodal learning is set to be the next big movement in AI because it mirrors how humans naturally process information through multiple senses. By integrating text, images, audio, and other data types, AI systems can understand and interact with the world in a more humanlike manner. This not only enhances the capabilities of AI but also makes it more accessible and useful in everyday applications.

For businesses, this means richer insights and more personalized customer experiences. For individuals, it translates to smarter, more intuitive interactions with technology. As we continue to generate and harness more diverse types of data, the potential for multimodal AI to revolutionize our world grows exponentially. This is why now is the time for both industries and individuals to start thinking multimodal, exploring how this technology can drive innovation and create a competitive edge in a rapidly evolving landscape.

I'll let you in on a secret. The future of AI extends far beyond the realm of GPTs, personal assistants, and chatbots that dominate current public discourse. AI is quietly revolutionizing the very fabric of technology itself, becoming an integral part of critical applications across various domains. From enhancing data analytics and bolstering cybersecurity to improving inspection and detection systems, refining search algorithms, and revolutionizing research and content creation, AI is reshaping how we interact with and leverage technology.

A prime example of this revolution is seen in the field of cybersecurity. Google Cloud's Chronicle SIEM (Security Information and Event Management) system uses AI and machine learning to detect and respond to security threats in real time. According to Google, this AI-powered system can analyze petabytes of security telemetry data in milliseconds, significantly enhancing threat detection capabilities.[10] This demonstrates how AI is not just an add-on but a core component in advancing technological capabilities.

At the heart of this AI revolution are large language models (LLMs), particularly multimodal LLMs, which are poised to fundamentally transform user interfaces in tech. These advanced models, capable of understanding and generating various forms of data including text, images, and potentially audio and video, will make technology more intuitive and accessible to a broader audience. By bridging the gap between human communication and machine understanding, multimodal LLMs have the potential to democratize access to complex technological tools and services.

A concrete example of this potential is Microsoft's Azure OpenAI Service, which integrates advanced language AI models into various business applications. One of their clients, CarMax, used this service to create a multimodal AI assistant that helps customers search for cars using natural language and images. This system enables users to ask complex questions about vehicles and even upload images for visual car searches, making the car-buying process more intuitive and user-friendly.[11] This case illustrates how multimodal LLMs can create more natural and efficient interfaces, potentially accelerating adoption and innovation across industries.

As these models continue to evolve, we can expect to see a new era of human–computer interaction that is more natural, efficient, and productive, ultimately accelerating innovation across all sectors of the tech industry.

Multimodal Learning and the Flywheel Effect

One of the most compelling aspects of multimodal learning is its potential to create a flywheel effect. In my experience at Amazon Web Services, I saw firsthand how this self-reinforcing cycle can drive exponential growth and innovation. Check out the flywheel shown in Figure 3.1.

FIGURE 3.1 The multimodal data flywheel.

Here's how it works:

- **More data types lead to better models.** As AI systems integrate more types of data, they become better at understanding and predicting complex scenarios. This improvement in model accuracy and robustness leads to more valuable insights and better decision-making.
- **Better models drive increased use.** When AI systems provide more accurate and relevant insights, they become more useful and widely adopted. This increased use generates even more data, which further enhances the models and continues the cycle.
- **Increased use generates more data.** As more users interact with multimodal AI systems, they produce a wealth of diverse data. This data is crucial for training and refining the AI models, making them even more effective and capable of handling new challenges.
- **Enhanced capabilities spur innovation.** With each iteration of the flywheel, AI systems become more capable and versatile. This continual improvement drives innovation, enabling businesses to explore new applications and opportunities that were previously unimaginable.

Actions for Technologists and Business Leaders

To fully leverage the power of multimodal learning, businesses need to rethink their approach to data and AI. Here are some key actions for business leaders to consider:

- **Think beyond text:** In strategic planning and decision-making, consider how multimodal data can provide deeper insights and better outcomes. Incorporate video, images, and sound into your data strategy to capture a more comprehensive view of your environment and customer interactions.
- **Prepare for new marketing dynamics:** As multimodal AI systems become adept at describing and interacting with products, marketers need to adapt. Consider how your products are represented and perceived through these AI lenses and develop strategies to ensure they are accurately and positively depicted. For example, ChatGPT is looking at encompassing ads. Imagine a prompt that I would write asking if I should wear pink for a speaking engagement. ChatGPT would of course respond "Yes, it is your signature color." And now it could also recommend checking out pink jackets at a particular store, showing video, and maybe even showing the jacket on me real time! Are you ready for this new world?
- **Invest in multimodal capabilities:** Evaluate and invest in AI technologies that can process and integrate diverse data types. This investment will position your business to capitalize on the advantages of multimodal learning and stay competitive in a rapidly evolving landscape.
- **Foster a culture of continuous learning:** Encourage your teams to experiment with and embrace multimodal AI. Create opportunities for learning and innovation, and foster a culture where employees are motivated to explore new technologies and applications.

The Future of AI Is Multimodal

Multimodal learning models represent a significant leap forward in the AI landscape, bridging the gap between human and machine understanding by integrating diverse data types. This approach not only enhances the capabilities of AI systems but also makes them more intuitive and effective in various applications. By embracing multimodal learning, businesses and individuals can unlock new levels of innovation and efficiency, paving the way for a future where AI seamlessly integrates into our daily lives.

As we continue to explore these groundbreaking trends and their implications, it becomes clear that the future of AI is not just about processing text or numbers—it's about creating systems that understand and interact with the world as we do through a rich tapestry of sensory inputs. The rise of multimodal learning marks the beginning of a new era in AI, one that promises to transform industries and redefine our relationship with technology.

CHAPTER

4

The Experiential Age Unfolds

Welcome to the experiential age, a transformative era defined by immersive, interactive, and deeply personalized experiences that revolutionize our engagement with the world. According to global technology company NTT Data, over 90% of businesses believe that enhancing customer experience will improve their bottom line.[1] Unlike the information age, which focused on data access and dissemination, or the digital age, which brought us unprecedented connectivity and automation, the experiential age emphasizes how we interact with and experience technology in multidimensional, sensory-rich environments. The experiential age marks a profound shift in how we perceive and interact with the world around us.

Customer experience (CX) is not just for trendy business-to-consumer (B2C) brands. In her groundbreaking book *Growth IQ: Get Smarter About the Choices That Will Make or*

Break Your Business (Portfolio), Tiffany Bova shatters this common misconception, asserting that CX is the secret weapon for a competitive edge in the 21st century—and it's just as crucial for business-to-business (B2B) as it is for B2C.

Many B2B companies fall into the trap of dismissing CX as mere hype, relevant only to consumer-facing businesses. But here's the kicker: it's even more vital in the B2B world.

Why?

Because in the complex, high-stakes arena of business-to-business interactions, a stellar customer experience can be the difference between a one-off transaction and a long-term, lucrative partnership.

In today's hypercompetitive market, product features and price points are easily matched. What's not so easy to replicate? The way you make your business customers feel throughout their journey with you. From the first sales call to ongoing support, every touchpoint is an opportunity to cement your position as not just a vendor, but a valued partner. So if you hadn't been excited for this chapter, it's time to sit up and take notice. Ignoring CX isn't just a missed opportunity—it's a fast track to obsolescence. In the digital landscape, where relationships are everything, CX isn't just important; it's your most powerful differentiator. And it's a place that AI can raise the bar.

The concept of the experiential age can be compared to stepping into the holodeck from *Star Trek*—a place where imagination becomes a reality, and any scenario can be vividly experienced. This era is characterized by the convergence of advanced technologies such as augmented reality (AR), virtual reality (VR), and artificial intelligence (AI).

Together, these technologies blur the lines between physical and digital worlds, creating spaces where users can engage with digital content in ways that feel natural and integrated into their real-world environments.

In this new age, our interactions with technology are no longer confined to screens and devices. Instead, they expand into our physical spaces, enabling us to experience digital content in a tangible, immersive manner. Whether it's walking through a virtual art gallery, participating in a holographic meeting, or navigating a digitally enhanced physical environment, the experiential age transforms how we perceive and engage with the world around us.

What Is the Experiential Age?

The experiential age is characterized by a shift from valuing material goods and information to prioritizing unique, memorable experiences. For example, a study highlighted by Neuroscience News found that experiences, irrespective of when happiness is measured—before, during, or after consumption—consistently provided greater happiness than material goods.[2] This is likely due to the lasting memories and emotional value that experiences create, whereas the perceived value of material items tends to diminish over time.

Additionally, AlixPartners' research indicates a lasting shift toward an experiential mindset among consumers, which is expected to continue even during economic downturns.[3] This shift has significant implications for various industries, particularly those related to dining and entertainment, as consumers increasingly seek meaningful and engaging experiences over material acquisitions. This evolution is reshaping how businesses approach consumer engagement, emphasizing the need to deliver unique and memorable experiences to meet the evolving demands of today's consumers.

In essence, the experiential age is about transforming the ordinary into the extraordinary. This era is built on the premise that people increasingly seek personal and immersive experiences over physical possessions—experiences that are not only immersive and interactive but also tailored to individual preferences and needs. This personalization is key to the experiential age, as it shifts the focus from generalized offerings to customized experiences that resonate deeply with consumers.

How the Experiential Age Is Different

The experiential age represents a significant departure from the industrial and information ages, fundamentally altering how value is created and experienced. While the industrial age focused on mass production and efficiency, and the information age on the acquisition and processing of knowledge, the experiential age is centered on the creation of value through immersive and meaningful experiences. This shift affects not only consumer behavior but also the strategic approaches businesses must adopt to stay competitive. And will affect us individually, too.

I recently had a discussion with Jeremiah Owyang, general partner at Blitzscaling Ventures, about how AI will save us time.[4] Current studies have shown that we spend about seven hours a day on the internet,[5] but imagine a future where AI agents take over laborious tasks for us. These tasks include managing repetitive emails, filling out expense reports, booking travel, scheduling calls, conducting internet research, and handling monotonous e-commerce activities. Although this transition won't be perfect and will require refinement, it promises to free up significant time for us.

It's interesting to see a future where AI will transform the way we interact with the internet. Information will be delivered through a few user interfaces where we manage our AI agents, reducing the need to traverse multiple websites. As AI agents become dominant, website owners will offer agent application programming interfaces (APIs) to provide information directly to these agents, streamlining processes. Although websites will still exist, they will evolve to feature AI-generated, personalized content for human visitors.

Large language models like ChatGPT and Claude will centralize user behavior in one app, integrating e-commerce seamlessly. Additionally, Google Search will adapt by integrating sponsored sentences to maintain advertiser revenues, blending them with generative AI search results. This shift is expected to revolutionize the digital landscape relatively soon, making our interactions with technology more efficient and personalized.

What would you do with seven hours a day back?

From Products to Experiences

In the industrial age, success was measured by the ability to produce goods efficiently at scale. Companies that mastered manufacturing and logistics dominated their industries. The information age then brought about a focus on data, information, and connectivity. The rise of the internet and digital technologies enabled businesses to gather, process, and leverage vast amounts of information, transforming how they operated and interacted with customers.

However, the experiential age transcends these paradigms by shifting the emphasis from products and information to the experiences that encompass them. Today, consumers are not just looking for high-quality products or comprehensive information; they seek experiences that engage their senses, evoke emotions, and create lasting memories. This is evident in the growing popularity of services and events that offer unique and personalized experiences, such as immersive theater productions, culinary tours, and adventure travel. For example, consider the difference between buying a pair of shoes in the past and today. Previously, the focus was on the product itself—its quality, durability, and price. Today, the shopping experience is equally important.

AI is set to revolutionize consumer experiences across industries. PWC research indicates that 45% of total economic gains by 2030 will stem from AI-enhanced products and services, fueling increased consumer demand.[6] This significant impact is expected because AI will enable the following:

- **Hyper-personalization:** AI algorithms will analyze individual preferences and behaviors to tailor products and services to each user's unique needs and desires.
- **Immersive experiences:** AI-powered virtual and augmented reality will create more engaging and interactive consumer experiences across sectors like retail, entertainment, and education.
- **Predictive offerings:** AI will anticipate consumer needs, presenting relevant products or services at the right time, enhancing convenience and satisfaction.
- **Dynamic pricing:** AI-driven pricing models will make products and services more accessible and affordable to a broader range of consumers.
- **Continuous improvement:** AI will enable rapid iteration and refinement of products based on real-time user feedback and use data.
- **Novel product categories:** AI will spur innovation, leading to entirely new types of products and services that address unmet consumer needs.

By driving these enhancements, AI is poised to dramatically increase the variety, attractiveness, and value of consumer offerings, ultimately stimulating demand and transforming the marketplace. Customers might visit a store that offers interactive displays where they can customize their shoes in real time or use AR to see how different styles look on their feet. This shift from a product-centric to an experience-centric approach reflects the core of the experiential age.

Recent research highlights a significant demographic shift toward preferring online experiences over offline ones, especially among younger populations. A survey by McKinsey[7] found that Gen Zers in Asia, particularly in countries like China and India, show a strong preference for online activities. They are more likely to shop online, engage with brands through digital platforms, and consume video content to make purchasing decisions.

This demographic is drawn to the convenience and efficiency of online shopping, with a majority favoring it over traditional in-store experiences. Additionally, PwC's Global Consumer Insights Pulse Survey[8] indicates that the trend toward online shopping has intensified post-pandemic, with many consumers globally not intending to return to their pre-pandemic shopping habits, further illustrating the shift toward digital consumption.

These findings underscore a significant movement, particularly among younger and tech-savvy consumers in regions like Asia, toward valuing their online lives more than their offline interactions, fundamentally reshaping consumer behavior and market strategies.

Evolution of Consumer Behavior

Consumer behavior is gradually shifting toward the experiential age, though this evolution is still in progress. So as you've seen, there's a growing trend where many consumers are beginning to prioritize experiences over material goods, but this shift is not yet universal or complete.

This emerging change is being driven by an increasing desire for deeper engagement and personalization among certain consumer segments. More and more people are showing a preference for spending their money on activities that offer memorable and unique experiences.

Examples of this trend include the following:

- Attending live events like concerts or festivals.
- Traveling to new destinations.
- Participating in immersive experiences, such as virtual reality adventures.

Imagine donning a pair of Apple Vision Pro glasses and finding yourself instantly transported into Alicia Keys' rehearsal studio. Today, with a demo delivered in the Apple Store, you can walk around her piano, listen to her voice's nuances, and even sense the studio's atmosphere. This isn't a distant fantasy; it's the kind of experience being created today, merging physical presence with digital engagement. Apple's retail stores have long been at the forefront of experiential retail. By integrating advanced technology like the Vision Pro glasses into their stores, Apple not only showcases the capabilities of their products but also creates an unforgettable experience for their customers. This blend of physical and digital realms enhances the shopping experience, making each visit to an Apple Store an adventure into the possibilities of their technology. By the way, the Vision Pro creates an AI Digital Twin to accomplish its feats!

Businesses are taking notice of this gradual shift and are increasingly looking to incorporate experiential elements into their offerings. This could involve creating more interactive shopping experiences, offering personalized services, or developing products that facilitate unique experiences. As technology continues to advance and social media amplifies the appeal of shareable experiences, we can expect this trend to continue growing.

As noted previously, this trend is particularly evident among younger generations, who value experiences as a means of self-expression and social connection. For example, instead of purchasing a high-end watch, many choose to invest in an unforgettable trip or a music festival that offers a sense of community and personal fulfillment. The rise of social media has further amplified this behavior, as sharing experiences has become a way to connect with others and build one's identity online.

Another example is concerts. Gaming platforms like Fortnite have redefined entertainment by hosting virtual concerts that attract millions of participants. A prime example is Fortnite's virtual concert by Travis Scott, which drew 12.3 million concurrent players, setting a record for the platform.[9] These events blend gaming with live music performances, creating unique experiences that go beyond traditional concert venues and reach a global audience. Similarly, Ariana Grande's Rift Tour in Fortnite attracted 78 million players, showcasing the massive appeal and potential of virtual concerts in the digital age.[10]

In the realm of retail, this change is manifesting in how stores design their spaces and engage with customers. Retailers are moving away from traditional store layouts to create environments that offer interactive and immersive experiences. For instance, a clothing store might host a virtual fashion show that enables customers to see garments in motion and order them directly from their seats. This level of engagement transforms the shopping process into an experience that is as important as the products themselves.

However, this shift toward the experiential age is an ongoing evolution rather than a complete transformation of consumer behavior at this point, and it is important to note that this shift is not uniform across all demographics or markets. Many consumers still place high value on material goods, and the balance between experiential and material consumption varies widely depending on factors like age, income, culture, and personal preferences.

Business Implications and Strategic Shifts

Although the experiential age is transforming many industries, it's crucial to recognize that not all products or services need to be turned into elaborate experiences. The key is to understand where enhanced experiences add value and where they might be unnecessary or even unwanted.

This is not as easy as it sounds. Per Accenture, over 88% of executives believe their customers' needs are evolving faster than their companies can adapt, and 64% of consumers wish companies would respond more swiftly to their changing demands.[11]

First, we will examine the approach to experiences and then the way AI can enhance the experience if that's the right path for customer value.

Balanced Approach to Experiences

Businesses must carefully consider where enhanced experiences truly add value and where they might be unnecessary or even detrimental to customer satisfaction. This critical understanding enables companies to strategically implement experiential elements, ensuring they meet customer needs without overwhelming them or compromising efficiency. Different sectors need to strike this balance: enhancing experiences where it matters most while maintaining simplicity and functionality where customers prefer it.

For example, there are differences among essential services, utilities, and time-sensitive services:

- **Essential services:** Some services, like getting a haircut, might not require extensive experiential elements. Many customers prefer efficiency and quality over an immersive experience for such routine tasks. A survey by ServiceNow found that 61% of consumers prioritize speed and efficiency in customer service interactions.[12]

- **Utility products:** For everyday items like household cleaners or office supplies, functionality often trumps experience. A study by McKinsey & Company showed that for utilitarian products, 73% of consumers prioritize price and quality over experiential factors.[13]
- **Time-sensitive services:** In sectors like health care or emergency services, the focus should remain on prompt, effective service delivery rather than creating elaborate experiences.

In fact, per a study by Medallia, there is a trend toward using AI to not only get educated on purchases but also on shopping for the best deals.[14] Generative AI is becoming part of the shopping journey. More than one-third of millennials and gen Zers say they've used AI for ideas about what to buy or where to shop. This includes comparisons of prices and quality.

However, even in these areas, subtle experiential improvements can enhance customer satisfaction without overcomplicating the core service. The following sections outline several key industry transformations happening today.

Fashion Retail Forty percent of consumers are willing to pay more for a product if they can experience it through AR.[15] Luxury fashion brand Gucci has embraced AR technology to enhance its digital shopping experience. Gucci launched an innovative AR feature in its mobile app, enabling customers to virtually try on sneakers from the comfort of their homes.

This AR product configurator works by using the user's smartphone camera. When activated, customers can point their phones at their feet, and the app overlays a 3D model of the selected Gucci sneakers onto the image. Users can cycle through different sneaker models and colorways, seeing in real time how each option would look on their feet.

The technology goes beyond simple visualization. It accurately represents the sneakers' materials, textures, and even how light interacts with different surfaces, providing a highly realistic preview. This level of detail helps customers make more informed purchasing decisions, potentially reducing return rates and increasing customer satisfaction.

Gucci's AR feature not only serves as a practical tool for online shoppers but also aligns with the brand's innovative image, appealing to tech-savvy luxury consumers. By bridging the gap between digital browsing and physical try-on experiences, Gucci has created a more engaging and interactive online shopping journey, setting a new standard in the luxury e-commerce space.

Banking and Finance The banking industry is known for its conservative approach to customer service. Today, banks are using digital channels to provide information and services. In the experiential age, leading banks like JP Morgan Chase are at the forefront of leveraging AI and machine learning (ML) to drive significant business value and enhance customer experiences.[16] In 2023, the financial giant expects to generate over $1.5 billion in business value from its AI and ML initiatives, capitalizing on an impressive 500 petabytes of data across 300 production use cases. This massive data use enables JPMorgan Chase to personalize products and experiences for its retail customers, creating more tailored and engaging interactions. Furthermore, the company is strengthening client relationships by employing advanced analytics and insights, enabling deeper understanding and more effective service delivery. This strategic use of AI and ML not only demonstrates JPMorgan Chase's commitment to technological innovation but also highlights how data-driven approaches can transform traditional banking services, improving both operational efficiency and customer satisfaction.

Retail Innovation Retail is rapidly evolving to meet the demands of the experiential age. Nike's House of Innovation stores are cutting-edge retail spaces designed to offer immersive and personalized shopping experiences, leveraging the latest in technology to enhance customer engagement. These flagship stores, located in cities like New York, Shanghai, and Paris, are equipped with features like AR, on-demand customization, and personalized product recommendations:

- **Augmented reality experiences:** Nike has integrated AR technology into its House of Innovation stores, enabling customers to visualize how different sneakers will look on their feet in various settings. This interactive feature helps customers make more informed decisions by providing a realistic preview of the products in a virtual environment.
- **Personalized shopping and on-demand customization:** Nike's stores also offer a high level of personalization, where customers can customize their products directly in-store. The integration of AI and data analytics enables Nike to tailor the shopping experience to individual preferences. Customers can use the Nike app to interact with products, access exclusive content, and even participate in community challenges. This focus on personalization extends to the ability to customize products on demand, making the shopping experience unique for each visitor.[17]
- **Innovative store design:** The House of Innovation stores are more than just retail spaces; they are designed to be

dynamic, adapting to the preferences and behaviors of local customers. The stores collect data through various Nike apps, which help in adjusting inventory and providing personalized recommendations. This creates a seamless blend of online and offline shopping experiences, where customers can engage with the brand in multiple ways—whether through self-service options or direct interaction with staff members.[18]

These innovations underscore Nike's commitment to creating memorable and engaging shopping experiences, blending technology with retail to foster deeper customer loyalty.

Balancing Experience and Efficiency

In the experiential age, striking the right balance between creating memorable experiences and maintaining operational efficiency is crucial for business success. This balance is further enhanced by adopting a business AI-first mindset, which leverages AI to optimize both experiences and operations. Although enhancing customer interactions can drive engagement and loyalty, it's equally important to ensure that these efforts don't compromise the core functionality of products or services.

AI can play a pivotal role in this balancing act, offering personalized experiences at scale while simultaneously improving efficiency. By integrating AI into their processes, businesses can make data-driven decisions about where and how to enhance experiences, predict customer preferences, and automate routine tasks. This AI-driven approach enables companies to create meaningful, tailored interactions without sacrificing the practicality and effectiveness that customers expect.

The Experience–Value Matrix

The following strategies offer a framework for businesses and AI First Leaders to navigate this delicate balance, helping them harness the power of AI to create impactful experiences and streamline operations:

- **Identifying core value:** Determine where your product or service sits on the spectrum between utility and experience.
- **Customer preferences:** Research what your specific customer base values most.
- **Selective enhancement:** Apply experiential elements strategically where they add the most value without compromising efficiency or core functionality.
- **Technology integration:** Use AR, VR, AI, and IoT to enhance experiences where appropriate, but avoid technological overkill in simple transactions.
- **Personalization versus privacy:** Although personalization can enhance experiences, respect customer privacy. A report by McKinsey & Company found that 40% of consumers are concerned about how companies use their personal data.[19]

This experience–value matrix, shown in Figure 4.1, helps evaluate and categorize products or services based on two key dimensions:

***X*-axis—Level of experience enhancement:** This represents how much a product or service is enhanced with experiential elements, incorporating aspects like technology integration (AR, VR, AI, IoT) and personalization.

***Y*-axis—Core value proposition:** This represents the fundamental utility or value that the product or service provides to the customer.

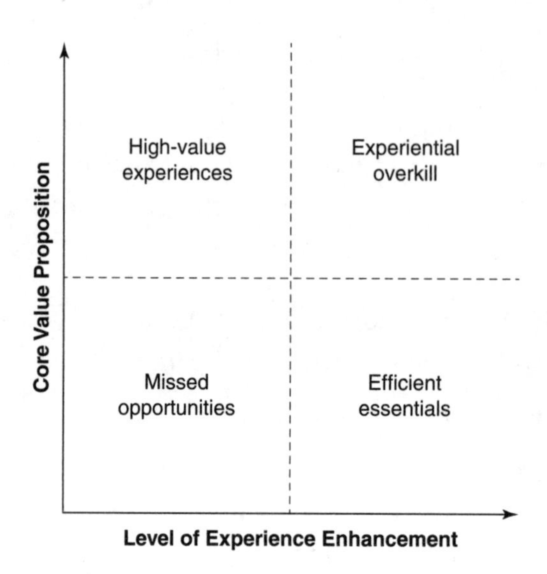

FIGURE 4.1 The experience–value matrix.

Here are the four quadrants of the matrix:

High-value experiences (top left): Products/services that offer high core value and are enhanced with meaningful experiences. These are ideal and should be the goal for most innovations.

Experiential overkill (top right): High in experiential elements but potentially compromising core value. This could represent overengineered solutions that might confuse or overwhelm customers.

Missed opportunities (bottom left): High in core value but lacking in experience. These represent areas where strategic enhancements could significantly improve customer engagement.

Efficient essentials (bottom right): Low in both core value and experience enhancement. These might be simple, utilitarian products or services where elaborate experiences aren't necessary or desired.

Using this matrix, businesses and AI First leaders can do the following:

- **Identify core value:** Plot where their current offerings sit on the matrix.
- **Analyze customer preferences:** Use research to understand where customers would prefer the offering to be on the matrix.
- **Plan selective enhancement:** Strategize moves toward the high-value experiences quadrant without overstepping into experiential overkill.
- **Guide technology integration:** Ensure tech additions move products/services upward or leftward on the matrix, not just rightward.
- **Balance personalization and privacy:** Consider how personalization efforts affect both axes, ensuring they add value without compromising trust.

This framework provides a visual and intuitive way to evaluate and strategize experience enhancements while keeping core values in focus.

By thoughtfully applying experiential elements where they truly add value, businesses can enhance customer satisfaction and loyalty without unnecessarily complicating simple transactions. The key is to create meaningful experiences that resonate with customers while maintaining efficiency and respecting individual preferences for simplicity in certain interactions.

Why Is the Experiential Age Important?

The experiential age marks a pivotal shift in how we interact with technology, consume products, and engage with brands. Its importance lies in its profound impact on various aspects of our lives, from personal fulfillment to economic growth. This era prioritizes the creation of meaningful, memorable experiences over the mere consumption of goods or information.

For example, Adobe Analytics research finds that online traffic to retail sites increased 304% year-over-year (YoY), and online traffic to travel sites jumped 553% YoY from generative AI tools, underscoring that consumers are leveraging conversational interfaces to support their shopping and travel experiences online.[20] For the AI-first thinker, this presents an unprecedented opportunity to leverage advanced algorithms and ML models to craft hyper-personalized, adaptive experiences at scale. By harnessing the power of AI, businesses can analyze vast amounts of data in real time, predicting customer preferences and behaviors to deliver experiences that feel intuitive and tailored to everyone, while simultaneously optimizing operational efficiency.

And the experiential age is driving innovation across sectors, fostering new business models and revenue streams. Generative AI is catalyzing innovative business models in brand interactions. Chatbots, currently the most widely adopted AI tool among US consumers, are reshaping customer service paradigms.[21] They're enabling brands to offer 24/7 personalized support at scale, significantly reducing operational costs while improving response times. Even at our startup, we are using customer support enhanced with AI to delivered more personalized experiences 24x7, enabling us to punch above our weight class. Beyond chatbots, text-based AI is creating new opportunities for dynamic, context-aware marketing communications.

AI-powered image generation is driving novel try-before-you-buy experiences. Virtual makeup try-ons and AI-assisted interior design visualizations are not only enhancing customer experiences but also opening new revenue streams and reducing return rates. These AI-driven innovations are redefining traditional industry boundaries, creating opportunities for cross-sector collaborations, and enabling brands to offer value-added services that were previously impractical or impossible.

It's redefining success metrics for companies, shifting focus from traditional key performance indicators to measures of customer engagement and satisfaction. An AI-first approach in this context involves not just implementing AI technologies but fundamentally rethinking business processes and customer interactions through an AI lens. This might involve using AI to create dynamic, responsive environments that adapt to user behavior in real time, or developing AI-driven platforms that can generate unique, personalized content or experiences on demand.

The AI strategist in the experiential age must balance the potential for groundbreaking innovations with ethical considerations, ensuring that AI-enhanced experiences respect privacy, promote inclusivity, and add genuine value to users' lives. By doing so, businesses can position themselves at the forefront of this transformative era, creating immersive, AI-powered experiences that not only meet but also anticipate customer needs, fostering deeper connections and driving long-term loyalty.

The Internet of Senses in the Experiential Age

As mentioned, the experiential age is introducing the Internet of Senses, where digital interactions engage all our senses, creating deeply immersive experiences. My brother and sister-in-law live in Denver, Colorado. One of the most innovative and immersive theme park experiences currently available is Meow Wolf's Convergence Station in Denver. This isn't your typical theme park with rides, but rather an interactive and surreal art installation that creates a truly unique, multisensory experience.

Here's what makes it special:

- **Immersive storytelling:** The installation tells the story of four alien worlds that have mysteriously converged in a cosmic event. Visitors become "memory travelers," exploring these worlds and uncovering a complex narrative.

- **Interactive art:** The four-story, 90,000-square-foot space is filled with over 70 unique installations created by more than 300 artists. Each room is a new, mind-bending experience that visitors can touch, climb on, and explore.
- **Multisensory experience:** The exhibits engage all senses with vibrant visuals, ambient sounds, textured surfaces, and even scents in some areas.
- **Technology integration:** Many exhibits incorporate technology, including responsive light installations, interactive projections, and even AI-driven experiences.
- **Nonlinear exploration:** There's no set path through Convergence Station. Visitors are encouraged to explore freely, discovering new details with each visit.
- **RFID technology:** Visitors receive RFID cards that allow them to interact with certain exhibits and track their progress through the story.

This attraction exemplifies the experiential age by creating a fully immersive, interactive environment that blends art, technology, and storytelling. It's a real-world example of how businesses are creating unique experiences that go beyond traditional entertainment models.

We are going to go beyond just seeing and hearing digital content. In the future, we can include touch, smell, and even taste. Please note many of these technologies are in the experimental stage but it's important that we know what's possible and what could be coming.

Here are some more real-world applications:

- **Touch (haptic feedback):** Haptic technology enables users to feel sensations in the virtual world. HaptX, a start-up, has developed gloves that let users feel the texture, shape, and movement of virtual objects. For example, architects can now "touch" their 3D building designs, feeling the smoothness of virtual walls or the roughness of stone textures.
- **Smell in VR:** Olorama Technology, a small Spanish company, has created a device that releases scents to match VR experiences. In a virtual wine tasting, users can smell the distinct aromas of different wines, enhancing the learning experience for sommeliers-in-training.
- **Digital taste:** Taste is the most challenging sense to replicate, but progress is being made. Nimesha Ranasinghe, a researcher at the University of Maine, has developed a system called *digital taste interface* that simulates basic tastes through electrical stimulation on the tongue. While still experimental, it opens possibilities for virtual food experiences.
- **Multisensory education:** zSpace, an edtech start-up, combines AR/VR with haptic feedback for interactive learning. Students can "dissect" virtual frogs, feeling the resistance as they make incisions, without the ethical concerns of using real animals.
- **AI-enhanced smell recognition:** Aryballe, a French company, has created a digital nose using AI. This device can identify and analyze odors, with applications ranging from quality control in food production to early disease detection based on breath analysis.

These innovations are just the beginning. Wouldn't it be cool to have technology that enables shoppers to feel the texture of clothes when shopping online and gauge the softness of a sweater or the stiffness of denim through their smartphone screens? I cannot wait!

As technology advances, we can expect even more seamless integration of our senses in digital experiences. The Internet of Senses is set to transform how we learn, shop, entertain ourselves, and even how we receive medical care, by creating digital experiences that feel increasingly real and engaging.

Strategic Actions for Embracing the Experiential Age

For businesses and AI First Leaders looking to thrive in the experiential age, several strategic actions can be undertaken. First, it is crucial to focus on understanding your customers deeply. This involves gathering insights into their needs, preferences, and behaviors through methods like surveys, focus groups, and data analytics. A thorough understanding of your target audience is essential for designing experiences that resonate and engage.

Next, emphasize the importance of experience design. Crafting compelling experiences requires creativity and innovation, ensuring that every touchpoint with your brand is memorable. Align these experiences with your brand values and customer expectations to create a consistent and impactful presence.

Technology plays a vital role in enabling and enhancing experiences. Invest in technologies like AR, VR, AI, and IoT, which can help create immersive and interactive engagements. For example, integrating AR into your product offerings can provide customers with a more engaging and informative experience, and AI can personalize interactions and recommendations based on individual user data.

Building emotional connections with customers is another critical component. Engage your audience on an emotional level through storytelling, personalization, and by delivering experiences that evoke positive emotions. This emotional engagement fosters loyalty and can turn customers into brand advocates.

Finally, continuously measure and improve your experiential strategies. Use metrics such as customer satisfaction, engagement rates, and return on investment to evaluate the success of your initiatives. Collect feedback and use it to iterate and enhance future experiences, ensuring that your approach remains relevant and effective.

AI-First Experiential Strategy Framework: PULSE

In the rapidly evolving landscape of the experiential age, businesses of all sizes can leverage AI to create transformative customer experiences. The PULSE framework—predictive personalization, ubiquitous integration, learning environments, symbiotic interactions, and ethical experience design—offers a road map for integrating AI into experiential strategies, regardless of a company's scale or resources (Figure 4.2).

- **Predictive personalization** forms the cornerstone of this approach. Small businesses can start by using AI to analyze customer data and predict preferences, tailoring their offerings accordingly. Medium-sized companies might implement more sophisticated systems that anticipate customer needs based on multiple data points, and large enterprises could develop complex AI models that create truly precognitive experiences, seeming to meet customer needs before they're even expressed.

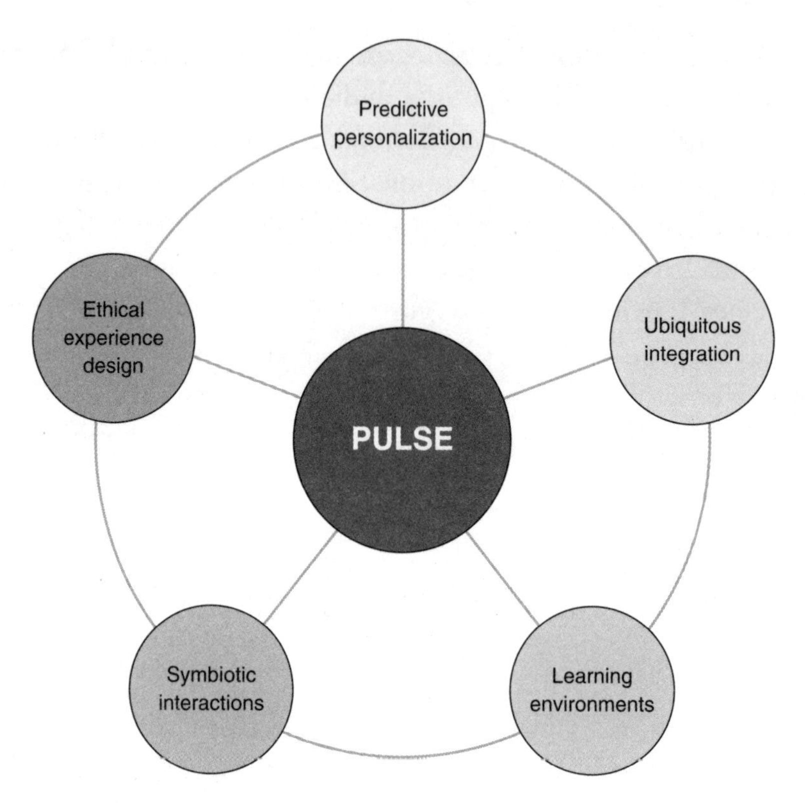

FIGURE 4.2 The PULSE framework.

- **Ubiquitous integration** challenges businesses to make AI an invisible yet omnipresent part of the customer experience. For a small local cafe, this might mean using AI to optimize their ordering system and inventory management. Medium-sized retailers could implement AI-powered ambient computing in their stores, subtly adapting the environment to customer preferences. Large corporations might create entire ecosystems where AI seamlessly connects various touchpoints, from online interactions to in-person experiences.
- **Learning environments** encourage businesses to create experiences that evolve with each interaction. A small

boutique could use AI to remember customer preferences and tailor the shopping experience over time. Medium-sized companies might implement more advanced systems that adapt not just to individual preferences but to collective behavior patterns. Large enterprises could create entire "living" spaces or platforms that continuously reconfigure based on user interactions.

- **Symbiotic interactions** focus on using AI to augment human capabilities rather than replace them. Small businesses could use AI assistants to enhance customer service, and medium-sized companies might implement AI copilots in their creative or problem-solving processes. Large corporations could develop sophisticated AI systems that work alongside humans in complex decision-making scenarios, each enhancing the other's capabilities.
- **Ethical experience design** is crucial for businesses of all sizes. Small companies can start by being transparent about their use of AI and ensuring user privacy. Medium-sized businesses might develop more comprehensive ethical guidelines for their AI use, and large enterprises could establish dedicated AI ethics boards and develop advanced systems for explaining AI decision-making to users.

Implementing this framework requires a shift in mindset across the organization. Small businesses can start by identifying one or two key areas where AI could enhance their customer experience and focus on those. Medium-sized companies might create cross-functional teams to implement AI across multiple touchpoints. Large enterprises could establish dedicated AI experience labs and integrate AI thinking into every aspect of their business strategy.

Regardless of size, all businesses should prioritize continuous evolution, contextual intelligence, and emotional resonance in their AI-driven experiences. They should also consider how to engineer serendipity—those delightful moments of discovery—into their AI systems and use AI for cognitive offloading, freeing up human creativity and higher-level thinking.

By adopting this AI-first mindset, companies of all sizes can create dynamic, evolving experiences that anticipate and shape customer expectations. In the experiential age, it's not just about using AI as a tool but about fundamentally rethinking how we create value and engage with customers in an AI-driven world. Whether you're a small start-up or a global corporation, the PULSE framework offers a pathway to creating truly transformative experiences that resonate in this new era.

CHAPTER 5

Everything Is Being Digitally Twinned

Welcome to the future, where everything from your coffee maker to entire cities has a digital twin. The term *digital twin* might sound like something out of science fiction, but it's very much a part of our present reality. Interestingly, although the concept has been around for a while, many people still find it a bit confusing. In fact, according to the Altair Global Survey, 22% of participants admitted they were unsure about what a digital twin is.[1]

The concept of Digital Twins is intrinsically linked with Artificial Intelligence (AI), as AI provides the analytical and predictive capabilities that bring these virtual models to life. Digital Twins leverage AI to simulate, analyze, and optimize their real-world counterparts, enabling businesses to make data-driven decisions with unparalleled precision. Adopting an AI First mindset is critical in this context, as it emphasizes the use of AI not just as a tool but as a core driver of innovation. This approach ensures organizations are prepared to integrate Digital Twins seamlessly into their workflows, unlocking efficiencies and creating smarter systems that learn and adapt over time.

As mentioned above, let's break it down. At its core, a digital twin is simply a virtual model of a physical object, process, or system. Think of it as a precise digital mirror that reflects its real-world counterpart. This can be as straightforward as a computer-aided design model of a mechanical part or as intricate as a digital replica of a complex manufacturing process involving artificial intelligence (AI). This fusion of physical and digital realms exemplifies the AI First principle while keeping human needs and experiences at the center of the technology.

In today's fast-paced digital world, digital twins are more than just cool tech—they are transformative tools that connect the physical and digital realms in ways we never thought possible. These virtual models enable us to simulate, predict, and optimize real-world objects and processes, providing a comprehensive and dynamic view of how they perform in real time. This predictive capability exemplifies how AI can augment human decision-making, creating a powerful partnership between human expertise and artificial intelligence. Over the past few years, the use of digital twins has skyrocketed, becoming a driving force behind innovation across various industries.

What Is a Digital Twin?

What makes digital twins fascinating is how they use data collected from various sources—like sensors and cameras—to create a real-time digital model that mirrors the actual state and behavior of whatever they are twinning.

Remember in the last chapter when I asked you to walk into an Apple Store and try out the Vision Pro headset? In that demo, you're essentially seeing digital twins of everything in the store. The products, the environment—they're all mirrored digitally to give you an immersive experience. Or think about riding in a Tesla. The roads that Tesla navigates are digita twins, created to help the car understand and drive autonomously. These examples show how Digital twins bridge the physical and digital worlds, creating dynamic models that enable us to simulate, monitor, and control real-world counterparts without the physical limitations.

Now, let's dig a bit deeper. Digital twins continuously integrate data, which means they are constantly updated to reflect the current state of their physical twins. This ongoing data flow lets us keep tabs on performance, predict when maintenance will be needed, and even test out improvements in a virtual space before making real-world changes. It's like having a crystal ball for engineers and operators to see how products and processes are performing and how they might behave under different conditions.

The applications for digital twins are vast and varied. They can help optimize the performance of complex machinery, improve the efficiency and sustainability of buildings, and even enhance urban infrastructure. Whether it's making sure that your car runs smoothly or designing a city that flows better, digital twins offer a powerful tool to bridge the gap between the physical and digital realms, driving innovation and efficiency across countless sectors.

Key Characteristics of Digital Twins

For me, digital twins are so powerful and versatile because of several core characteristics:

Real-time data integration is a fundamental characteristic of digital twins. Imagine your physical object or system continuously feeding data to its virtual counterpart. This constant stream of information ensures that the digital twin remains an accurate and up-to-date representation of its physical sibling. Whether it's a car engine, a manufacturing process, or even an entire city, this real-time data keeps the digital twin perfectly in sync with the real world. For example, in a manufacturing setting, sensors on machinery can send data to the digital twin, enabling it to reflect the current operational status and any immediate changes. This real-time integration demonstrates how AI First Technology can enhance human decision-making capabilities.

Beyond just mirroring the present, digital twins excel in simulation and analysis. They can model and scrutinize the behavior of their physical counterparts, offering a powerful way to predict future states and identify potential issues before they occur. Think of it as having a crystal ball that lets you foresee problems and test solutions in a virtual environment. This capability is invaluable in industries like aerospace, where engineers can simulate how different components of an aircraft will perform under various conditions without ever leaving the ground.

The ability to optimize and control is another standout feature of digital twins. This means they don't just show you what's happening—they also provide insights on how to improve efficiency and reliability. For instance, a digital twin of a power plant can continuously analyze performance metrics, suggesting adjustments to optimize energy output and reduce downtime.

A key enabler of these advanced capabilities is AI and machine learning (ML). These technologies empower digital twins to not only learn from the data they collect but also adapt and evolve over time. This results in deeper insights and more accurate predictive capabilities. Imagine a digital twin of a vehicle fleet that uses AI to learn from each vehicle's performance data, continuously improving its ability to predict maintenance needs and optimize routes for fuel efficiency.

Finally, digital twins are increasingly finding their place in the metaverse, where they contribute to creating immersive and interactive experiences that bridge the digital and physical worlds. This integration means you can interact with digital twins in a virtual environment that mirrors reality. For example, urban planners can use a digital twin of a city within a virtual space to simulate traffic patterns, visualize the impact of new infrastructure, and make informed decisions that enhance urban living.

In essence, digital twins are not just static models but dynamic, evolving systems that reflect, analyze, and enhance the real world in real time. Their ability to integrate data continuously, simulate future scenarios, optimize performance, learn and adapt to AI, and provide immersive experiences makes them invaluable across myriad applications. Whether it's improving industrial processes, advancing health care, or transforming urban planning, digital twins are at the forefront of innovation, driving efficiency and creating new possibilities.

How Is a Digital Twin Different from Business as Usual?

Digital twins mark a significant shift from traditional business practices that often rely on static models and retrospective analysis. In the conventional approach, decisions are typically based on historical data and periodic reports, leading to reactive management. Digital twins, however, offer a dynamic, real-time perspective that enables continuous monitoring and immediate responses to changing conditions. This is the power of using Digital Twinning with an AI First mindset. You are always looking at where AI and machine learning models can add value to your business.

Take manufacturing as an example. Traditionally, maintenance schedules are based on fixed intervals or historical performance, often leading to unnecessary maintenance or unexpected breakdowns. With a digital twin, the factory can continuously monitor machine performance and predict when maintenance is needed, optimizing the process and reducing costs.

In retail, traditional inventory management might involve periodic stock checks and forecasts based on past sales. This method can lead to overstocking or stockouts. By contrast, a digital twin of the inventory system can provide real-time insights into stock levels and predict future demand, ensuring that the right products are available at the right time.

Digital twins also excel in simulating and analyzing complex systems. Traditional models might not fully capture the interactions between different components of a system. Digital twins, however, can simulate these interactions in detail, leading to more accurate predictions and better-informed decisions. For instance, urban planners using a digital twin of a city can simulate traffic flows, noise levels, and the impacts of new developments, enabling them to make smarter, more effective decisions. This exemplifies how an AI First approach pushes beyond conventional analysis - using advanced simulations to solve problems that were previously too complex to tackle.

The Rise of Digital Twins in Banking and Finance

In an era of rapid technological advancement, the banking and financial services industry has emerged as an unexpected pioneer in the adoption of digital twin technology. Traditionally associated with the design and optimization of physical products, digital twins—virtual representations of real-world objects or processes—have found a new home in the world of finance, revolutionizing how financial institutions operate and serve their customers. This transformation aligns perfectly with an AI First mindset, where financial institutions aren't just digitizing existing processes, but fundamentally rethinking how AI can reshape their core operations.

A recent global survey by Altair[2] has shed light on this surprising trend. The banking, financial services, and insurance (BFSI) sector stands among the leading adopters of digital twin technology, with a staggering 71% of respondents reporting its use in their organizations. This high adoption rate is matched only by the automotive and heavy equipment industries, sectors where one might more naturally expect to find such technology.

What's driving this widespread adoption? The answer lies in the unique challenges facing the financial sector today. From fending off new competitors to meeting ever-increasing consumer expectations, from navigating complex regulatory landscapes to combating sophisticated criminal activities, financial institutions are under immense pressure to innovate and deliver exceptional products and services. Digital twins have emerged as a critical tool in this battle, helping organizations to optimize processes, monitor behavior in real time, and predict future trends with unprecedented accuracy.

The applications of digital twin technology in finance are diverse and impactful. Over half of the surveyed BFSI organizations use digital twins to optimize business processes, and 51% leverage them for real-time behavior monitoring and predictive analytics. This focus on monitoring and prediction is particularly crucial in finance, where it can be applied to prevent fraud, understand customer behavior, track satisfaction levels, and make more informed lending decisions. This exemplifies how AI First leaders think differently - they don't just ask how AI can improve existing processes, but how it can reveal entirely new possibilities. In fraud detection and lending, for instance, they start by asking "What could we achieve if AI were helping to make these decisions?" rather than "How can AI help our current decision-making?"

Perhaps most striking is the BFSI sector's emphasis on using digital twins for personalization. The Altair survey revealed that financial institutions were the most likely of any industry to cite the "personalization of products and services" as the area where digital twins had the greatest positive impact. This aligns perfectly with the growing demand for tailored financial products and services in today's market.

The value of digital twins extends beyond operational efficiency and customer service. A remarkable 93% of BFSI respondents reported that digital twin technology helps them create more sustainable financial products and processes. This finding is particularly significant given the recent surge in consumer interest for greener banking products and services that promote sustainable practices and investments.

As we look to the future, it's clear that digital twin technology will play an increasingly vital role in shaping the landscape of banking and finance. With 97% of current users in the BFSI sector describing the technology as important to their organization, and 71% considering it very important, digital twins are fast becoming an indispensable tool for financial institutions looking to stay competitive in a rapidly evolving industry.

The adoption of digital twins in finance represents more than just a technological shift; it signifies a fundamental change in how financial institutions approach problem-solving, innovation, and customer service. As the technology continues to evolve and mature, we can expect to see even more sophisticated applications emerge, further transforming the way we think about and interact with financial services in the digital age.

Why Digital Twinning Is Important

Digital twinning is becoming a game changer across various sectors, driving significant economic, cultural, and technological impacts.

From an economic perspective, digital twins are revolutionizing how businesses operate, leading to substantial cost savings and productivity boosts. Instead of relying solely on physical prototypes, which are expensive and time-consuming to produce, engineers can use digital twins to simulate and refine their designs in a virtual environment. This not only speeds up the development process but also makes it more cost-effective.

Culturally and socially, digital twins are reshaping how we interact with our environment and manage our health. In health care, they enable personalized medicine by enabling doctors to create digital replicas of patients' organs or even entire bodies. These replicas can be used to simulate treatments and monitor health conditions in real time, leading to more precise and effective care. In urban planning, digital twins help cities run more efficiently by managing resources better and planning infrastructure projects that enhance residents' quality of life. For example, a city could use a digital twin to simulate traffic flow and optimize road networks, reducing congestion and improving air quality.

The technological advancements that support digital twins are nothing short of impressive. They are powered by a synergy of AI, the IoT, and advanced simulation technologies. AI and ML amplify the capabilities of digital twins. They enable these virtual models to learn from data, adapt to changes, and provide predictive insights that were previously unimaginable. This means digital twins can continuously improve their accuracy and effectiveness over time. IoT plays a critical role by supplying the real-time data needed to keep digital twins in perfect sync with their physical counterparts. Sensors and connected devices feed constant streams of information into the digital twin, ensuring it reflects the latest state of the physical object or system. Simulation technologies add another layer, enabling detailed and realistic modeling of complex systems, which supports their optimization and control.

The future of digital twins is incredibly promising. We are on the brink of even more profound advancements as these technologies become more integrated and sophisticated. Expect to see deeper integration with augmented reality and virtual reality, making digital twin experiences more immersive and interactive. This could enable users to step into a virtual world that mirrors the real one, where they can interact with digital twins in a more natural and engaging way. Moreover, digital twins might evolve to become more autonomous, using AI to make decisions and take actions without human intervention. This could be crucial for developing smart cities and autonomous vehicles, where real-time data and decision-making are vital. As digital twins continue to develop, their role in shaping the future of technology and business will only grow, offering limitless possibilities for innovation and efficiency.

Case Studies and Examples of Digital Twins

Digital twins are transforming industries in ways we might have only dreamed of a few years ago. Let's dive into some compelling examples across different sectors to see how digital twins are making a real impact.

Health Care: Precision and Personalization

Imagine a scenario where doctors can monitor a patient's heart condition in real time through a digital twin created using advanced imaging and sensor technology. This isn't science fiction—it's happening now. Digital twins in health care are revolutionizing how we diagnose, treat, and manage patient care.

Take the case of a digital twin of a patient's heart. This virtual model enables doctors to simulate different treatments, understand how the heart is functioning in real time, and plan personalized care strategies that are tailored to the individual's unique needs. The result? More accurate diagnoses and more effective treatments.

Siemens Healthineers has developed a technology called the Cardiac Twin.[3] The Cardiac Twin is a patient-specific 3D heart model that combines anatomical and functional patient data. It uses advanced imaging techniques, including MRI and CT scans, along with AI algorithms to create a detailed digital representation of a patient's heart. The technology enables doctors to simulate various treatment options and predict outcomes, helping in treatment planning and decision-making. It can be used for planning complex procedures, such as valve replacements or other cardiac surgeries. The Cardiac Twin can also be used for ongoing monitoring of a patient's heart condition, allowing for adjustments to treatment plans as needed. It's worth noting that although Siemens Healthineers is a leader in this field, other companies like Philips Healthcare and GE Healthcare are also working on similar digital twin technologies for health care applications.

Beyond this, digital twins enable continuous remote monitoring and telemedicine, providing vital care for patients with chronic conditions or those living in remote areas where regular hospital visits might not be feasible.

Automotive: Redefining Vehicle Design and Maintenance

The automotive industry is undergoing a radical transformation thanks to digital twins. Think about Tesla's approach to vehicle maintenance and design.[4] Each Tesla car has its own digital twin that collects and mirrors data for real-time monitoring and diagnostics. This digital model helps predict when maintenance is needed, optimizing battery performance and enhancing the car's autonomous driving capabilities. But it doesn't stop there. Digital twins also streamline the design and testing of new vehicles. Engineers can simulate different driving scenarios and optimize vehicle performance in a virtual environment before a single physical prototype is built. This not only speeds up the development process but also significantly cuts costs.

Retail: Enhancing Customer Experiences

In the retail world, digital twins are creating immersive and interactive shopping experiences that blend the physical and digital realms seamlessly. Imagine stepping into an Apple Store, but instead of being there in person, you're exploring it virtually through a digital twin. Apple uses these virtual models to provide an online shopping environment where customers can navigate the store, view products in 3D, and make purchases as if they were actually there. This creates a richer, more engaging experience for customers. Retailers also leverage digital twins to optimize their inventory and supply chain operations, ensuring that products are available when and where customers want them, which enhances customer satisfaction and operational efficiency.

Supply Chain: Optimization

Mars, the global powerhouse in confectionery, pet care, and food products, has embraced digital twin technology to revolutionize its supply chain management. Leveraging advanced IoT services and AI, Mars has created a comprehensive virtual replica of its vast network of 160 manufacturing facilities.[5] This innovative approach enables the company to monitor and optimize its operations in real time, processing data from production machines across its global infrastructure.

The AI-infused digital twin has yielded significant improvements in operational efficiency, notably enhancing production capacity and implementing predictive maintenance strategies that have markedly increased machine uptime. Furthermore, the technology has proven instrumental in reducing waste, particularly in addressing packaging inconsistencies that previously led to product losses. By harnessing the power of digital twins, Mars exemplifies how traditional industries can adapt cutting-edge technologies to streamline complex supply chains, improve productivity, and minimize environmental impact. This case study underscores the transformative potential of digital twins in large-scale manufacturing and supply chain optimization, setting a benchmark for other global enterprises to follow.

Agriculture: Optimization of Crops

Farmers Edge, a medium-sized agricultural technology company, uses digital twins in combination with AI to help farmers optimize their crop production. They create digital replicas of farms using satellite imagery, weather data, soil sensors, and other IoT devices.[6]

AI analyzes the digital twin data to predict crop yields, detect early signs of crop stress or disease, and optimize irrigation and fertilizer use. Farmers can simulate different scenarios (e.g., changing planting dates or crop varieties) to make informed decisions. The system provides real-time alerts and recommendations, allowing for quick responses to changing conditions.

This application of digital twins helps small and medium-sized farms increase productivity, reduce waste, and make more sustainable farming decisions.

Dentistry: Simulation of Treatment

Digital twin technology is making significant strides in the field of dentistry. This technology involves creating virtual replicas of a patient's oral structures. These digital twins enable dentists to simulate various treatment scenarios, improving diagnosis, treatment planning, and patient outcomes.

For example, the digital twin can be used to anticipate the results of dental procedures, helping dentists to optimize their approaches before actual treatment. This ensures a higher level of precision and personalization in dental care. The technology not only enhances clinical practices but also boosts patient engagement by enabling patients to visualize and understand their treatment plans better.[7]

My dentist in Scottsdale, Arizona, just used digital twinning technology on me during my last visit. It was fascinating to see how this technology can be used for great value in small businesses, too.

Consumer Electronics: Innovating Product Development

The consumer electronics industry is harnessing the power of digital twins to drive innovation and streamline product development. Imagine a leading electronics company using a digital twin to design and test a new transparent TV. Engineers can simulate various design choices and performance scenarios in the digital twin, optimizing the product before ever building a physical prototype. This approach not only reduces development costs but also accelerates the time to market. Additionally, digital twins are employed to replicate marketing processes, enabling businesses to simulate different strategies and optimize their impact on customer engagement and sales.

City-State Planning: Creating a Smart Nation

Another real-world example of a digital twin in action involves one of my favorite cities in the world: Singapore. In 2014, Singapore embarked on an ambitious project as part of its Smart Nation initiative: the creation of a comprehensive digital twin of the entire city-state. Known as *Virtual Singapore*, the aim of this project is to develop a dynamic 3D model of the country that can be used for urban planning, disaster management, and public service improvements.[8] This digital twin of the city represents one of the most complex and large-scale applications of the technology to date, offering valuable insights into the core computing power required for maintaining real-time digital twins.

The foundation of Virtual Singapore's data collection system is a network of over 1,600 sensors deployed across the city. These sensors continuously gather real-time data on various urban parameters including traffic flow, weather conditions, air quality, and energy use. Supplementing this sensor network, data is also collected from public transportation systems, buildings, and mobile devices, creating a rich, multidimensional data ecosystem.

To process this vast amount of data, Singapore leverages the computational power of the National Supercomputing Centre, Singapore's petascale supercomputer, ASPIRE 1. With a peak performance of 1.286 petaFLOPS and 13 petabytes of storage, ASPIRE 1 provides the necessary horsepower to handle the complex calculations and simulations required for maintaining the digital twin in real time.

The software backbone of Virtual Singapore is Dassault Systèmes' 3DEXPERIENCE platform. This sophisticated system integrates myriad data sources and provides powerful simulation capabilities, enabling city planners and officials to interact with and analyze the digital twin effectively. To support the high-speed, low-latency data transmission necessary for real-time updates, Singapore has implemented a nationwide 5G network, ensuring that data from IoT devices reaches the central system with minimal delay.

Although the supercomputer forms the core of the processing power, the project also uses cloud computing services for scalable storage and processing. This hybrid approach allows for flexibility in handling varying computational loads. Additionally, edge computing devices are deployed in critical areas such as traffic management, enabling real-time decision-making with minimal latency where immediate responses are crucial.

The applications of this digital twin are diverse and impactful. Urban planners use the model to simulate the effects of new buildings on wind flow, shadows, and traffic patterns before construction begins, leading to more informed city development. In emergency scenarios, the twin can simulate various evacuation scenarios, helping to optimize the allocation of emergency resources. The model also plays a crucial role in energy management, monitoring and predicting consumption patterns to optimize the city's power grid.

However, the implementation of such a comprehensive digital twin is not without challenges. Integrating diverse data sources into a coherent model required the development of standardized data formats and application program interfaces (APIs). Privacy concerns necessitated the implementation of strict data anonymization protocols and transparent data use policies. The enormous computational demands for real-time updates are managed through distributed computing and continuous upgrades to the supercomputing infrastructure.

Despite these challenges, the early results of Virtual Singapore have been promising. The digital twin has been successfully used to optimize the placement of solar panels across the city, increasing renewable energy generation. It has also improved emergency response times by 5–7% through better route planning and has contributed to reducing urban heat island effects by informing building placement decisions.

The Virtual Singapore project exemplifies the significant computing power required to maintain a real-time digital twin of an entire city. It demonstrates how a combination of supercomputing resources, extensive sensor networks, advanced software platforms, and cutting-edge networking technologies can come together to create a powerful tool for urban management and planning. As digital twin technology continues to evolve, the lessons learned from this project will undoubtedly inform and inspire similar initiatives around the world.

These examples show just a glimpse of how digital twins are reshaping industries. From personalized health care and advanced automotive design to immersive retail experiences and smarter city planning, digital twins are driving innovation and efficiency across the board. These examples demonstrate how digital twins, combined with AI, can provide significant benefits to small, medium, and large businesses across different industries. They enable more precise decision-making, improved efficiency, and the ability to simulate various scenarios without real-world risks.

As this technology continues to evolve, its applications will only expand, offering even more opportunities to bridge the physical and digital worlds in transformative ways.

Strategic Actions for Embracing Digital Twins

To embrace digital twin technology effectively, consider these strategic actions. This strategic framework aligns closely with the concepts discussed in Chapters 1–4, particularly those focusing on multimodal interactions and enhanced customer experiences, while also addressing the accelerated pace of technological advancement driven by AI.

- **Explore real-world experiences:** Visit companies that are leading in digital twin technology. Engage with their processes to understand how they leverage digital twins to drive innovation and efficiency.

- **Involve your team:** Encourage your team to explore digital twin technologies firsthand. Organize visits to tech expos, innovation labs, or digital twin-enabled environments to inspire new ideas and approaches.
- **Invest in technology and training:** Invest in the technologies needed to create and support digital twins, such as AI, IoT, and simulation software. Provide training for your team to ensure they have the skills to leverage these technologies effectively.
- **Develop a digital twin strategy:** Create a clear strategy for how digital twins will be used in your business. Identify key areas where digital twins can add value and develop a road map for implementation.
- **Focus on integration and scalability:** Ensure your digital twin solutions integrate with your existing systems and processes. Plan for scalability to accommodate future growth and technological advancements.
- **Measure and improve:** Continuously evaluate your digital twin initiatives' performance. Use metrics like operational efficiency, cost savings, and customer satisfaction to measure success and identify improvement areas.

At its core, the framework emphasizes the importance of real-world engagement and continuous learning. Exploring real-world experiences encourages organizations to immerse themselves in practical applications of digital twin technology. This hands-on approach resonates with the multimodal concept discussed in Chapter 3 because it enables teams to experience firsthand how digital twins can integrate various sensory inputs and outputs to create more comprehensive and intuitive representations of physical systems. By visiting leading companies and engaging with their processes, teams can gain invaluable insights into how digital twins are transforming customer experiences across different industries.

The idea of involving your team dovetails seamlessly with the previous discussions on the importance of cross-functional collaboration in delivering exceptional customer experiences. By encouraging team members to explore digital twin technologies through tech expos and innovation labs, organizations foster a culture of innovation and adaptability. This approach is crucial in the context of AI-driven acceleration, where the rapid pace of technological advancement requires teams to be agile and continuously update their skills and knowledge.

The framework's emphasis on investing in technology and training addresses the critical need for organizations to keep pace with the rapidly evolving technological landscape. As discussed in Chapter 3, the integration of AI and multimodal interfaces is revolutionizing customer interactions. By investing in the necessary technologies (AI, IoT, simulation software) and providing comprehensive training, organizations can ensure they have the tools and expertise to create digital twins that offer rich, multisensory experiences to customers.

Developing a clear digital twin strategy is essential for aligning technological capabilities with business objectives. This strategic approach enables organizations to identify key areas where digital twins can add the most value, particularly in enhancing customer experiences. By creating a road map for implementation, companies can ensure that their digital twin initiatives are purposeful and aligned with broader customer experience goals.

The focus on integration and scalability within the framework is particularly relevant in the context of multimodal experiences and AI-driven acceleration. As customer interactions become increasingly complex and multifaceted, digital twins must be capable of integrating seamlessly with existing systems while also being scalable to accommodate rapid technological advancements. This aspect of the framework ensures that organizations can create cohesive, end-to-end customer experiences that evolve with changing technologies and customer expectations.

The final component of the framework addresses the need for continuous evaluation and refinement. In the fast-paced world of AI and digital experiences, the ability to quickly assess the performance of digital twin initiatives and make necessary improvements is crucial. This iterative approach aligns with the agile methodologies often employed in developing multimodal interfaces and AI-driven systems, ensuring that digital twin implementations remain effective and relevant in meeting evolving customer needs.

Of course, you need to select the right technology partner as well. Before selecting a partner, clearly define your organization's specific needs and objectives for digital twin implementation. Look for partners with proven expertise in digital twin technology, AI, IoT, and relevant industry-specific knowledge. Their technical capabilities should match or exceed your project requirements.

The framework provides a holistic strategy for organizations to harness the power of digital twins in an AI-first world. It acknowledges the multimodal nature of modern customer experiences and the need for rapid adaptation in the face of AI-driven acceleration. By following this framework, organizations can create digital twin implementations that not only enhance operational efficiency but also deliver immersive, personalized experiences that resonate with customers in the digital age. The framework's emphasis on continuous learning, strategic investment, and ongoing improvement ensures that organizations remain at the forefront of digital innovation, ready to leverage emerging technologies to create ever more sophisticated and engaging customer experiences.

The era of digital twins is here, transforming how we interact with and understand the world around us. By creating virtual replicas of physical objects and processes, digital twins enable us to simulate, analyze, and optimize in ways that were previously unimaginable. From health care to automotive, urban planning to consumer electronics, the applications of digital twins are vast and varied. As we continue to explore this technology's potential, it's clear that the future is digital and it's twinned. Embracing digital twins offers a pathway to greater innovation, efficiency, and customer engagement, positioning businesses at the forefront of the digital revolution.

CHAPTER

6

Tokenization of Everything

Welcome to the age where everything, from your favorite plushie to sprawling real estate, can be represented digitally on a blockchain. This concept, known as *tokenization*, is reshaping how we think about ownership and value in the digital era.

For AI-First leaders, tokenization represents more than just a technological shift - it's a fundamental reimagining of how value and ownership can be represented and transferred in an AI-driven world. These leaders understand that combining AI with tokenization creates powerful new possibilities for automation, verification, and value creation.

During my recent visit to the World Economic Forum in Davos, tokenization was one of the hottest topics of discussion among global leaders and business innovators. But what is it and how does it differ from traditional business practices? Let's start with a definition.

What Is Tokenization?

Let's start with the basics: Imagine you have a plushie that you adore. By tokenizing this plushie, you create a digital record of its ownership that resides on a blockchain. This digital token serves as a unique identifier for the plushie, proving that it's yours. Now, you can transfer, trade, or even sell this digital record, just as you would the physical item.

In simpler terms, tokenization is the process of converting rights to an asset into a digital token stored on a blockchain. This token can represent physical or digital assets, from real estate properties to digital art. By embedding the value and ownership of these assets into a secure and immutable blockchain record, tokenization transforms how we manage and exchange assets.

Blockchain and tokenization work hand in hand to revolutionize how we represent and transfer value in the digital world. *Blockchain* provides a secure, transparent, and decentralized ledger system where all transactions are recorded and verified across a network of computers. *Tokenization* leverages this blockchain infrastructure to convert rights to real-world assets or concepts into digital tokens. These tokens, securely tracked on the blockchain, can represent anything from real estate and artwork to financial instruments and voting rights.

AI-First leaders particularly value this combination because it creates a foundation for intelligent automation. While blockchain provides the trusted infrastructure, AI can analyze token movements, predict market trends, and optimize token-based systems in ways that would be impossible for humans to manage at scale.

The immutable nature of blockchain ensures that token ownership and transfers are recorded accurately and permanently, whereas its decentralized structure enables peer-to-peer token transactions without the need for traditional intermediaries.

Together, blockchain and tokenization create a powerful system for digitizing, securing, and trading various forms of value in a more efficient and accessible manner.

Key Characteristics of Tokenization

Tokenization is a game changer, and several core characteristics highlight why it's such a revolutionary concept. At its heart, tokenization transforms physical and digital assets into tokens that exist on a blockchain, providing a precise and tamperproof digital footprint. Imagine having a digital certificate that not only proves you own a piece of real estate or a rare piece of art but also records every transaction involving that asset. This secure and immutable record on the blockchain ensures that ownership details can't be altered, providing a high level of trust and preventing fraud.

One emerging term you'll hear in discussions about tokenization is *onchain*. Just like the term *online* became ubiquitous, often unhyphenated and seamlessly integrated into our lexicon, onchain is rapidly becoming a commonplace term. It refers to activities or transactions that are recorded on a blockchain. When something is onchain, it means it's part of this secure, transparent ledger, where every change is logged and verifiable.

Transparency is another key benefit of tokenization. Every transaction and change in ownership is meticulously recorded on the blockchain, creating a clear, traceable history of the asset. This is particularly valuable in sectors where verifying the provenance and authenticity of goods is essential, like in luxury goods or the art market. When a buyer knows that every previous owner of a valuable watch or painting is verifiable, it boosts confidence and trust in the transaction.

AI-First leaders see this transparency as more than just a feature - it's a strategic advantage. They leverage AI to analyze the rich data generated by tokenized transactions, extracting insights that can inform business strategy and identify new opportunities. This combination of tokenization's transparency with AI's analytical capabilities creates a powerful feedback loop for continuous improvement.

Efficiency is drastically improved through tokenization as well. Traditional asset transfer methods often involve a lot of paperwork and intermediaries, slowing down the process and increasing costs. Tokenization streamlines this by reducing the need for such intermediaries, leading to quicker, more efficient transactions. Imagine being able to transfer the ownership of a house with just a few clicks, bypassing the usual lengthy legal procedures. All of this can be managed onchain, making the process transparent and secure.

Tokenization also democratizes investment opportunities by breaking down traditionally illiquid assets into smaller, tradable tokens. This fractional ownership model makes it possible for more people to invest in high-value assets like real estate or art, which were previously accessible only to wealthy individuals or large institutions. It enhances market liquidity and opens up new avenues for smaller investors to participate. When these transactions happen onchain, they are secure, verifiable, and accessible to anyone with internet access.

Smart contracts, a pivotal aspect of tokenization, add another layer of functionality. These are self-executing contracts with the terms directly written into code. They automatically enforce agreements and execute transactions when predefined conditions are met. This automation not only increases operational efficiency but also reduces the risk of human error or disputes. For instance, a rental agreement tokenized on the blockchain could automatically transfer funds to the landlord when the tenant pays rent, streamlining the process and reducing the need for manual intervention. Everything is recorded onchain, providing a clear, tamperproof record of all actions.

The integration of artificial intelligence (AI) and blockchain technology is what makes tokenization so powerful. AI enhances the management and analysis of tokenized assets, providing insights and optimizing processes that were previously labor-intensive. Meanwhile, blockchain offers a secure, transparent ledger essential for recording and verifying ownership and transactions.

Together, AI and blockchain enable a seamless and efficient system for managing and exchanging tokenized assets, paving the way for innovative applications across various industries. As the term *onchain* becomes as ubiquitous as online, it represents the shift toward a future where digital transactions and ownership records are seamlessly and securely integrated into our everyday lives. Traditional business leaders might see blockchain just as a way to record and track ownership. But AI-First leaders think differently. They see how AI can spot patterns in all this data to prevent fraud, predict market trends, and create new business opportunities. It's like having a brilliant analyst working 24/7 to turn all this information into valuable insights and automatically catch any problems before they happen.

However, these leaders also recognize a critical challenge: as AI becomes more powerful at generating content and interactions, people will increasingly question what's real and authentic. While AI drives efficiency, it may also create distrust and weaken human connections. This is where tokenization becomes especially valuable - it can provide verified proof of authenticity, whether for digital content, credentials, or transactions. AI-First leaders understand this balance: using AI to drive innovation while using tokenization to maintain trust and verify what's genuine in an increasingly AI-generated world.

Why Tokenization Is Important

Tokenization is driving substantial economic benefits by enabling businesses to enhance operations, reduce costs, and boost productivity. As mentioned previously, in the real estate sector, tokenizing property deeds streamlines transactions, reduces the need for intermediaries, and cuts down on administrative costs. This not only makes property transactions faster and more affordable but also opens up the market to a wider range of buyers and investors.

In the world of finance, tokenization is revolutionizing how assets are traded and managed. Digital tokens can be easily traded on various platforms, unlocking liquidity for traditionally illiquid assets such as real estate, art, and even intellectual property. This enhanced liquidity creates new investment opportunities and allows for more dynamic and flexible asset management.

Beyond economic benefits, tokenization is transforming how we interact with and understand ownership. In the fashion industry, for instance, tokenization is being used to ensure the authenticity of luxury goods. By attaching a digital token to each item, brands can provide customers with a verifiable record of the product's provenance and authenticity, protecting them from counterfeits and maintaining the value of genuine products.

In the realm of digital identity, tokenization enables individuals to securely store and manage their credentials on the blockchain. This can include anything from educational certificates to rental agreements. By tokenizing these documents, individuals can easily verify their authenticity and ownership, simplifying processes like applying for a job or renting an apartment.

Case Studies and Examples of Tokenization

Tokenization is reshaping how we interact with and manage various assets across different sectors. AI First leaders should start to see blockchain data as a new valuable source for their AI models. Every transaction, transfer, and verification becomes a data point that can reveal customer behavior, market trends, and business risks. This combination helps leaders spot problems early and identify new business opportunities they might have missed. Let's dive into some real-world examples to see how this onchain technology is making a significant impact and why it's a game changer for customers and users.

Space Debris Management

In the vast expanse of space, debris from old satellites and defunct spacecraft poses a growing threat. Traditionally, tracking and managing this space junk has been a monumental challenge. However, NASA and other space agencies are now exploring the use of tokenization to tackle this issue.[1] Each piece of space debris can be assigned a unique digital token on the blockchain. This token not only identifies the debris but also records its ownership and the responsible party for its removal. This means that instead of just floating aimlessly, each piece of debris becomes an accountable entity. Moreover, this innovative approach could turn space debris into valuable, tradeable assets, creating a new market for recycled space materials. Imagine the potential economic benefits of repurposing this space junk into useful resources.

Authenticity in Fashion

In recent years, the luxury goods industry has faced growing challenges with counterfeiting and authenticity verification. To combat these issues, several high-end brands have turned to blockchain technology and tokenization.

A prime example of this trend is the Aura Blockchain Consortium, a groundbreaking initiative formed by luxury powerhouses LVMH (Louis Vuitton), Prada Group, Richemont (Cartier), and OTB Group (Diesel).[2] This consortium represents a collaborative effort to harness the power of blockchain for creating secure and transparent authentication systems. By working together, these traditionally competitive brands are setting a new standard for product verification in the luxury sector. The Aura Blockchain Consortium's approach enables participating brands to tokenize their products, creating a unique digital identity. This digital token contains crucial information about the product's origin, materials, and journey through the supply chain, all stored immutably on the blockchain. For consumers, this means unprecedented access to verified information about their luxury purchases, enhancing trust and brand loyalty.

One of the consortium members leading the charge in implementing this technology is Vacheron Constantin, a prestigious watch brand under the LVMH umbrella. Vacheron Constantin has integrated blockchain into its production process in a way that showcases the practical applications of this technology. As each luxury timepiece is completed at the company's Geneva factory, critical product information is uploaded and stored on the blockchain.

This information might include details about the watch's components, craftspeople involved in its creation, and unique serial numbers. By tokenizing this data, Vacheron Constantin offers its customers a transparent and tamperproof verification mechanism. Potential buyers or current owners can easily authenticate their watches by accessing this blockchain-stored information, effectively combating counterfeiting and providing peace of mind. This use of tokenization not only enhances the value proposition of Vacheron Constantin's products but also sets a new standard for transparency and authenticity in the luxury watch industry, potentially influencing practices across the broader luxury goods sector.

By assigning a digital token to each piece of clothing, brands can create a verifiable record of authenticity and ownership on the blockchain. This digital proof ensures that buyers are getting the real deal and not a counterfeit. Unlike traditional methods, where authenticity might be confirmed by receipts or expert opinions, this onchain verification is secure and tamperproof. This system can be extended to other high-end goods, ensuring that items retain their value and authenticity in the resale market, making the shopping experience more trustworthy for customers.

"Given this fashion example, AI First leaders in any industry could start exploring how combining AI with blockchain verification creates business value. Consider how every verified interaction could generate data for AI to analyze - revealing customer behavior, spotting market trends, and identifying new opportunities. In a world where digital trust becomes increasingly vital, this combination helps leaders both protect their brand and gain deeper market insights"

Sustainability

Sustainability is becoming a crucial factor for consumers, and brands are increasingly claiming their products are made sustainably. But how can customers be sure? Tokenization provides a solution.

The TREE Token represents an innovative approach to combining cryptocurrency with environmental conservation. This crypto-impact fund for forestry and climate aims to make a significant impact on global reforestation efforts.[3]

With an ambitious goal of leveraging 100 million euros over five years, the project plans to plant 100 million trees and plants in agroforestry climate projects. This massive undertaking is expected to sequester an impressive 33 million tons of CO_2 equivalent, making a substantial contribution to climate change mitigation.

What sets the TREE Token apart is its unique approach to funding. By tokenizing these sustainable assets, it opens up investment opportunities to the public, enabling individuals to coinvest in climate-positive agroforestry projects. This democratization of investment in environmental projects not only helps to fund large-scale conservation efforts but also provides potential financial benefits to investors, with expected returns of 3–7% per year. The TREE Token thus creates a win-win scenario, aligning financial interests with environmental goals and potentially accelerating the pace of reforestation efforts globally.

Another great example of using new technology for sustainability comes from COSOLAR, a community-owned solar power project in Rio de Janeiro, Brazil. In May 2022, COSOLAR teamed up with a company called Things Go Online to create a digital system for tracking their solar energy production.[4] This system uses a special type of online record-keeping technology that's very secure and can't be altered once information is added. It's like a digital ledger that everyone can see but no one can change without everyone knowing.

With this system, COSOLAR can accurately measure and record how much clean energy it produces. This digital record helps prove that the energy is coming from solar power and enables COSOLAR to be rewarded for producing clean energy. It's a bit like getting points on a loyalty card, but for generating solar power.

This approach makes it easy for anyone to see how much sustainable energy COSOLAR is producing, which helps build trust and encourages more investment in clean energy. The success of this project in Brazil shows how this kind of digital tracking could be used in other places around the world to help promote and support clean energy production. It's a creative way of using modern technology to help tackle climate change and encourage more people to invest in and use renewable energy. AI First leaders recognize that sustainability isn't just about tracking data - it's about proving real impact. When AI analyzes blockchain records of environmental initiatives, it can show which efforts truly make a difference and where to focus next.

Real Estate Ownership

Buying property often involves navigating a maze of paperwork and intermediaries. Tokenization is streamlining this process.

The application of tokenization in real estate offers a compelling example of how this technology can transform traditional markets. In February 2022, a significant milestone was reached when the first home in the United States was sold as a non-fungible token (NFT). The property, a 2,164-square-foot house in Gulfport, Florida, was auctioned for approximately $654,000. This transaction, facilitated by blockchain company DeFi Unlimited and real estate tokenization platform Propy, demonstrated the practical application of blockchain technology in property sales.[5]

Propy uses blockchain technology to tokenize real estate, making property transactions more secure, transparent, and efficient. Through its platform, Propy enables real estate to be represented as a digital asset, or token. This process involves creating a digital certificate of ownership, which is stored on the blockchain as an NFT.

Propy Keys are NFTs that symbolize ownership of a property by representing shares or full ownership rights to the physical asset. When a property is tokenized using Propy, it is typically held by a legal entity. The NFT linked to this entity grants the holder ownership of the property indirectly, bypassing traditional real estate transaction hurdles and enabling quicker and simpler property transfers globally. This approach enhances liquidity in the real estate market and opens up opportunities for fractional ownership, enabling multiple investors to own shares in a property.

The process of this sale illustrates the key benefits of tokenization in real estate. Instead of transferring a physical deed, the NFT represented ownership of an LLC that held the property rights. This digital approach streamlined the transaction process, reducing the need for extensive paperwork and intermediaries. The entire sale was completed in just over an hour through an online auction, a stark contrast to traditional real estate transactions that often take weeks or months.

Furthermore, this method opens real estate investment to a global market, enabling buyers from anywhere in the world to participate with ease. The transparency and security provided by blockchain technology ensure that all transaction details are recorded immutably, reducing the potential for fraud and disputes. This case demonstrates how tokenization can increase liquidity in the real estate market, simplify property transfers, and potentially democratize access to real estate investment opportunities.

Event Ticketing

The excitement of attending a big event like the Super Bowl can be marred by the risk of counterfeit tickets. The National Football League (NFL) has tackled this issue by implementing tokenized tickets. Each ticket is represented by a digital token on the blockchain, which serves as proof of the holder's attendance. This system drastically reduces ticket fraud and provides a verifiable record of participation. Fans can also keep these digital tokens as collectible memorabilia, adding a unique value to their event experience. Unlike traditional paper or even standard digital tickets, these onchain tokens are secure and tamperproof, ensuring a smoother and more secure ticketing process.

In addition, in collaboration with bands like Avenged Sevenfold, Ticketmaster has implemented NFT ticketing through the band's Deathbats Club NFT collection.[6] These NFTs offer fans exclusive access to live shows, preshow experiences, and premium seats. This approach enables artists to maintain better control over ticket distribution, reduce fraud, and enhance fan engagement by providing exclusive perks to NFT holders.

The 2024 Paris Olympic Games also used NFT tickets to enhance security, prevent counterfeiting, and provide operational efficiencies.[7] NFT tickets will not only ensure unique ownership verification and real-time tracking of transfers but also offer additional benefits such as dynamic pricing and automated royalties from resales. This innovative use of blockchain technology is expected to set a new standard for major global events.

Car Titles and More

The automotive industry is undergoing a significant transformation, with tokenization, blockchain, and AI at the forefront. These technologies are revolutionizing the way we handle car titles, turning an often cumbersome, paper-based process into a streamlined, secure digital system. CHAMP Titles, Inc., an Ohio-based start-up, exemplifies this innovative approach, leading the charge in the onchain revolution for vehicle documentation.

At the core of this transformation is the powerful combination of blockchain and AI. Blockchain technology creates a secure, immutable digital ledger for vehicle titles. This means that every transaction, transfer of ownership, or update to a vehicle's history is recorded in a tamperproof manner. The result is a drastic reduction in fraud risk and a significant increase in transparency throughout the vehicle's life cycle. Tokenization takes this a step further by representing each vehicle title as a unique digital asset, or token, on the blockchain. This allows for easy transfer of ownership and instant verification of a vehicle's status.

AI complements these technologies by enhancing decision-making processes for title applications. Machine learning algorithms can quickly analyze vast amounts of data, identifying patterns and flagging potential issues that might take human workers hours or days to detect. This dramatically speeds up processing times, reducing what once took weeks to mere minutes or hours.

The benefits of this technological integration extend far beyond state motor vehicle departments. Car dealers can complete sales more quickly and with greater confidence in the vehicle's history. Lenders can process auto loans faster and with reduced risk. Fleet managers gain real-time insights into their vehicle inventory. Insurance carriers can access accurate, up-to-date vehicle information, potentially leading to more precise policy pricing. Even service providers benefit from having a clear, accessible record of a vehicle's maintenance history.

CHAMP Titles' success in partnering with states like New Jersey, West Virginia, Illinois, and Kentucky demonstrates the growing recognition of these technologies' value.[8] As more states adopt these innovative solutions, we can expect to see a nationwide shift toward more efficient, secure, and transparent vehicle title management.

This revolution in car title management showcases the broader potential of tokenization, blockchain, and AI across various industries. By digitizing assets, securing transactions, and enhancing decision-making processes, these technologies are paving the way for more efficient, transparent, and fraud-resistant systems in numerous sectors beyond automotive. As this trend continues, we can anticipate similar transformations in real estate, intellectual property rights, and other areas where secure, verifiable ownership records are crucial.

California is also pioneering the use of blockchain to tokenize car titles, allowing vehicle ownership records to be stored and transferred digitally. This innovation simplifies the buying and selling process and provides a tamperproof record of vehicle history. Similarly, tokenization can revolutionize how we handle various documents and credentials, from rental agreements to educational certificates. Storing these records onchain ensures they are secure, easily accessible, and verifiable, streamlining many administrative processes in our daily lives. AI First leaders will look beyond single-industry solutions. The lessons learned from tracking car ownership can apply to any business that needs to verify and manage valuable assets. AI helps spot these opportunities and automate the entire process.

Art and Digital Collectibles

The art world is undergoing a digital transformation through NFTs. Artists can now tokenize their creations, turning them into unique digital tokens that serve as certificates of ownership and authenticity. This enables artists to sell their digital works directly to collectors, bypassing traditional galleries and auction houses. NFTs also create new opportunities for digital collectibles that can be traded and owned just like physical items. This onchain approach not only provides a new revenue stream for artists but also offers collectors a secure and verifiable way to own and trade digital art, something that was not possible with conventional methods.

A notable example of art being tokenized is Pablo Picasso's painting, "Fillette au béret."[9] This 1964 masterpiece was tokenized by Sygnum Bank, enabling 50 investors to collectively own the artwork by purchasing 4,000 tokens. This form of fractional ownership democratizes access to high-value art pieces, enabling a broader range of investors to participate in the art market.

Another significant example is the digital artwork, "Everydays—The First 5,000 Days" by the artist Beeple, which was sold as an NFT for $69.3 million at a Christie's auction, highlighting the immense potential value in tokenizing digital art.

Education Credentials

Universities or other educational institutions can issue tokens representing degrees, certifications, or completed courses. These digital credentials are tamperproof and easily verifiable by potential employers. The blockchain stores the complete educational history, making it simple for students to share their credentials and for employers to verify them. This system could reduce credential fraud and streamline the hiring process.

An example of education being tokenized can be seen with Learning Machine, a company that has partnered with the MIT Media Lab to develop the Blockcerts open standard for creating, issuing, viewing, and verifying blockchain-based educational certificates. This initiative enables educational institutions to issue credentials, such as diplomas and certificates, as digital tokens. These tokens provide a secure and verifiable way for individuals to store and share their academic achievements, making the process more transparent and resistant to fraud. Tokenizing educational credentials not only enhances security but also simplifies verification processes, enabling employers and other institutions to easily authenticate a candidate's qualifications.

This approach to tokenizing education helps democratize access to verified credentials, making it easier for people from all backgrounds to demonstrate their skills and knowledge. By using blockchain technology, these digital certificates are stored in a decentralized manner, ensuring that they are immutable and accessible long-term.

Music Royalties

Artists can tokenize future royalties from their songs or albums. Each token represents a fraction of the royalty rights. Fans or investors can purchase these tokens, essentially buying a share of the song's future earnings. When the song generates revenue through streaming, sales, or licensing, token holders receive their proportional share. This model provides artists with up-front capital and enables fans to directly support and benefit from their favorite musicians' success.

An example of music royalties being tokenized is DJ 3LAU's initiative through his platform, Royal.[10] Royal allows artists to tokenize their music royalties, creating limited digital assets that represent a share of the royalties generated by a song. Fans and investors can buy these tokens, effectively purchasing a stake in the future earnings of a song. This approach not only provides artists with immediate funding but also enables fans to financially benefit from the success of the music they support. By using blockchain technology, Royal ensures transparency and accuracy in royalty distribution, reducing the reliance on traditional intermediaries.

Another example is the use of NFTs by artists like Kings of Leon, who released their album "When You See Yourself" as an NFT.[11] This tokenization approach enabled fans to buy unique digital collectibles linked to the album, creating new revenue streams and deepening fan engagement. These examples highlight how tokenization in the music industry can empower artists, create closer connections with fans, and provide new ways to monetize creative work.

Supply Chain Traceability

Products can be tokenized at each step of their journey through the supply chain. Each token contains information about the product's location, condition, and handling. This creates a transparent and immutable record of the product's journey from manufacturer to consumer. For industries like food or pharmaceuticals, this can provide crucial information about sourcing, quality control, and authenticity. Consumers can easily verify the origins and journey of their purchases.

An example of food sources being tokenized is through the work of the company Silal Fresh, which uses blockchain technology to enhance traceability in its food supply chain.[12] By tokenizing food items, Silal Fresh can provide a transparent, immutable record of each product's journey from farm to table. This process improves food safety by enabling quick identification of the source of any contamination, thus aiding in faster recalls and reducing waste. The use of blockchain in this way also ensures that consumers can trust the authenticity and quality of their food because they can track its entire history through a simple scan of a QR code.

Voting Rights

Organizations can tokenize voting rights for shareholders or members. Each token represents a certain number of votes or a specific voting power. This system enables secure and transparent digital voting for corporate governance, community decisions, or other collective choice scenarios. Smart contracts can automatically tally votes and execute decisions based on predefined rules, increasing efficiency and reducing the potential for disputes in voting processes.

One notable example of tokenized voting took place in the town of Tsukuba, Japan. In August 2018, Tsukuba became the first Japanese city to introduce a blockchain-based voting system, enabling citizens to vote on local development programs.[13] The voting process used a digital identity verification system linked to Japan's "My Number" national identification cards, ensuring that only eligible voters could participate. This system aimed to enhance transparency and security, reduce the risk of fraud, and provide a more efficient way to manage and tally votes.

South Korea's test of blockchain election systems focuses on improving transparency and curbing fraud.[14] A small-scale trial proved successful, but scalability remains a challenge. Greenland (population 56,000) used blockchain in its 2021 elections, showing potential for smaller-scale elections as well as areas in need of improvement.

These international examples further show the potential benefits and current limits of blockchain voting.

In all these cases, tokenization represents a significant advancement over traditional methods. By moving these processes onchain, we gain security, transparency, and efficiency that were previously unattainable. This shift not only levels up the experience for customers and users but also opens new markets and opportunities, transforming how we interact with assets in our daily lives.

The Future of Tokenization and AI

We think of tokenization as a way to turn almost anything of value into a digital token—like transforming a property deed into a digital version that's easy to trade. Now, picture AI as a super-smart computer brain that can learn and make decisions. When we combine these two powerful tools, we're opening up a world of new possibilities.

Here's what this team-up will mean for all of us:

- **Smarter decision-making:** AI can help us make better choices about which tokens to buy or sell by analyzing tons of information quickly.

- **Easier access for everyone:** Tokenization makes it simpler for anyone to invest in things that were once out of reach, like expensive real estate or rare art. AI can make this process even smoother by personalizing recommendations.
- **More trust in digital transactions:** By using secure blockchain technology (which is like a super-safe digital ledger), tokenization makes online deals more trustworthy. AI can spot any unusual activity, making things even safer.
- **New ways to use and trade value:** Together, these technologies might create entirely new markets. Imagine being able to easily trade tokens that represent your skills or time!
- **Helping the planet:** We could use this combo to tackle big issues like climate change, by creating and trading tokens that represent environmental efforts.

As these technologies get better and work together more closely, they'll become easier for everyone to use. You won't need to be a tech expert to benefit from them.

Of course, there are challenges to overcome, like making sure these systems are fair and protecting people's privacy. But the potential benefits are huge. We're moving toward a future when managing and exchanging value of all kinds—whether it's money, property, or even ideas—could be as easy as sending a text message. So, although it might sound like science fiction, the combination of tokenization and AI is already starting to change our world. It's an exciting time, and we're all part of this digital revolution.

Here's what I imagine the future might look like someday with everything being tokenized:

Sandy woke up to the gentle chime of her smart home system.

"Good morning, Sandy," it said. "Your tokenized solar panels generated excess energy last night. The tokens have been automatically traded for credits on your grocery account."

She smiled, thinking about how far technology had come. Just a few years ago, the idea of her roof making her money while she slept would have seemed like science fiction.

As She got ready for work, she checked her phone. Her AI financial advisor had rebalanced her token portfolio overnight. It had sold some of her real estate tokens—tiny fractions of properties around the world—and bought into a promising new biodiversity project in the Amazon. Sandy loved how she could invest in saving the planet, even with a modest income.

On her way to the office, Sandy passed a construction site. She pointed her phone at it, and an augmented reality overlay appeared, showing her the tokenized ownership structure of the project. On a whim, she bought a small stake in the building. It was no more complicated than liking a post on social media.

At work, a tech writer specializing in blockchain and tokenization, was excited about a new project. She was documenting a revolutionary process where job seekers could tokenize their skills and experience, creating verifiable digital résumés. It fascinated her how this technology was making hiring processes more efficient and reducing fraud.

During her lunch break, Sandy visited a virtual reality art gallery. She admired a beautiful digital sculpture and decided to buy a fraction of it. The token representing her ownership was automatically added to her digital wallet. She loved that she could own a piece of art that existed only in the digital world.

As she walked home, Sandy passed a local park. Her phone notified her that the city was issuing tokens to fund the park's expansion. She bought a few, knowing they'd give her voting rights on future park decisions. It felt good to have a say in her community's development.

That evening, as She relaxed at home, she reflected on how tokenization had changed her life. She was able to invest in things she cared about, had more control over her assets, and felt more connected to her community and the world at large. The system wasn't perfect—there were still concerns about privacy and the digital divide—but overall, she felt that tokenization had made the world more accessible and inclusive.

As she drifted off to sleep, Sandy wondered what new possibilities tomorrow's tokens would bring. In this new world, it seemed like anything was possible. She looked forward to writing about these developments and helping others understand this exciting new technology.

AI First leaders face a critical balancing act: while they must imagine a future where AI and blockchain reshape every business transaction, they need to start with solving real problems today. Begin by identifying places where trust and verification matter in your current business - whether that's in supply chains, customer interactions, or internal processes - and explore how combining AI analysis with blockchain verification could create immediate value. This practical foundation will help you build toward those bigger future possibilities.

Strategic Actions for Brands Considering Tokenization

For brands looking to leverage tokenization, several strategic actions are essential. Start by evaluating which of your assets could benefit from tokenization. Consider factors such as the asset's value, transferability, and potential for fractional ownership. Not all assets are suitable for tokenization, so focus on those that align with your strategic goals and offer clear value in being digitized.

Understanding the regulatory environment is crucial because tokenization involves navigating complex legal and regulatory landscapes. Ensure compliance with local and international regulations and seek legal counsel to understand the implications of tokenizing your assets. This step is vital to avoid legal pitfalls and ensure that your tokenization initiatives are sustainable.

Investing in robust blockchain technology is also critical. Choose a blockchain platform that offers security, scalability, and interoperability to support your long-term needs. The right technology foundation is essential for successfully implementing and managing tokenized assets.

Educating your stakeholders about the benefits and implications of tokenization is equally important. Transparency and education are key to gaining trust and ensuring a smooth transition to tokenized assets. Inform your customers, partners, and employees about how tokenization works and what advantages it offers.

Finally, explore new business models and revenue streams enabled by tokenization. Consider how tokenization can facilitate fractional ownership, create digital collectibles, or enhance loyalty programs. These new opportunities can help your brand stay competitive and innovative in a rapidly evolving digital landscape.

Leadership Actions for Embracing Tokenization and AI

Navigating the tokenization landscape reveals surprising insights that aren't immediately obvious. As business AI-first leaders, understanding these nuances can be game changing.

Following are some aha moments I've encountered in my journey with tokenization and AI.

The Paradox of Transparency

Although tokenization promises increased transparency, it can create new forms of opacity. For instance, when we tokenized our supply chain, we discovered that the sheer volume of data made it harder, not easier, to spot irregularities. The aha moment came when we realized we needed AI to make sense of this tokenized data. AI algorithms could identify patterns and anomalies that humans simply couldn't see, turning overwhelming transparency into actionable insights.

The Talent Conundrum

Contrary to popular belief, successful tokenization doesn't always require a team of blockchain experts. I've found that diverse teams often drive the most innovative tokenization solutions. The key is having people who can bridge the gap between traditional business processes and tokenized systems. For example, we had a marketing specialist who, after some basic blockchain training, came up with a brilliant, tokenized loyalty program that our tech team hadn't considered. The lesson? Don't just hire for technical skills; look for adaptable minds.

The Regulatory Paradox

Here's a counterintuitive insight: stringent regulations can accelerate tokenization adoption. When we faced strict data protection laws, it forced us to innovate. We developed a tokenization system that not only complied with regulations but also provided better data security than traditional methods. This "forced innovation" ended up giving us a competitive edge. The takeaway? Don't view regulations as obstacles but as catalysts for creative tokenization solutions.

The Scalability Surprise

Many assume that blockchain-based tokenization systems are inherently scalable. In reality, we found that scaling tokenized systems often hit unexpected bottlenecks. The aha moment came when we realized that AI could help predict and manage these bottlenecks before they occurred. By using machine learning to optimize our tokenized processes, we achieved scalability that wasn't possible with tokenization alone.

The Identity Revolution

One of the most profound realizations was how tokenization and AI together are redefining digital identity. We started a project to tokenize customer identities for easier verification. What we didn't expect was how this would enable entirely new business models. By combining tokenized identities with AI-driven predictive analytics, we could offer hyper-personalized services that were previously unimaginable. The lesson? Tokenization isn't just about improving existing processes; it's about unlocking entirely new possibilities.

The Collaboration Catalyst

Perhaps the most surprising insight was how tokenization broke down organizational silos in unexpected ways. When we tokenized our internal processes, different departments suddenly had unprecedented visibility into each other's operations. This transparency, combined with AI-driven insights, fostered spontaneous collaborations. Teams that had never worked together before were now joining forces to solve complex problems. The takeaway? Tokenization can be a powerful tool for organizational transformation, far beyond its technical applications.

Leading in the age of tokenization and AI isn't just about understanding the technology; it's about recognizing these hidden dynamics and leveraging them for transformative change. By staying alert to these less obvious aspects, leaders can guide their organizations to not just adopt tokenization but to reimagine their entire business paradigm.

Tokenization is reshaping how we view and interact with assets, offering unprecedented opportunities for security, efficiency, and innovation. As you explore the potential of tokenization for your brand, consider how it can enhance your offerings, streamline operations, and open new markets. The future is digital, and tokenization is at the forefront of this transformation. By embracing tokenization, brands can position themselves at the cutting edge of the digital economy, ready to leverage the full potential of this revolutionary technology.

CHAPTER

7

The Convergence Concept

In the realm of technology, *convergence* refers to the powerful integration of multiple advanced technologies like artificial intelligence (AI), blockchain, spatial computing, and quantum computing. This integration is not just about these technologies existing side by side, but about creating a dynamic synergy that amplifies the capabilities of each. By combining these technologies, businesses can unlock new opportunities and achieve efficiencies that were previously unimaginable.

AI First leaders understand that convergence isn't just about adopting multiple technologies - it's about reimagining their entire business through the lens of these combined capabilities. Where others see individual tools, they see opportunities to create entirely new business models and customer experiences.

For example, AI has been transformative in analyzing and learning from vast amounts of data, enabling smarter decision-making and automation. However, when AI is integrated with blockchain, it gains an added layer of security and transparency.

Blockchain's immutable ledger ensures that the data AI uses is authentic, tamperproof, and traceable, which is crucial for maintaining trust and integrity in data-driven processes.

Furthermore, the introduction of quantum computing into this mix takes things to an entirely new level. Quantum computing can process complex computations at unprecedented speeds, significantly enhancing the efficiency and power of AI models. This means that tasks that once took days or even weeks can now be completed in a fraction of the time, opening new possibilities for real-time data analysis and decision-making.

But convergence goes beyond just technology. It encompasses cultural and community shifts as well. For instance, the rise of remote work during the COVID-19 pandemic accelerated the adoption of digital tools and platforms, changing how we interact and collaborate. (We have a converging crisis!) This cultural shift toward digital-first interactions has created a fertile ground for converging technologies to thrive because businesses and individuals alike seek more efficient and integrated solutions to navigate this new landscape.

Today, I work from home as part of a remote unicorn start-up, leveraging a convergence of advanced technologies to stay connected and productive. One of the key tools I use is Salesforce's Einstein, an AI-powered assistant that helps with various tasks such as market research and data analysis. Einstein quickly processes large datasets and provides actionable insights, which saves me considerable time and enhances my decision-making processes.

For communication, I rely on Lavender, an AI-driven email tool that optimizes my email outreach by providing real-time suggestions and analytics, making my communication more effective. Whisper, another indispensable tool, helps with translation, ensuring that language barriers are seamlessly overcome.

In addition to AI, augmented reality (AR) and virtual reality (VR) technologies play a crucial role in maintaining a sense of presence and connection during virtual conferences and meetings. I remember attending my first virtual conference in the metaverse a few years ago. Donning a VR headset, I found myself immersed in a digital environment where I could interact with colleagues and industry experts as if we were in the same room. The experience was not only engaging but also opened new possibilities for networking and collaboration, breaking down geographical barriers that had previously limited our interactions. Today, the metaverse is embedded with AI from avatars to actions.

By integrating these technologies, I manage to maintain efficiency, security, and a high level of engagement, demonstrating the profound impact of technology convergence in the modern remote work landscape.

Additionally, convergence can lead to societal benefits such as reducing the amount of work required to sustain our lifestyles, thereby enabling more time for creative and fulfilling pursuits. For instance, with the integration of AI and automation, repetitive and mundane tasks can be handled more efficiently, freeing up human resources for more strategic and innovative roles. Quantum computing could revolutionize health care by accelerating drug discovery and personalized medicine, and blockchain could ensure the security and integrity of medical records.

In essence, convergence is about harnessing the strengths of multiple technologies to create something greater than the sum of its parts. It's about finding innovative ways to solve complex problems, streamline processes, and drive growth and innovation. By embracing convergence, businesses can stay ahead of the curve and position themselves for long-term success in an increasingly digital and interconnected world. This convergence isn't just about technological integration; it's about the convergence of ideas, cultures, and communities, enabling us to navigate and thrive in a future where collaboration and adaptability are key.

Why Does Convergence Matter?

I believe that technological convergence is important and is affecting every one of us personally today and our businesses.

Let me explain.

Convergence multiplies experiential changes, making each innovation more impactful. Imagine using a smart home device that integrates AI, blockchain, and Internet of Things (IoT). AI can manage your home's energy consumption by learning your habits, blockchain can ensure the security and privacy of your data, and IoT connects all your devices seamlessly. When these technologies work together, the overall experience is exponentially better than using each technology in isolation. You get a smarter, safer, and more interconnected home environment that significantly enhances your daily life.

It also accelerates the rate of change that we have to manage and helps our teams manage through. Convergence accelerates the rate of change, driving rapid advancements and efficiencies. Think about how fast technology evolves; now imagine that pace doubled or tripled. For example, in health care, AI can analyze patient data to predict illnesses, blockchain can secure patient records, and quantum computing can process complex genetic information quickly. This integration speeds up research and development, leading to faster medical breakthroughs and more effective treatments. It's like putting technological progress on a fast track, benefiting everyone involved.

In addition, it enhances system resilience. Integrating diverse technologies enhances the resilience of systems, making them more adaptable to disruptions. For instance, in supply chain management, combining AI for predictive analytics, blockchain for transparent tracking, and IoT for real-time monitoring creates a robust system. If a disruption occurs, such as a delay in shipping, the system can quickly adapt by finding alternative routes or suppliers, minimizing the impact.

Like Waze, the satellite navigation software that adds resilience to our lives by finding the quickest route around a problem traffic area, imagine what such technology can do for a supply chain. This resilience is crucial in today's fast-paced, unpredictable world where adaptability can be a significant competitive advantage.

And it also accelerates the need for cross-disciplinary collaboration. Convergence fosters innovation by encouraging cross-disciplinary collaboration. It brings together experts from different fields to create hybrid solutions that tackle complex challenges. For example, a team of AI researchers, blockchain developers, and quantum physicists working together can develop a new secure voting system. AI ensures accuracy, blockchain provides transparency and security, and quantum computing processes vast amounts of data rapidly. This collaboration not only solves a significant problem but also pushes the boundaries of what's possible when different disciplines converge.

Finally, convergence opens up new markets and opportunities by enabling the development of innovative products and services. For instance, combining AI with blockchain and quantum computing can create a new platform for digital identities. This platform could revolutionize online transactions, making them more secure and efficient, and could be used in various applications from e-commerce to government services. By integrating these technologies, businesses can create new products that didn't exist before, tapping into new customer bases and revenue streams.

Convergence is not just a buzzword; it's a powerful force that multiplies the impact of innovations, accelerates progress, enhances system resilience, fosters collaboration, and opens new markets.

How Convergence Is Affecting Our World Today

The convergence of advanced technologies like AI, blockchain, and quantum computing is driving groundbreaking innovations across various industries. Following are several compelling examples of how these technologies are converging to create significant impacts.

Smart Agriculture

In smart agriculture, a powerful trio of technologies is reshaping farming practices: AI, IoT, and blockchain. This convergence brings unprecedented efficiency and sustainability to the agricultural sector.

Here's how it works:

- AI analyzes vast amounts of data collected by IoT sensors in fields.
- Sensors monitor soil moisture, crop health, and weather conditions.
- Blockchain ensures data transparency and security.

This synergy enables precise farming techniques. Farmers make data-driven decisions to reduce water use, optimize fertilization, and improve crop yields. The result? A more productive and sustainable approach to agriculture.

Dimitra, a global agriculture technology company, exemplifies this transformative power. Operating in 68 countries with over 100,000 users, Dimitra integrates AI, IoT, and blockchain to provide comprehensive insights. Its approach empowers farmers to enhance control over crops and livestock. It helps implement precision agriculture techniques. It reduces costs and improves productivity.

Despite the benefits, adoption remains low. McKinsey reports only 39% of farmers use farm-management software. A mere 18% use precision agriculture techniques. Asia lags particularly in adoption rates.[1]

Several barriers contribute to slow uptake:

- High implementation costs.
- Lack of personalized services.
- Logistical challenges in rural areas.

The true power of this convergence lies in creating a highly optimized, data-driven farming ecosystem. AI algorithms, fed by IoT sensor data, provide real-time insights on crop health and soil conditions. Blockchain ensures produce traceability from seed to sale, potentially increasing market value.

This system enables smart contracts that automatically execute actions. For instance, irrigation systems could trigger when soil moisture drops below a certain level. The outcome is increased yields, reduced waste, and improved food safety.

However, significant concerns arise. Questions of data ownership and privacy loom large.[2] There's fear that large agri-tech companies could exploit the vast amounts of data generated. Smaller farms might struggle to keep up with the technological complexity. As agriculture becomes increasingly digitized, cybersecurity becomes a pressing issue. There's also the risk of losing traditional farming knowledge.

Innovative solutions are emerging to address these challenges:

- Onchain data cooperatives enable farmers to pool data while maintaining collective control.
- Open-source initiatives develop accessible AI and blockchain tools for smaller farms.

- Agricultural education now includes data literacy and tech skills.
- Governments are developing regulatory frameworks to protect farmers' data rights.

As these technologies mature, we're likely to see more user-friendly interfaces and plug-and-play solutions. This will lower the barrier to entry for all farmers.

The convergence of AI, blockchain, and IoT has the potential to create a more transparent, sustainable, and equitable food system. We can work toward a future when technology empowers rather than divides. The goal? To cultivate a landscape where traditional farming wisdom and cutting-edge technology grow side by side.

In this future, farmers large and small can thrive. Consumers can trust their food sources. Our agricultural practices can nurture rather than deplete our planet.

The path forward requires careful tending. But the seeds of technologically enhanced, sustainable agriculture have been planted. With continued innovation, collaboration, and thoughtful implementation, we can harvest the full potential of these transformative technologies.

Energy Management

Combining AI, blockchain, and IoT in energy management systems can create more efficient and sustainable energy grids. AI predicts energy consumption patterns, IoT devices monitor real-time energy use, and blockchain facilitates secure and transparent energy transactions. This convergence allows for better energy distribution, reduces wastage, and enables peer-to-peer energy trading. Consumers can sell excess energy generated from renewable sources directly to others, promoting sustainable energy practices. If only AI existed, predictive analytics would be possible, but without IoT, real-time monitoring would be limited. Without blockchain, energy transactions might lack the necessary security and transparency, hindering the growth of decentralized energy markets.

For example, Bia Energy, based in Colombia, is an energy trader focusing on providing smart meters and a consumption analysis platform to businesses. It uses AI to analyze energy consumption data, IoT devices for real-time monitoring, and blockchain for secure and transparent energy transactions. This integrated approach enables businesses to optimize their energy use, reduce waste, and facilitate peer-to-peer energy trading, thus promoting sustainable energy practices.

In addition, start-ups are entering this space. GridX, a German start-up, develops IoT solutions for the energy sector, connecting and controlling energy generation and storage systems to form decentralized virtual power plants. It employs AI for predictive analytics and real-time data processing, IoT for monitoring and managing energy flows, and blockchain for ensuring secure and transparent transactions within the energy network. This convergence helps in better energy distribution, reducing costs, and enabling efficient peer-to-peer energy trading.

In the realm of renewable energy, Vortex Bladeless is reimagining wind power. This Spanish start-up is developing wind energy generators without traditional blades, aiming to address issues like noise pollution and wildlife hazards associated with conventional turbines. Its innovative approach, however, requires advanced technology to succeed.[3]

Vortex Bladeless uses a platform from Altair to revolutionize its development process. This shows the power of selecting the right partners throughout this process.

Here's how the convergence of AI and IoT is driving innovation:

- **Data collection:** IoT monitoring boards fitted to prototypes gather real-time data on wind speed, oscillation patterns, and energy output. This constant stream of information forms the foundation for analysis and improvement.
- **AI-powered analytics:** Altair's platform employs machine learning algorithms to analyze the collected data. These AI systems identify patterns and suggest optimizations that human engineers might miss, accelerating the refinement of designs.
- **Digital twins:** Virtual replicas of physical aerogenerators enable extensive testing without the need for multiple physical prototypes. This capability significantly reduces development time and costs.
- **Predictive maintenance:** By analyzing performance data, the AI system can predict when maintenance is needed before issues arise, reducing downtime and extending equipment lifespan.

The impact of this technological convergence on Vortex Bladeless has been substantial:

- Development cycles have shortened from months to weeks.
- Energy production efficiency has improved through AI-driven optimizations.
- Overall costs have decreased, making bladeless wind energy more competitive.
- Environmental impact has been reduced, with quieter operation and lower risk to wildlife.

This story illustrates the power of AI and IoT convergence in driving innovation. By harnessing these technologies, Vortex

Bladeless is not only advancing its unique approach to wind energy but also contributing to the broader evolution of the renewable energy sector. As we face global energy challenges, such innovations demonstrate how technology can help us develop more efficient, environmentally friendly power sources.

The Vortex Bladeless story teaches us that the future of renewable energy lies not just in new mechanical designs but also in the intelligent application of data and analytics. It shows how AI and IoT can work together to transform ideas into reality, potentially reshaping our approach to harnessing natural resources for energy production.

Health Care Diagnostics

AI, blockchain, and quantum computing are revolutionizing health care diagnostics. AI analyzes medical images and patient data to detect diseases early. Blockchain secures patient records, ensuring data privacy and integrity. Quantum computing accelerates complex genetic analyses and drug discovery processes. Early and accurate diagnosis, personalized treatment plans, and faster drug development are possible with this convergence. Patients receive better care, and health care providers can offer more effective treatments. If only AI existed, diagnostics would improve, but data security and privacy might be compromised. Without quantum computing, the speed of genetic analyses and drug discovery would be significantly slower, delaying advancements in personalized medicine.

One company using AI and blockchain is Mediledger, a blockchain network used by major pharmaceutical companies and hospitals to track drug supply chains, enhancing patient safety by ensuring drug authenticity and reducing counterfeits. It incorporates AI for predictive analytics and IoT for real-time tracking.

Another real-world example of combining AI, blockchain, and quantum computing in health care is seen with the Cleveland Clinic. The Cleveland Clinic has partnered with IBM to leverage quantum computing for accelerating health research.[4] This collaboration focuses on using quantum computing to enhance drug design and genetic analysis, significantly speeding up the process and providing more accurate results. IBM's quantum systems, integrated with AI for data analysis and blockchain for securing patient data, demonstrate how these technologies converge to revolutionize health care diagnostics and treatment.

Financial Services

In financial services, AI, blockchain, and quantum computing combine to enhance security, efficiency, and decision-making. AI detects fraudulent transactions, blockchain secures financial records, and quantum computing optimizes portfolio management and risk assessment. This convergence creates a more secure, transparent, and efficient financial system. Financial institutions can offer better services, reduce fraud, and make more informed investment decisions. If only AI existed, fraud detection would improve, but without blockchain, the security of financial records would be at risk. Without quantum computing, the optimization of complex financial models would be slower, affecting the quality of financial services.

One company combining AI, blockchain, and quantum computing in the financial services sector is HSBC. HSBC has explored various use cases, such as cybersecurity, fraud detection, and natural language processing. It leverages AI for advanced data analytics, blockchain for securing transactions with quantum-hardened cryptographic keys, and quantum computing for enhancing fraud detection and risk management processes.[5]

HSBC's initiatives include using Quantum Origin, a platform that generates cryptographic keys using quantum computers, providing stronger security for financial transactions. Additionally, it is exploring quantum machine learning to improve fraud detection and quantum natural language processing to enhance customer service.

And it's not just industries but functional areas will change, too.

Marketing

AI algorithms now predict consumer needs with uncanny accuracy, using data from vast IoT networks. Personal AI assistants filter marketing messages, ensuring relevance and value for each individual.

Augmented reality has transformed the advertising landscape. Every surface can become a personalized ad space, visible only to the intended viewer. This creates immersive, context-aware experiences that feel more like helpful suggestions than intrusive marketing.

Blockchain technology has ushered in a new era of data privacy and value exchange in marketing. Consumers now control their personal data, choosing what to share with brands. In return, they receive direct compensation for their attention and data through micro-transactions.

Key impacts of this convergence include the following:

- Hyper-personalized marketing experiences.
- Improved data privacy and consumer control.
- Ethical marketing practices enforced by regulations.
- Real-time strategy adjustments based on global sentiment analysis.

The concept of market segments has evolved into "segments of one," with every interaction uniquely tailored to the individual. This precision targeting, combined with immersive experiences and transparent data practices, has created more meaningful and valuable interactions between brands and consumers.

Unilever's embrace of AI, IoT, and blockchain in marketing is nothing short of revolutionary.[6]

Imagine knowing exactly what a customer wants before they do. That's the power of AI in marketing. Unilever uses AI to do the following:

- Analyze vast amounts of data quickly.
- Predict consumer trends.
- Personalize ads for individual customers.

This means Unilever can create ads that feel like they're speaking directly to you. No more one-size-fits-all commercials!

IoT devices, like smart fridges or connected packaging, give Unilever real-time data about how people use their products. It's like having a direct line to customers' habits and preferences. This information helps Unilever create products people actually want and market them at just the right moment.

Blockchain might sound complicated, but for Unilever, it's all about trust and transparency. By using blockchain in ad buying, Unilever ensures that their ads are seen by real people, not bots. It's like having a foolproof receipt for every ad placement. This saves money and builds trust with customers.

The real magic happens when Unilever combines these technologies. AI analyzes data from IoT devices to predict trends, and blockchain ensures the resulting ads are delivered honestly and efficiently. It's a powerful trio that's transforming how Unilever connects with customers. For Unilever, this tech cocktail means smarter spending, happier customers, and a big leap ahead of the competition.

In plain English? Unilever can now market to you like a friend who knows you really well, instead of a stranger shouting from a billboard. That's pretty exciting stuff!

Sales

The sales profession has also been transformed by AI, IoT, and blockchain technologies. AI now handles routine tasks such as lead qualification and initial outreach. This frees human sales professionals to focus on building complex relationships and solving intricate problems.

VR and AR have blurred the lines between in-person and remote sales. Salespeople can create immersive product demonstrations, enabling clients to experience products in their own environments before they're even manufactured.

Blockchain-powered smart contracts have streamlined the sales process. Deals are automatically executed when predefined conditions are met, dramatically reducing sales cycles and eliminating friction points.

The IoT has created new sales paradigms:

- Products can initiate their own sales processes for replacements or upgrades.
- AI sales assistants provide real-time insights during client interactions.
- Predictive analytics enable remarkably accurate sales forecasting.

The role of salespeople has evolved into that of "value architects." They use AI-enhanced insights to craft complex solutions that address both current needs and anticipated future challenges.

This convergence in sales has resulted in faster cycles, more complex solution building, and an increased focus on relationship building. The seamless integration of technology has made sales processes more efficient and effective than ever before.

Carrefour, the French retail giant, is shaking things up with some cool tech tricks.[7] Here's what they're doing:

- Using blockchain to track where food comes from.
- Letting AI figure out what deals you'll love.
- Employing smart devices to keep shelves stocked.

So why is this such a big deal? Let's break it down.

Imagine knowing exactly where your veggies came from, from farm to fork. That's what Carrefour's blockchain does. It's like having a digital diary for each product. Customers love this because it builds trust. When people trust a store, they're more likely to shop there. It's that simple.

Now, think about getting a coupon for your favorite snack just when you're craving it. Spooky? Nope, just AI doing its thing. Carrefour uses AI to predict what you might want to buy. This means happier customers and more sales. Win-win!

Last, Carrefour uses IoT (that's tech-speak for smart devices) to manage inventory. No more empty shelves or wasted food. It's like having a crystal ball that tells them exactly what to stock and when.

Put it all together, and you've got a shopping experience that's more personal, more trustworthy, and more efficient. For Carrefour, this means loyal customers, less waste, and bigger profits. In the cutthroat world of retail, that's not just nice to have—it's a game changer. Carrefour isn't just selling groceries anymore; they're selling a smarter way to shop.

In both marketing and sales, the fusion of technology has created a landscape of precision targeting, immersive experiences, and frictionless transactions. The result is a more dynamic, responsive, and value-driven marketplace.

Immersive Retail Experiences

The convergence of AI, blockchain, spatial computing, and IoT is transforming the retail sector. AI personalizes shopping experiences by analyzing consumer behavior, spatial computing creates immersive virtual shopping environments, IoT tracks inventory and consumer interactions in real time, and blockchain secures transaction data. This convergence enables retailers to offer highly personalized and interactive shopping experiences, both online and in physical stores. Customers can virtually try on clothes, view products in 3D, and receive tailored recommendations, enhancing their overall shopping experience. If only AI existed, personalized recommendations would be possible, but without spatial computing, the immersive experience would be missing. Without IoT, real-time tracking of inventory and consumer behavior would be limited, and without blockchain, transaction security could be compromised.

One company currently leveraging AI, blockchain, spatial computing, and IoT for an immersive shopping experience is H&M.[8] H&M has experimented with an AR app that enables customers to see digital fashion models wearing the latest clothing collections when they point their smartphone cameras at in-store signs. This innovative use of augmented reality enhances the shopping experience by making it interactive and engaging, enabling customers to visualize products in a new way.

Additionally, home improvement retailer Lowe's showcased its use of AI, AR, and IoT to enhance omnichannel commerce.[9] By integrating these technologies, Lowe's aims to unify the in-store and online shopping experiences. This includes AI-powered chatbots for customer assistance, AR devices for product visualization, and IoT-enabled smart inventory management systems that streamline operations and improve customer engagement.

Advanced Urban Planning

Urban planning is being revolutionized by the convergence of AI, blockchain, spatial computing, and IoT. AI analyzes urban data to optimize city planning, spatial computing creates detailed 3D models of urban environments, IoT sensors monitor real-time city dynamics, and blockchain ensures transparent and secure data management. This convergence enables more efficient and sustainable city planning. Urban planners can visualize and simulate city changes in 3D, make data-driven decisions to improve infrastructure, and ensure that all data is secure and transparent. If only AI existed, data analysis for city planning would improve, but without spatial computing, detailed 3D visualization and simulation would be absent. Without IoT, real-time monitoring of city dynamics would be limited, and without blockchain, data security and transparency could be compromised.

One real-world example of such convergence in urban planning is the city of Helsinki, Finland. Helsinki uses these technologies to enhance city planning and improve residents' quality of life. AI analyzes urban data for optimal planning, spatial computing creates detailed 3D models for visualization, IoT sensors monitor real-time city dynamics, and blockchain ensures secure and transparent data management. This convergence enables efficient and sustainable urban development, ensuring data integrity and fostering community engagement.

This convergence of AI, IoT, and blockchain has not just improved existing systems—it has fundamentally reshaped how society functions. Privacy concerns and the digital divide have been addressed through strict regulations and global initiatives to ensure technology access. The result is a world that's more connected, efficient, and equitable than ever before.

As we stand in this transformed world of the future, we realize that the true power of these technologies lies not in their individual capabilities, but in their seamless integration into the very fabric of our lives. The convergence revolution has ushered in an era of unprecedented innovation, sustainability, and human potential.

Brands and Leaders Need to Pay Attention

In my leadership journey, I've seen firsthand how embracing convergence can drive success. Brands and leaders should adopt an AI First mindset by continuously monitoring emerging technologies and fostering a culture of innovation. This proactive approach enables organizations to stay ahead and leverage new opportunities. For example, during my time at IBM, we combined AI and quantum computing to develop more efficient data analysis methods, showcasing the power of convergence.

I'm an advisor to several start-ups and I've seen them use these technologies to "punch above their weight." They have leveraged AI to create a 24/7 operation that rivals much larger competitors. They implemented an AI system that analyzes data from multiple sources—voice calls, emails, and tweets—to provide round-the-clock customer support and generate valuable insights. This AI assistant handles basic inquiries, prioritizes urgent matters, and even predicts customer needs based on patterns in the data.

They also integrated blockchain technology to securely manage sensitive customer information, which has become a key differentiator. As a result, their small team can provide responsive, personalized service at any hour, significantly improving customer satisfaction and helping us win contracts with larger enterprises. This AI-driven approach has enabled them to compete successfully against industry giants despite limited resources.

Encouraging cross-disciplinary collaboration is essential. By integrating experts from various fields, we can develop innovative solutions that harness the combined strengths of multiple technologies. Creating collaborative workspaces and promoting teamwork are vital to achieving this.

Agility is key in a rapidly evolving landscape. Brands should implement agile strategies, breaking down projects into manageable tasks and iterating based on feedback. This approach enabled us to quickly adapt and innovate, keeping us flexible and responsive to change.

Data security and ethics are paramount. As convergence intensifies, ensuring robust data protection and promoting ethical practices in AI and blockchain applications is crucial. Prioritizing transparency and responsibility builds trust with users.

Engaging with stakeholders is essential for successful convergence. By involving customers, employees, partners, and regulators in our initiatives, we gained valuable insights and built trust. Regular updates and collaborative decision-making processes were key in aligning our efforts with broader societal goals.

Leveraging partnerships and ecosystems amplifies the potential of convergence. Collaborating with technology providers and research institutions provided access to new knowledge and resources.

Leaders as AI-First Thinkers in the Age of Technological Convergence

As we navigate the intricate landscape where AI converges with spatial computing, blockchain, IoT, and other emerging technologies, leaders must evolve into convergence-savvy, AI-first thinkers.

This shift isn't just about adopting new tools; it's a fundamental reimagining of leadership in a hyper-connected, AI-driven world. Here's how you can lead the way in your organization:

- **Cultivate a holistic understanding:** Don't silo your knowledge. Instead, strive to grasp how AI can enhance blockchain's security, how it can make sense of vast IoT data streams, or how it can create more immersive spatial computing experiences. This interconnected perspective is crucial for identifying breakthrough opportunities.
- **Foster a culture of convergent innovation:** Encourage your teams to think beyond single-technology solutions. Set up cross-functional "convergence labs" where AI experts collaborate with blockchain developers, IoT specialists, and spatial computing designers. The next big innovation might arise from the intersection of these fields.
- **Develop a keen eye for convergence-driven disruption:** AI alone is powerful, but AI combined with blockchain and IoT could revolutionize supply chains. AI melded with spatial computing could transform remote work. Stay alert to how these technological synergies might upend your industry.
- **Prioritize ethical considerations in convergent systems:** As AI interacts with blockchain's immutability or IoT's pervasive data collection, new ethical challenges emerge. Establish a multidisciplinary ethics board that can navigate the complex implications of these converging technologies.
- **Embrace radical transparency:** As AI systems increasingly intertwine with blockchain, IoT, and spatial computing to make complex decisions, maintaining trust becomes paramount. Communicate openly about how these converging technologies are being used in your organization. Share both successes and challenges. Use blockchain to

create immutable records of AI decision-making processes. Leverage IoT and spatial computing to provide real-time, immersive visualizations of your AI systems at work. This unprecedented level of transparency will not only build trust with stakeholders but also attract top talent who value ethical and open technological practices.

- **Reimagine data strategies for a convergent world:** AI thrives on data, but how does this change when that data is secured by blockchain or sourced from countless IoT devices? Develop comprehensive data strategies that leverage the strengths of each technology while respecting privacy and security.
- **Build partnerships across technological domains:** The true power of convergence often lies beyond any single organization's capabilities. Forge alliances with companies specializing in blockchain, IoT, or spatial computing. Create ecosystems where AI can be the connective tissue between diverse technological capabilities.
- **Invest in convergence-ready infrastructure:** Ensure your organization's technical backbone can support the integration of AI with other emerging technologies. This might mean upgrading to 5G for better IoT connectivity or investing in quantum-resistant blockchain systems.
- **Cultivate "convergence translators" within your organization:** These individuals should be able to bridge the gap between different technological domains, helping teams understand how AI can be leveraged across various platforms and systems.
- **Embrace iterative development in convergent projects:** The interaction between AI and other technologies can yield unpredictable results. Adopt agile methodologies that allow for rapid prototyping and frequent reassessment of project goals.

- **Position yourself as a thought leader in technological convergence:** Share your experiences and insights. Engage with policymakers to help shape regulations that foster innovation while protecting societal interests. The leaders who thrive will be those who can articulate a vision of how converging technologies can solve grand challenges.

The path to becoming an AI First leader looks different depending on your business scale:

- For small businesses, start by identifying one critical process where data validation matters - perhaps customer verification or supply tracking. Start with simple AI tools and learn from these interactions.
- Mid-sized companies might begin by examining their data streams across departments. Look for places where AI could analyze blockchain-verified transactions to spot trends, reduce risks, or improve customer experience.
- Large enterprises should consider how combining AI with blockchain could transform entire business units. Start with areas where trust is crucial - whether that's in supply chains, customer relationships, or partner networks. Remember that IOT can provide data where data scarcity exists.
- Regardless of size, the key is starting with real business problems while keeping an eye on future possibilities. The goal isn't to adopt technology for its own sake, but to solve today's challenges while building the foundation for tomorrow's opportunities.

The future is not just AI-driven; it's convergence-powered. Now, let's tackle some of the challenges we might encounter.

CHAPTER

8

Challenges Brought on by AI

Artificial intelligence (AI) has brought us remarkable advancements. AI has been shown to improve the diagnostic accuracy for conditions like multiple sclerosis by 44% and can detect lung nodules 26% faster than manual inspections, identifying 29% of previously missed nodules.[1]

But like any new technology, it introduces a set of challenges that must be addressed. These challenges are integral to understanding and navigating the complexities of AI.

"For example, A tragic case involving a 14-year-old boy from Florida has sparked concerns about the safety of AI chatbots. The teen developed an emotional attachment to a Character. AI chatbot modeled after a "Game of Thrones" character, which engaged in intimate and suggestive conversations. Shortly before his suicide, the AI bot allegedly encouraged him to "come home," raising questions about the platform's safeguards for vulnerable users. This incident has led to a lawsuit against Character.AI and its parent company, Google, highlighting the ethical and regulatory challenges of AI companions."

Teaching my dad to use ChatGPT was an adventure in itself. He's always been a bit of a tech adventurer, and once I showed him how the AI could answer questions, provide information, and even help with troubleshooting, he was hooked.

One day, he decided to test ChatGPT by asking for help with replacing a part on his car. To his delight, the AI provided step-by-step instructions and identified the issue accurately. My dad was thrilled and began using ChatGPT for various small tasks around the house. He discovered that sometimes ChatGPT made up "stuff" as he called it.

However, the real surprise came when he used ChatGPT to check some symptoms he was experiencing. He had been feeling unwell and decided to list his symptoms to see what ChatGPT would suggest. The AI indicated that his symptoms might be related to cancer. My dad scheduled a doctor's appointment immediately but it turned out to be just a simple flu. The lack of strong training (and use in this case) highlights that you need the right data to determine the right answers.

This experience underscored the incredible potential of AI in everyday life, from practical tasks to health concerns. It also highlighted the importance of combining AI with human judgment. Although AI can be an invaluable tool, it's crucial to seek professional advice for medical issues. My dad's journey with ChatGPT was a powerful reminder of how technology, when used wisely, can make a significant difference in our lives and also some of the challenges we can face.

In this chapter, I'll cover six critical challenges facing AI today:

- **Trust:** The need for transparency and reliability in AI systems.
- **Hallucinations:** Addressing errors and inaccuracies in AI outputs.

- **Data scarcity:** Overcoming limitations in available data for AI training.
- **Societal impact:** Navigating job displacement and potential biases in AI.
- **Environment concerns:** There is a risk to sustainability.
- **Copyright concerns:** The implications here will be important.

Each of these challenges presents unique obstacles to the widespread adoption and effective implementation of AI technologies. By examining these issues in depth, we can better understand the current state of AI and the steps needed to harness its full potential while mitigating associated risks.

The Current Trust Deficit in AI

The rapid advancement of AI has ushered in a new era of technological capabilities, promising transformative changes across various sectors. However, with great power comes great responsibility—and great skepticism. The lack of trust in AI systems poses a significant challenge to their widespread adoption and effective implementation.

Building trust in AI systems is crucial for their successful adoption and responsible use. At the World Economic Forum in Davos, I encountered the Edelman Trust Barometer, which highlighted the state of trust in technology and AI.

Although technology remains the most trusted business sector globally, it was the only sector in the Trust Barometer that did not see a year-over-year increase in trust. This is concerning because as AI becomes ubiquitous, it also faces declining trust levels. AI-specific trust has dropped from 62% to 54% over the past five years.[2]

Trust issues in AI stem from several key factors:

- Lack of transparency in decision-making processes aka the Black Box Problem.
- Incidents of AI errors and biases.
- Concerns about privacy and data security.
- Fear of job displacement.

Let's explore these challenges with real-world examples.

The Black Box Problem

AI systems often operate as black boxes, making decisions through processes that are opaque to users. This lack of transparency can lead to distrust and resistance to adoption. The complexity of AI algorithms makes it difficult for nonexperts to understand how decisions are made, leading to skepticism about the fairness and reliability of these systems.

These two examples came from the United Kingdom (UK). The UK government's use of an AI algorithm to predict A-level results during the COVID-19 pandemic led to widespread controversy. The algorithm, which considered factors like a school's historical performance, was accused of unfairly downgrading students from disadvantaged backgrounds. The lack of transparency in how the algorithm made its decisions fueled public outrage and ultimately led to the government abandoning the system.[3]

A notable example is a study led by the University of Cambridge, which found that AI techniques in medical imaging can lead to false positives and false negatives, potentially resulting in incorrect diagnoses and treatment decisions.[4] This highlights the importance of human oversight and the need for further refinement of these technologies.

AI Errors and Biases

High-profile cases of AI errors or biased decisions have further eroded public trust. These incidents highlight the potential for AI to perpetuate and even amplify existing societal biases, raising serious ethical concerns about the deployment of AI in sensitive areas such as hiring, criminal justice, and health care.

For example, AI's application in hiring processes has also raised concerns about fairness and bias. A well-known case involved Amazon's AI recruiting tool, which was found to be biased against women. The system, which was designed to automate the hiring process, ended up discriminating against female candidates because it was trained on résumés submitted to the company over a 10-year period, which were predominantly from men.[5]

This incident underscores the critical need for careful monitoring and evaluation of AI systems to ensure they promote fairness and do not perpetuate existing biases.

Privacy and Data Security Concerns

Because AI systems require vast amounts of data to function effectively, concerns about data privacy and security have become paramount. The collection, storage, and use of personal data by AI systems raise questions about individual privacy rights and the potential for data breaches or misuse.

For example, Samsung faced backlash when it was revealed that their AI-powered smart TVs were collecting and analyzing users' viewing habits without clear consent. This case highlighted the ongoing challenges in balancing AI capabilities with user privacy in consumer electronics.[6]

OpenAI faced scrutiny over its data practices when it was revealed that ChatGPT was using personal data from various websites to train its language model without explicit consent. This raised concerns about the privacy implications of large language models and the potential misuse of personal information.[7]

The AI photo editing app Lensa came under fire for its privacy policies. Users discovered that the app's terms allowed it to use their uploaded photos and AI-generated images for any purpose, including training future AI models. This incident highlighted the complex privacy issues surrounding AI-powered apps and the data they collect.[8]

These examples demonstrate that as AI technology advances, so do the challenges related to data privacy and security. They highlight the need for clearer regulations, more transparent data practices, and increased user awareness about how their data is being used in AI systems.

Fear of Job Displacement

Although AI promises increased efficiency and productivity, it also raises fears about job displacement. The potential for AI to automate tasks traditionally performed by humans has led to concerns about widespread unemployment and economic disruption. This fear is particularly acute in industries where routine tasks are prevalent, such as manufacturing, customer service, and data entry.

A World Economic Forum report predicted that by 2025, 85 million jobs might be displaced by the shift in labor division between humans and machines. However, it also forecasted the emergence of 97 million new roles adapted to the new division of labor among humans, machines, and algorithms. This suggests a complex transition period when job markets will need to adapt, and workers will need to acquire new skills to remain competitive.[9]

The fear of job displacement is not just about unemployment but also about the changing nature of work itself. As AI takes over routine tasks, human workers might need to focus more on skills that AI cannot easily replicate, such as creativity, emotional intelligence, and complex problem-solving. This shift requires significant adaptations in education and training systems to prepare the workforce for an AI-driven economy.

Building Trust: The Way Forward

To address these challenges and build trust in AI systems, leaders and organizations must prioritize the following:

- **Transparency:** Implement explainable AI models and open-source algorithms.
- **Fairness:** Actively work to identify and mitigate biases in AI systems.
- **Privacy protection:** Adopt robust data protection measures and be transparent about data use. And even more protection for vulnerable users.
- **Human–AI collaboration:** Emphasize how AI can augment human capabilities rather than replace them.
- **Education:** Invest in public awareness and education about AI's capabilities and limitations.

By addressing these concerns head-on, we can work towards a future when AI is not only powerful but also trustworthy and beneficial to society. The path to widespread AI adoption is paved with challenges, but with responsible development and deployment, we can harness its full potential while ensuring it aligns with human values and societal needs.

IBM Watson: A Milestone in AI Trust and Public Perception

While discussing challenges in AI trust, it's crucial to acknowledge significant milestones that have shaped public perception. One such landmark event was IBM's Watson competing on the quiz show *Jeopardy!* During my tenure at IBM, which included Watson's *Jeopardy!* performance, it wasn't just about showcasing AI's capabilities but also about explaining how Watson processed and analyzed information to arrive at the correct answers. This transparency helped build trust in Watson's capabilities.

IBM Watson, a question-answering computer system, made history when it competed against former *Jeopardy!* champions Ken Jennings and Brad Rutter. Watson demonstrated its ability to understand natural language questions, search its vast database, and provide accurate answers faster than its human competitors. The AI system won the competition, showcasing the potential of AI to process and analyze information at superhuman speeds.

The key aspects of Watson's *Jeopardy!* performance include the following:[10]

- **Natural language processing:** Watson could understand and respond to complex, questions in natural language.
- **Speed and accuracy:** The AI system could process vast amounts of information and provide accurate answers within seconds.
- **Broad knowledge base:** Watson demonstrated knowledge across a wide range of topics, from history and literature to science and pop culture.

There was a positive impact from Watson's success on AI trust and perception:

- **Positive demonstration:** Watson's success on *Jeopardy!* was a powerful demonstration of AI's capabilities, helping to build public trust in AI technology.
- **Transparency efforts:** IBM made efforts to explain how Watson worked, which helped demystify AI for the general public. This transparency was crucial in building trust.
- **Limitations revealed:** Despite its impressive performance, Watson also made some errors that highlighted the limitations of AI, reminding the public that these systems are not infallible.

- **Ethical considerations:** The event sparked discussions about the ethical implications of AI, including questions about fairness in competition between humans and machines.
- **Future potential:** Watson's performance hinted at the potential applications of AI in fields requiring rapid information processing and decision-making, such as health care and finance.

The Watson *Jeopardy!* event was a pivotal moment in AI history, simultaneously showcasing the technology's potential and sparking important discussions about its implications. It demonstrated that with proper development, transparency, and public engagement, AI systems could earn public trust and acceptance.

As AI continues to evolve, it is crucial to address these risks to fully harness its benefits while ensuring reliability and fairness.

Hallucinations in AI Output

AI's tendency to produce hallucinations—generating incorrect or fabricated information—poses a significant challenge that must be addressed. A hallucination in the context of AI refers to instances when an AI system provides responses or outputs that are not based on actual data or facts. These hallucinations are a significant concern because they can lead to misinformation, especially when AI is used in applications that require high accuracy, such as medical advice, legal information, or scientific research.

Key points on AI hallucinations include the following:

- **Frequency:** Studies have shown that hallucination rates can vary significantly across different AI models. AI hallucinations are infrequent but constant, making up between 3% and 10% of responses to the queries—or prompts—that users submit to generative AI models.[11]

- **Why hallucinations happen:** Hallucinations can occur due to several reasons:
  - Incomplete or biased training data.
  - Unclear or ambiguous prompts from users.
  - The inherent design of language models to predict the next word in a sequence without necessarily understanding context or factual accuracy.
- **Mitigation strategies:** To reduce hallucinations, AI developers are exploring techniques such as the following:

  - Fine-tuning models with domain-specific data.
  - Improving prompt engineering.
  - Implementing retrieval-augmented generation, where the AI is restricted to respond based on a specific, verified database.

These measures help ensure that the responses are grounded in real-world knowledge and are less likely to be hallucinatory.

A Real-World Example

To illustrate the real-world impact of AI hallucinations, I want to share this personal example. Recently, I helped my daughter with a school essay assignment in which her teacher allowed the use of ChatGPT. As we worked through the essay, we discovered that ChatGPT had provided numerous incorrect answers. This led to a valuable teaching moment about the importance of fact-checking and not blindly trusting AI-generated information. We had to verify each piece of information provided by ChatGPT, which was time-consuming but crucial for ensuring the accuracy of her work.

This experience highlights several key points:

- AI hallucinations can occur even in educational settings, potentially misleading students.

- Critical thinking and fact-checking skills are essential when using AI tools.
- The responsibility of verifying AI-generated information often falls on the user.
- AI hallucinations can significantly affect the efficiency and reliability of using AI for research and learning.

A side note about AI and education. A survey conducted in May 2024 for the Walton Family Foundation shows that knowledge of and support for AI in education is growing among parents, teachers, K–12 students, and college students. More than 80% of each group said it has had a positive impact on education.[12]

The study further showed that AI has become deeply integrated into the education system, with increased awareness and regular use among teachers, parents, and students. Despite a slight uptick in negative views, the overall perception of AI in education remains positive, especially among those who have personally used the technology. There's a general consensus on the beneficial applications of AI in schools.

However, a significant gap exists between AI's widespread use and institutional readiness. Most K–12 stakeholders report that their schools lack formal AI policies, fail to provide necessary teacher training, and aren't adequately preparing students for AI-centric careers. This policy vacuum has led to unauthorized and unguided AI use, with students, parents, and teachers often navigating AI integration independently.

Interestingly, all stakeholders express a preference for thoughtful, encouraging AI policies rather than the current unstructured approach. This situation highlights a critical need for educational institutions to develop comprehensive AI strategies that align with the growing demand and positive sentiment toward AI in education.

Recognizing AI hallucinations is crucial because it directly affects the trustworthiness and reliability of AI systems. When users rely on AI for critical information, such as in health care, education, or legal fields, the consequences of AI hallucinations can be severe.

The Way Forward for AI-First Business Leaders

As a business leader aspiring to be an AI-first thinker, addressing the challenge of AI hallucinations requires a multifaceted approach that balances innovation with responsibility. Here's how you can lead the way in your organization:

- **Invest in AI literacy:** Start by investing in AI literacy programs for your team. This doesn't mean everyone needs to become a data scientist, but they should understand the basics of how AI works, its capabilities, and its limitations. Organize workshops, bring in experts, and encourage ongoing learning about AI technologies. This knowledge will empower your team to use AI tools more effectively and critically.
- **Implement robust verification processes:** Develop a culture of "trust but verify" when it comes to AI-generated content. Establish clear protocols for cross-checking AI outputs, especially for critical business decisions. This might involve using multiple AI tools, consulting human experts, or creating custom verification algorithms tailored to your industry.
- **Foster collaboration between AI and human expertise:** Rather than viewing AI as a replacement for human intelligence, position it as a powerful tool that enhances human capabilities. Encourage your teams to work alongside AI, using their domain expertise to guide and refine AI outputs.

This collaborative approach can significantly reduce the risk of uncaught AI hallucinations while boosting overall productivity.

- **Engage in responsible AI partnerships:** When selecting AI vendors or partners, prioritize those who are transparent about their AI's limitations and actively work on reducing hallucinations. Don't hesitate to ask tough questions about their AI models' accuracy rates, training data, and safeguards against misinformation. Your choice of partners can significantly affect the trustworthiness of the AI solutions you implement.
- **Develop AI-assisted decision-making frameworks:** Create decision-making frameworks that intelligently combine AI insights with human judgment. This could involve developing a tiered system where AI recommendations are weighted differently based on the criticality of the decision and the AI's known reliability in specific domains.
- **Embrace continuous learning and adaptation:** The field of AI is rapidly evolving, and so should your approach to it. Stay informed about the latest developments in AI technology, particularly advancements in reducing hallucinations. Be prepared to adapt your AI strategies as new tools and best practices emerge.

By adopting these strategies, you can position your organization at the forefront of AI innovation while responsibly managing the risks associated with AI hallucinations. Remember, being an AI-first leader doesn't mean blindly embracing every new AI technology. It means thoughtfully integrating AI into your business processes in ways that enhance human capabilities, drive innovation, and maintain the trust of your customers and stakeholders.

Lack of Data

In the age of AI-first, it's all about the data. Lack of data is one of the most significant challenges in developing and deploying effective AI systems. Data is the fuel that powers machine learning models, and without sufficient, diverse, and high-quality data, AI systems can produce biased, inaccurate, or incomplete results. In fact, there are increasingly articles about "data scarcity".

One stark example of the consequences of insufficient data is the gender gap in medical research. Until 1993, women were not mandatorily included in clinical research in the United States. This exclusion created an estimated 17-year data gap. For instance, a liver disease prediction tool, effective in 77% of cases overall, failed to diagnose correctly in 44% of cases involving women due to the lack of female-specific data. This gap underscores the importance of inclusive data collection to ensure AI systems work equitably for all populations.[13]

The scarcity of data can lead to significant blind spots in AI models. For example, McKinsey reports that 19% of respondents from companies using AI cited inadequate data infrastructure as a significant barrier to their AI initiatives. Furthermore, AI models often rely on historical data that might not accurately reflect current realities, exacerbating biases and inaccuracies in predictions and decisions.[14]

Addressing the lack of data involves several strategies.

Synthetic Data

One promising approach is the use of synthetic data—artificially generated data that mimics real-world data. Synthetic data can help fill gaps in training datasets, providing more comprehensive input for AI models. This method is particularly useful when real data is scarce, sensitive, or difficult to collect. However, ensuring the quality and representativeness of synthetic data remains a challenge.

Key benefits of synthetic data include the following:

- Filling gaps in underrepresented categories.
- Protecting privacy by avoiding the use of real personal data.
- Enabling the creation of edge cases that are rare in real-world data.

However, ensuring the quality and representativeness of synthetic data remains a challenge. Leaders must invest in robust validation processes to ensure synthetic data accurately reflects real-world scenarios.

And make sure you balance synthetic and real data: although synthetic data and augmentation are powerful tools, they should complement, not replace, real-world data.

Data Labeling

Another critical strategy is improving data labeling processes. High-quality labeled data is essential for supervised learning models. Companies can employ a combination of human annotators and automated labeling tools to enhance the accuracy and efficiency of this process. Moreover, leveraging advanced techniques such as active learning, where the model iteratively queries the most informative data points for labeling, can maximize the impact of limited labeling resources.

Data Diversity

The importance of data diversity cannot be overstated. AI models trained on homogeneous data are likely to perform poorly in diverse real-world scenarios. Organizations should strive to collect and incorporate diverse datasets that reflect the full spectrum of potential use cases. This approach helps mitigate biases and ensures the AI system's robustness across different contexts and populations.

The AI Index Report highlights that although large AI models are being trained on vast datasets, issues of bias and fairness remain prevalent.[15] Efforts to improve the fairness and transparency of AI models are ongoing, but there is still a significant gap between model performance and ethical considerations. Researchers and practitioners must continue to develop and implement metrics and standards to evaluate and mitigate these biases effectively.

Collaboration on Data Sharing

Fostering collaboration across sectors can help address data scarcity. Partnerships with academia, industry, and government can facilitate data sharing and collective efforts to build comprehensive datasets. Such collaborations can also promote the development of standardized frameworks for data collection, management, and sharing, ensuring consistency and quality across different AI applications.

Transfer Learning

Transfer learning is a powerful technique that enables AI models to leverage knowledge gained from one task to improve performance on a different, but related, task. This approach is particularly valuable when dealing with limited data in specific domains.

For example, a model trained on a large dataset of general images can be fine-tuned with a smaller dataset of specific medical images, resulting in a more accurate diagnostic tool. Transfer learning can significantly reduce the amount of domain-specific data needed to achieve high performance.

Benefits of transfer learning include the following:

- Reduced training time and computational resources.
- Improved performance on tasks with limited data.
- Ability to leverage pretrained models for new applications.

Data Augmentation Techniques

Data augmentation involves creating new training examples by applying various transformations to existing data. Although synthetic data generation creates entirely new data points, augmentation modifies existing ones.

Common data augmentation techniques include the following:

- **For images:** Rotation, flipping, scaling, cropping, or adding noise
- **For text:** Synonym replacement, back translation, or text generation
- **For audio:** Adding background noise, changing pitch, or time stretching

These techniques can effectively increase the size and diversity of training datasets, helping AI models generalize better to new, unseen data.

An Example of Adaptability: American Magic

Even if you have all the known data, a focus on adaptability is crucial. For example, the New York Yacht Club (NYYC) American Magic team collaborated with Altair to leverage AI for a competitive edge in the upcoming America's Cup. This partnership has led to the creation of an advanced AC75 yacht capable of reaching speeds over 55 miles per hour. Altair's AI technology processes vast amounts of sailing data from current and previous events to identify patterns and optimize routes. By combining this data with self-learning algorithms, the team developed a yacht that performs specific maneuvers efficiently and learns to sail the fastest routes. This blend of AI and human expertise is crucial in maximizing the yacht's potential, demonstrating the power of data in enhancing performance.[16]

However, despite the technological advancements and meticulous data analysis, unpredictable elements like weather conditions can still significantly affect the competition. Although teams have access to historical weather data for Barcelona, where the competition will be held, they cannot accurately predict the exact wind and sea state they will encounter during the America's Cup. This uncertainty highlights the limitations of even the most advanced AI systems, emphasizing the need for adaptability and real-time decision-making in response to changing conditions. The case of NYYC and Altair underscores the importance of combining robust data analysis with the flexibility to navigate unpredictable elements in high-stakes scenarios.

Tackling the challenge of insufficient data in AI requires a multifaceted approach, including the use of synthetic data, improved labeling processes, increased data diversity, and cross-sector collaboration. By addressing these issues, we can build more reliable, fair, and effective AI systems that benefit everyone.

The Way Forward for AI-First Leaders in Data

As an AI-first leader, addressing data scarcity is crucial for the success of your AI initiatives. Here's a concise road map to navigate this challenge:

- **Prioritize data strategy:** Develop a comprehensive data strategy that aligns with your business goals. Identify key data sources, gaps, and quality issues within your organization.
- **Invest in data infrastructure:** Allocate resources to build robust data collection and storage systems. This foundation is essential for effective AI implementation.
- **Embrace synthetic data:** Explore the use of synthetic data to augment your existing datasets, especially in areas where real data is scarce or sensitive.
- **Foster data partnerships:** Collaborate with industry peers, academic institutions, or data providers to access diverse and complementary datasets.
- **Implement data governance:** Establish clear protocols for data management, ensuring privacy, security, and ethical use of data across your organization.
- **Cultivate a data-driven culture:** Encourage data literacy among your teams and promote a culture that values data-driven decision-making.
- **Leverage advanced techniques:** Explore methods like transfer learning and few-shot learning to maximize the value of limited data. Few-shot learning is a machine learning approach that aims to learn new tasks or recognize new classes of objects from just a few examples, similar to how humans can quickly learn new concepts without needing hundreds or thousands of examples.

- **Monitor and adapt continuously:** Regularly assess the performance and biases of your AI models, adapting your data strategy as needed.

By focusing on these key areas, you can build a strong foundation for AI success, even in the face of data scarcity. Remember, the goal is not just to accumulate more data, but to ensure you have the right data to drive meaningful insights and actions for your business.

Fear of Job Elimination

If you believe the headlines, AI has already taken over. It's ubiquitous, with everyone from students using ChatGPT to complete assignments, to businesses laying off workers in favor of intelligent automation. But the stats tell a different story. A report reveals that only 7% of people in the United States use generative AI daily.[17] The stark contrast between AI hype and actual use is revealing. Although generative AI dominates headlines, most people have barely scratched its surface, using it only once or twice. This adoption gap exposes critical issues of awareness, accessibility, and perceived value in everyday life. It's a sobering reminder that despite the AI revolution's promise, its real-world integration lags far behind the buzz. This disconnect challenges us to bridge the gap between AI's potential and its practical application for the average person.

A popular sentiment I've seen circulating is the desire for AI to handle mundane tasks, not the creative ones. Science fiction and fantasy author Joanna Maciejewska's quote on X (formerly Twitter) captures this well: "I want AI to do my laundry and dishes so that I can do art and writing, not for AI to do my art and writing so that I can do my laundry and dishes."[18] As of this writing, it had over 3.1 million views. This resonates with many who fear job displacement and emphasizes the potential of AI to enhance human creativity rather than replace it.

The fear of AI eliminating jobs is a significant concern. Historical trends show that technological advancements often bring initial job displacement but eventually create new job opportunities. The printing press, the steam engine, and computers all faced similar scrutiny. AI is expected to automate repetitive tasks, potentially displacing certain jobs, but it can also create new roles that require advanced skills in AI management and development. According to the World Economic Forum, AI could displace 85 million jobs by 2025 but create 97 million new ones.[19]

Far from being a job thief, AI is emerging as a powerful ally for many professionals, especially creatives. It's not about replacement, but enhancement. AI's potential to amplify creativity remains largely untapped, offering exciting possibilities for innovation. By embracing AI as a collaborator rather than a competitor, we can offload mundane tasks and free ourselves to focus on what truly matters—the essence of creative thinking.

This shift in perspective opens doors to new forms of expression and efficiency, pushing the boundaries of what's creatively possible. Jaron Lanier, computer scientist and composer, captures this sentiment well: "AI should be a tool that enhances human creativity, not a replacement for it," he says. "We need to rethink our approach to AI development to ensure it supports and amplifies our creative endeavors rather than undermining them."[20]

The future of creativity lies in the synergy between AI and human ingenuity. By developing AI systems that complement rather than replace human creativity, we can unlock unprecedented potential. AI excels at handling repetitive tasks, generating initial concepts, and processing vast amounts of data. This frees human creatives to focus on what they do best: refining ideas, adding important touches, and making intuitive leaps that machines can't replicate. As Jensen Huang, CEO of NVIDIA, aptly points out in the NVIDIA Blog, this collaboration heralds a new era of innovation. It's not about AI versus humans, but AI with humans, leading to a revolutionary blend of efficiency and inspiration in creative work. "The future is generative ... which is why this is a brand-new industry. The way we compute is fundamentally different. We created a processor for the generative AI era."[21]

The AI revolution demands a parallel revolution in workforce development. With over 120 million workers slated for retraining in the next three years, the urgency to upskill is clear. This isn't just about job preservation; it's about unlocking human potential. By investing in AI-focused education and training, we're not merely adapting to change—we're embracing it. This proactive approach empowers individuals to work symbiotically with AI, enhancing their capabilities and opening new career vistas. The result? A workforce that's not threatened by AI, but emboldened by it, ready to drive innovation and productivity to unprecedented heights.

The Way Forward: Navigating AI's Impact on Employment

As leaders in the AI era, we face a daunting challenge: balancing optimism with hard truths. The reality is stark—AI will disrupt employment significantly, and cost-cutting will likely drive initial adoption.

For example, Amazon CEO Andy Jassy has reported significant benefits from the company's AI assistant, Amazon Q, which has saved the company an estimated $260 million in annualized efficiency gains and the equivalent of 4,500 developer years of work. The AI tool has dramatically reduced the time needed for tasks like upgrading applications, with 79%

of AI-generated code reviews being shipped without changes. Despite initial challenges with accuracy, Amazon has improved the tool's performance through expanded human review. Jassy emphasized the tool's impact on tedious but critical software development tasks, enhancing security and reducing infrastructure costs. Amazon plans to continue expanding Amazon Q's capabilities, viewing it as a game changer for the company's productivity and efficiency.[22]

Following are some suggestions on how to navigate this complex landscape:

- **Embrace radical honesty:** Acknowledge openly that AI will lead to job losses. Transparency builds trust and prepares your workforce for change.
- **Prioritize strategic adaptation:** Identify roles most at risk and develop transition plans. This isn't about preserving every job but about strategic workforce evolution.
- **Invest in reskilling selectively:** Focus reskilling efforts on roles that complement AI, not compete with it. Be discerning—not every position can or should be saved. And note that it is the employee's responsibility too to ensure that are constantly upgrading their skills.
- **Foster an innovation mindset:** Encourage employees to identify new AI-enabled business opportunities. This can create new roles while driving company growth.
- **Cultivate ethical AI practices:** Develop guidelines for responsible AI implementation. This can mitigate negative impacts and enhance your company's reputation.
- **Engage in policy dialogue:** Participate in discussions about AI regulation and social safety nets. Business leaders have a crucial role in shaping a sustainable AI future.

- **Plan for social impact:** Consider the broader societal effects of AI-driven job displacement. Explore partnerships with educational institutions or local governments to support community transition.
- **Communicate a compelling vision:** Articulate how AI will transform your industry and the new opportunities it will create. Help your team see beyond immediate disruptions.
- **Lead with empathy:** Recognize the fear and uncertainty your employees face. Provide support resources and clear communication channels.
- **Prepare for resistance:** Expect and plan for pushback. Develop strategies to address concerns and misconceptions about AI's impact.

Remember, as leaders, our role is not to sugarcoat the AI revolution but to guide our organizations through it with clarity, strategy, and responsibility. The path ahead is challenging, but with thoughtful leadership, we can harness AI's potential while mitigating its negative impacts.

Although the fear of AI eliminating jobs is valid, it's crucial to adopt a balanced perspective. AI will undoubtedly transform the job market, but with proactive measures such as retraining programs, transparent communication, and ethical practices, we can navigate this transformation successfully. The key lies in leveraging AI's potential to enhance human capabilities and create new opportunities, ultimately leading to a more dynamic and innovative workforce.

Environmental Issues: The Risk for Sustainability

AI technologies pose significant environmental challenges. The deployment and operation of AI systems require substantial computational power, which translates into high energy consumption and carbon emissions. Some of the key challenges associated with the environmental impact of AI are outlined in the following sections.

High Energy Consumption

Training large-scale AI models, such as deep learning algorithms, involves extensive computational resources. The process can consume massive amounts of electricity, often generated from fossil fuels, leading to a significant carbon footprint.

Recent research has highlighted the significant environmental impact of training large AI models. For example, training a model like ChatGPT, which has 175 billion parameters, consumed approximately 1,287 megawatt-hours of electricity and resulted in carbon emissions of about 502 metric tons. This emission level is comparable to the annual emissions of about 112 gasoline-powered cars.[23]

The energy demand continues to rise as AI applications become more complex and widespread.

Data Centers and Cooling Needs

AI operations rely heavily on data centers, which house servers running 24/7. These data centers require substantial cooling systems to prevent overheating, further increasing energy use. According to some estimates, data centers already consume about 1% of the global electricity supply, and this number is expected to grow as the demand for AI services increases.[24]

Resource Intensity

The production of AI hardware requires raw materials like rare earth elements, which involve environmentally damaging mining processes. The extraction of these materials often leads to habitat destruction, soil degradation, and pollution of water resources, highlighting the environmental cost embedded in AI technologies.[25]

The Way Forward for Leaders Regarding the Environmental Impacts

Is there anything you can do as a business leader for the environment? Yes, there are several strategies to mitigate the environmental impacts of AI while still leveraging its capabilities:

- **Invest in energy-efficient AI hardware:** Select and invest in energy-efficient hardware specifically designed to reduce power consumption. NVIDIA and other chip manufacturers are increasingly offering products optimized for energy efficiency, which can significantly reduce the environmental footprint of AI operations. Leaders should prioritize these options when upgrading or purchasing new AI infrastructure.
- **Optimize AI workloads:** Implement techniques that optimize AI workloads to reduce energy consumption. This can involve using more efficient algorithms, reducing the size and complexity of models, and using techniques like model pruning or quantization. These approaches help maintain performance while lowering the computational power required.
- **Adopt sustainable data center practices:** Partner with data centers that use renewable energy sources. Because AI operations are highly reliant on data centers, shifting to those powered by wind, solar, or other renewable energy sources can drastically cut down carbon emissions. Furthermore, employing cooling technologies that minimize energy use can also make a substantial impact.

- **Implement life cycle analysis for AI hardware:** Conduct life cycle assessments of AI hardware to understand the environmental impact from production to disposal. By doing so, leaders can make informed decisions about procurement, use, and recycling of hardware, focusing on minimizing the environmental footprint. Encouraging suppliers to adopt sustainable mining and manufacturing practices can also be part of a broader strategy.
- **Engage in carbon offset programs:** For emissions that cannot be directly eliminated, investing in carbon offset programs can help balance the environmental impact. Companies can fund renewable energy projects, reforestation, or other initiatives that capture or reduce carbon emissions elsewhere.
- **Promote research and development in green AI:** Invest in or collaborate with research institutions to develop new technologies and methods for more sustainable AI. This includes innovations in hardware, software, and data processing techniques that prioritize low energy consumption and reduced environmental impact.
- **Build an AI governance framework with sustainability goals:** Develop an internal governance framework that integrates sustainability into the AI strategy. This framework should include setting clear, measurable goals for reducing the environmental impact of AI operations, regular reporting on progress, and continuous improvement based on the latest technologies and practices.

It will also be important in how you engage with customers and employees, who are very passionate about these topics.

- **Transparency with stakeholders:** Clearly communicate the steps the company is taking to minimize the environmental impact of AI to customers, investors, and employees. This includes publishing sustainability reports, setting public sustainability goals, and providing updates on progress.

- **Employee engagement and training:** Educate employees about the environmental impacts of AI and encourage their participation in sustainability initiatives. Empowering employees with the knowledge and tools to contribute to the company's sustainability efforts can foster a culture of responsibility and innovation.

By taking these proactive steps, business leaders can ensure that their AI strategies not only drive innovation and growth but also contribute to a more sustainable and responsible future. Balancing technological advancement with environmental stewardship is not just an ethical imperative but also a strategic advantage in a world increasingly concerned with sustainability.

Copyright Concerns

AI has introduced complex challenges, particularly in the realm of copyright. Because AI systems are increasingly capable of generating content that resembles human creativity—such as text, images, music, and videos—questions about intellectual property rights and the ethical use of content have become urgent. This has led to a surge in lawsuits and growing concerns over deep fakes, making AI and copyright a contentious issue.

Unauthorized Use of Copyrighted Material

One of the primary concerns is the unauthorized use of copyrighted material by AI systems. Many AI models are trained on vast datasets scraped from the internet, which often include copyrighted works. This raises issues about whether the use of these materials without explicit permission constitutes a violation of copyright law.

For example, there have been numerous legal cases involving companies like OpenAI and Google, where content creators argue that their work has been used without consent to train AI models. The legal landscape is murky because current copyright laws did not anticipate the advent of AI, leading to uncertainty about the fair use of such materials.[26]

Ownership of AI-Generated Content

Another challenge lies in determining the ownership of AI-generated content. If an AI system generates a piece of art, a song, or a written article, who owns the copyright? Is it the creator of the AI, the user who inputs the prompts, or does the content have no owner at all?

The lack of clear legal guidelines on this issue has led to disputes and lawsuits. For instance, artists and authors have raised concerns about AI-generated works that mimic their style, claiming that this infringes on their intellectual property rights.[27]

Deep Fakes and Misinformation

Deep fakes—realistic, AI-generated videos or audio that manipulate appearances and voices—have become a significant issue in mainstream media. These deep fakes can be used to create convincing but entirely fabricated content, posing risks to privacy, reputation, and security. The rise of deep fakes has led to a wave of lawsuits and legal actions aimed at curbing their spread. Celebrities, politicians, and everyday individuals have fallen victim to deep fakes, which can be used for disinformation, defamation, or harassment.

Remember when the internet was captivated by a viral image of Pope Francis wearing a stylish white puffer jacket? This unexpected fashion statement quickly spread across social media, only to be revealed as a deep fake—an AI-generated image that never actually happened. The incident highlighted the growing presence of deep fakes and their ability to blur the lines between reality and digital manipulation, raising concerns about the potential for misinformation.[28]

Around the same time, I attended a red carpet event in Hollywood, choosing to wear a puffer jacket as a unique fashion statement. Given Los Angeles's reputation for warm weather, I didn't bring an appropriate jacket and so had to wear the only thing I had with me: a white puffer jacket. My choice was unexpected, and it caught the attention of photographers and attendees alike. However, when pictures of me at the event began circulating, some people speculated that my image was also fake, influenced by the recent deep fake of the Pope. The coincidence made it seem like reality was imitating digital fabrication.

These events underscore how the rise of deep fakes is affecting public perception and reality. The viral image of the Pope and the ensuing reactions to my own fashion choice show that people are increasingly skeptical of what they see, questioning the authenticity of even real-world events. This emphasizes the need for awareness and critical thinking as we navigate a world where digital and real are becoming ever more intertwined.

Legal and Ethical Implications

The legal system is struggling to keep pace with these rapid technological advancements. Current copyright laws are often inadequate to address the nuances of AI-generated content and the ethical implications of deep fakes. As a result, there is a growing call for updated legislation that specifically addresses AI and copyright issues. Some proposed solutions include creating new categories of intellectual property for AI-generated works, implementing stricter regulations on the use of copyrighted material for AI training, and developing ethical guidelines to prevent the misuse of AI for creating harmful content.

The Way Forward for Business Leaders with an AI Mindset: Navigating Copyright Challenges

As AI technology evolves, business leaders must navigate the complex landscape of copyright issues that arise from the use of AI-generated content. Managing these challenges effectively requires a proactive and strategic approach that balances innovation with legal and ethical responsibilities.

Here are my suggestions on how business leaders can address copyright concerns in the context of AI:

- **Implement clear policies on data use:** Business leaders should establish and enforce clear policies regarding the data used to train AI models. It's essential to ensure that all data used for training is sourced ethically and legally, respecting the copyrights of original content creators. This includes obtaining licenses or permissions when using copyrighted material and avoiding unauthorized scraping of data from the internet. By setting strict guidelines on data use, companies can minimize the risk of copyright infringement and legal disputes.
- **Develop robust AI ethics guidelines:** Creating and adhering to robust AI ethics guidelines can help companies navigate the ethical implications of AI use. These guidelines should address issues such as the ownership of AI-generated content, the use of copyrighted materials, and the potential for AI to create harmful or misleading content, such as deep fakes. Establishing an ethics committee or advisory board

can provide oversight and ensure that AI practices align with both legal standards and corporate values.

- **Leverage legal and technical solutions:** To protect against copyright violations and the misuse of AI-generated content, business leaders should leverage both legal and technical solutions. This includes investing in technologies that can detect and prevent the use of copyrighted material without permission, such as digital watermarking and content recognition systems. Additionally, businesses should stay informed about emerging laws and regulations related to AI and copyright, ensuring compliance and preparing for potential legal challenges. For example, one company that I am on the board of is Authentrics. They help identify risks in any material that could be considered questionable.
- **Foster collaboration and education:** Business leaders should foster collaboration with legal experts, policymakers, and industry peers to shape the future of AI and copyright regulation. By participating in industry groups and advocacy efforts, companies can help develop fair and effective policies that protect intellectual property rights while encouraging innovation. Moreover, educating employees, especially those involved in AI development, about copyright laws and ethical practices can help prevent inadvertent infringements.
- **Maintain transparency and accountability:** Maintaining transparency with customers, stakeholders, and the public about the use of AI and the measures taken to respect copyright laws is crucial. This can build trust and demonstrate a company's commitment to ethical AI practices. Leaders should also implement accountability mechanisms to monitor AI use and address any potential copyright issues that arise. Regular audits and reporting can help ensure that AI activities remain compliant with legal and ethical standards.

As AI continues to transform industries, business leaders with an AI mindset must take a proactive approach to managing copyright challenges. By implementing clear policies, developing ethical guidelines, leveraging legal and technical tools, fostering collaboration, and maintaining transparency, companies can harness the power of AI responsibly. Addressing these challenges not only helps protect intellectual property rights but also supports the sustainable growth of AI technologies in a legally and ethically sound manner.

Enhanced Responsible AI Framework

To help address these challenges, not eliminate them but to mitigate them, I created the responsible AI framework of things to think through. To address the complex challenges posed by AI, a comprehensive responsible AI framework must be adopted, ensuring the integration of key ethical, legal, and societal considerations. This framework, shown in Figure 8.1, focuses on general principles but also incorporates specific issues such as trust, hallucinations, data scarcity, societal impact, environmental concerns, and copyright.

Ethics and responsibility
Regulation and compliance
Education and skills development
Research and development
Data management and security
Innovation and application
Infrastructure and compute power
Public perception and engagement
Investment and funding
International collaboration and competition

FIGURE 8.1 The responsible AI framework.

Ethics and Responsibility

Central to responsible AI is the commitment to ethical practices. This includes ensuring that AI systems are transparent, reliable, and trustworthy. Building trust requires making AI decisions understandable to users and stakeholders. Additionally, addressing hallucinations—instances where AI generates inaccurate or misleading information—is crucial. Implementing rigorous validation and verification processes can help ensure that AI outputs are accurate and reliable.

Regulation and Compliance

Compliance with evolving laws and regulations is essential for managing copyright concerns, which are increasingly relevant as AI systems generate content that might infringe on intellectual property rights. Business leaders must establish protocols to ensure that AI systems respect copyright laws and that the use of data for training AI models is lawful and ethical. This includes obtaining proper licenses and respecting the rights of content creators.

Education and Skills Development

To effectively address data scarcity, investing in education and skills development is critical. Training data scientists and AI developers to collect, curate, and augment data responsibly can help overcome limitations in available data for AI training. Additionally, educating employees on the ethical implications of AI, including biases and societal impact, ensures that the workforce is equipped to handle the broader consequences of AI deployment.

Research and Development

Continuous research is needed to develop AI technologies that are both innovative and ethical. Addressing hallucinations and improving data management are key research areas. By focusing on creating AI systems that can handle data scarcity effectively and produce accurate outputs, companies can advance AI while mitigating potential risks. Research should also focus on understanding and reducing AI's environmental impact, developing sustainable computing methods, and energy-efficient algorithms.

Data Management and Security

Responsible data management is foundational to trustworthy AI. This involves not only protecting data privacy and ensuring security but also addressing data scarcity. Developing methods to enhance data diversity and representativeness can help improve AI model performance. Additionally, robust data management practices are necessary to maintain the integrity of the data used for training and deploying AI systems.

Innovation and Application

Encouraging innovation in AI must be balanced with ethical considerations, particularly concerning societal impact and environmental sustainability. AI applications should be designed to enhance societal benefits, such as improving health care and education. Environmental concerns should also be addressed by developing AI applications that are energy-efficient and by using infrastructure powered by renewable energy sources.

Infrastructure and Compute Power

As the demand for computational resources grows, investing in sustainable infrastructure is critical. This includes using energy-efficient data centers and exploring alternative energy sources to power AI operations. By reducing the environmental footprint of AI, companies can contribute to global sustainability goals and demonstrate their commitment to responsible innovation.

Public Perception and Engagement

Building trust with the public is essential for the successful adoption of AI. Engaging with stakeholders, including consumers, policymakers, and the general public, fosters a dialogue about the ethical use of AI. Transparency in AI operations and clear communication about the steps taken to ensure ethical and responsible AI use are crucial for gaining public trust.

Investment and Funding

Funding for AI should prioritize projects that align with ethical standards and societal benefits. Investment in research that addresses the challenges of trust, hallucinations, data scarcity, and environmental sustainability will drive the development of responsible AI solutions. Public and private sector collaboration can enhance funding opportunities for initiatives that focus on ethical AI.

International Collaboration and Competition

Global cooperation is necessary to establish standards and best practices for responsible AI. This includes harmonizing regulations to address copyright concerns and data management and working together to mitigate the environmental impact of AI. International collaboration can help create a shared framework for ethical AI development, balancing competition with a commitment to societal well-being.

By addressing these critical areas, the enhanced responsible AI framework provides a comprehensive approach to managing the opportunities and challenges presented by AI. It ensures that AI technologies are developed and used in ways that are ethical, sustainable, and beneficial to society.

It's normal to have fears and challenges when faced with new technology. Throughout history, every groundbreaking advancement has brought with it a mix of excitement and apprehension. The printing press, steam engines, and the internet were all met with skepticism and fear before becoming integral to our daily lives.

AI is no different. The unknowns about AI's impact on jobs, privacy, and society are valid concerns that need to be addressed through thoughtful dialogue and proactive measures. Understanding these fears is the first step toward building a responsible framework for AI integration.

CHAPTER

9

How to Become an AI-First Leader

I am an artificial intelligence (AI)-first leader. AI-first leaders not only drive technological advancements but also inspire their organizations to thrive in an increasingly AI-driven world. They are the trailblazers, the ones who aren't afraid to push the envelope and explore uncharted territories. These leaders inspire teams by communicating their vision for AI, simplifying complex concepts, and igniting excitement. They create a culture of curiosity, where employees feel encouraged to ask questions, experiment, and learn continuously.

They model curiosity and adaptability, embracing fresh ideas and continuous learning. They foster a culture where innovation thrives, and calculated risks drive growth. By fostering a sense of purpose and showing how AI can solve real-world problems, they inspire their teams to think creatively and push the boundaries of what's possible.

The urgency to become an AI-first leader in today's rapidly evolving business landscape cannot be overstated. We are witnessing an unprecedented acceleration in AI adoption across industries, with transformative implications for businesses worldwide.

The latest McKinsey Global Survey on AI reveals striking trends[1]:

- Sixty-five percent of respondents report their organizations regularly use generative AI.
- This nearly doubles the adoption rate from just 10 months prior.
- Three-quarters predict generative AI will lead to significant or disruptive industry changes.

This exponential growth underscores AI's swift integration into core business operations. For companies lagging in AI adoption and leadership, the consequences could be severe. They risk diminished competitiveness, missed opportunities for innovation, and potential obsolescence in increasingly AI-driven markets.

The imperative for leaders to embrace an AI-first mindset is critical. Those who fail to adapt risk being left behind in an era when AI is not just an advantage but a necessity for survival and growth.

However, the journey to becoming an AI-first leader isn't one-size-fits-all. The approach should be tailored to each business's specific needs, values, and context. Some businesses, such as those dealing with highly sensitive information, traditional crafts, or operating in niche local markets, might need to approach AI adoption more cautiously or selectively.

For example, at a San Diego farmer's market, I encountered a stall selling hand-carved wooden items. I picked up an intricately crafted bowl, admiring its craftsmanship. "Now this is something you cannot make with AI," I commented to the artisan. He agreed, then surprisingly added, "That's right, but I customize all my marketing using AI social media tools." This interaction highlighted an interesting juxtaposition of traditional craftsmanship and modern technology in small business operations.

The key for AI-first leaders is thoughtful integration that aligns with the organization's core values and enhances its unique strengths. This might mean using AI for back-office efficiency in privacy-critical services, or applying it to customer insights in artisanal businesses while preserving traditional crafting methods. Even for organizations that don't see an immediate need for AI, staying informed about developments in the field is crucial.

True AI-first leadership is about understanding these critical areas, making strategic decisions about where and how to implement AI, and being prepared to adapt as the technology evolves. By doing so, leaders can harness the power of AI to drive innovation and growth, while remaining true to their organization's mission and values. In this rapidly changing landscape, the most successful AI-first leaders will be those who can balance the push for innovation with the specific needs and values of their organization.

What Does It Mean to Be an AI-First Leader?

From my experience, being an AI-first leader is about more than just implementing AI technologies; it's about inspiring and guiding my organization through the complexities and opportunities presented by AI. By fostering collaboration, inclusivity, and a culture of continuous learning, I ensure that my team is well-equipped to navigate the fast-paced world of AI. This approach not only drives technological advancements but also positions our organization for sustained growth and innovation.

AI-first leaders are adept at communicating the broader impact of AI on their industry and society. They articulate how AI initiatives align with the company's mission and values, creating a sense of shared purpose. By involving their teams in the journey toward AI integration, they build a collective enthusiasm and commitment to driving change. This inclusive approach ensures that everyone feels a part of the AI revolution, motivated to contribute to the organization's success in meaningful ways.

From my experience, AI-First leadership is not a solitary journey. Collaboration is key. Leaders must create opportunities for diverse perspectives to be heard and valued. This diversity leads to stronger, more innovative solutions. This means creating opportunities for diverse perspectives to be heard and valued, ultimately leading to more robust and innovative solutions. By building a strong, unified team committed to the shared goal of AI integration, these leaders set the stage for sustainable growth and innovation.

It's important to note that being an AI-First leader isn't limited to the role of Chief AI Officer.[2] Managers, employees, and team leaders at every level can embody AI-First leadership.

I'll share some of my learning about what AI-first leadership is about and how I see AI-first leadership really making an impact.

Implementing AI in Business Strategy

Integrating AI into the core business strategy is a fundamental step for AI-first leaders. This involves identifying areas where AI can create the most impact, such as customer service, operations, and product development. Leaders should develop a clear AI road map that aligns with the organization's overall objectives, outlining specific goals, timelines, and metrics for success. Regularly reviewing and adjusting this road map ensures that the organization remains agile and responsive to technological advancements and market changes.

To start, leaders need to conduct a thorough analysis of the business to pinpoint areas where AI can drive significant improvements. For example, in customer service, AI can be used to create chatbots that handle routine inquiries, freeing up human agents to focus on more complex issues. In operations, AI can optimize supply chain management by predicting demand and reducing waste. In product development, AI can accelerate innovation by analyzing market trends and consumer preferences, leading to the creation of more targeted and successful products.

The AI Road Map Once these areas are identified, the next step is to develop a comprehensive AI road map. This road map should detail the specific AI initiatives to be undertaken, the expected benefits, and the resources required. It should also include clear timelines for implementation and milestones to measure progress. By setting realistic and measurable goals, organizations can track their AI journey and make necessary adjustments to stay on course.

A critical component of the AI road map is ensuring alignment with the organization's overall strategic objectives. This means that AI initiatives should not be pursued in isolation but should support and enhance the broader goals of the company. For instance, if an organization's primary objective is to improve customer satisfaction, AI initiatives should be focused on enhancing the customer experience through personalized services and faster response times.

In addition to strategic alignment, the road map should also address potential challenges and risks associated with AI implementation. This includes considerations about data privacy, security, and ethical use of AI. By proactively addressing these issues, organizations can mitigate risks and build trust with stakeholders.

Regular review and adjustment of the AI road map are essential to keep pace with the rapid advancements in AI technology and changing market dynamics. This iterative process involves continuously monitoring the performance of AI initiatives, gathering feedback, and making data-driven decisions to refine strategies. For example, if an AI model used in customer service is not performing as expected, leaders should be prepared to tweak the algorithm, retrain the model with new data, or explore alternative solutions.

Implementing AI in business strategy requires a systematic and holistic approach. By identifying key areas for AI application, developing a detailed road map, ensuring strategic alignment, addressing challenges, fostering innovation, and investing in training, AI-first leaders can drive significant value and position their organizations for long-term success in the AI era. But always start with a small projects. Launch pilot projects that showcase AI's potential while embedding ethical practices and leveraging high-quality data. Use these successes to integrate AI across departments for greater impact.

Overcoming Resistance to AI Adoption Resistance to AI adoption often stems from valid concerns about job security, skill obsolescence, and changes to established workflows. To address these challenges effectively, organizations should focus on three key actions:

- **Implement comprehensive retraining programs:** Develop initiatives that upskill both leaders and employees. This dual approach ensures leadership understands AI's potential and challenges while equipping staff members with skills to work alongside AI systems. Make sure the employees know that they have a role to play in upskilling themselves.

- **Create AI integration teams:** Form cross-functional groups including skeptics and enthusiasts to guide AI implementation. This approach ensures diverse perspectives are considered and helps identify genuine concerns and opportunities.
- **Provide clear transition paths:** For roles likely to be significantly affected by AI, develop and communicate concrete plans for redeployment or career transitions. This honest approach acknowledges potential job losses while demonstrating a commitment to employee welfare.

By focusing on these actionable strategies, organizations can address AI adoption challenges head-on, balancing technological advancement with workforce concerns.

Driving Measurable Impact

Ultimately, the success of AI initiatives lies in their ability to drive measurable impact. AI-first leaders must focus on setting clear objectives and metrics for their AI projects, continuously monitoring progress, and making data-driven decisions. They should prioritize AI applications that deliver tangible business value, such as improving customer experience, increasing operational efficiency, or driving revenue growth. Regularly communicating the impact of AI initiatives to stakeholders helps build momentum and support for ongoing AI investment.

The first step in driving measurable impact is to establish clear and achievable objectives for AI initiatives. These objectives should align with the overall strategic goals of the organization and should be specific, measurable, attainable, relevant, and time-bound. For example, an AI-first leader might set an objective to reduce customer service response times by 20% within six months using AI-powered chatbots. By setting precise targets, leaders can provide direction and focus for their

AI projects. Klarna, a Swedish buy-now-pay-later company, has effectively utilized AI to reduce operational costs, demonstrating a clear return on investment (ROI). In the first quarter of 2024, Klarna decreased its sales and marketing spending by 11%. AI contributed to 37% of this reduction, equating to annual savings of approximately $10 million.[3]

Once objectives are set, it's crucial to define the key performance indicators (KPIs) that will be used to measure success. KPIs should be directly linked to the business outcomes that the AI initiatives are expected to affect. For instance, if the goal is to enhance customer experience, relevant KPIs might include customer satisfaction scores, Net Promoter Scores, and the number of support tickets resolved by AI. By identifying the right KPIs, organizations can track the performance of their AI initiatives and gauge their effectiveness.

Continuous monitoring and evaluation are essential to ensure that AI projects stay on track and deliver the expected results. AI-first leaders should implement robust monitoring systems that collect real-time data on AI performance. This data should be analyzed regularly to identify trends, detect issues, and make informed decisions.

For example, if an AI system is not meeting its performance targets, leaders might need to adjust the model, retrain it with new data, or explore alternative solutions. This iterative approach helps to refine AI systems and maximize their impact. AI leaders emphasize the importance of data-driven decision-making. This involves using AI to analyze vast datasets and derive actionable insights, which can significantly improve business operations.[4]

Data-driven decision-making is a hallmark of successful AI-first leaders. By leveraging data insights, leaders can make informed choices about where to allocate resources, which projects to prioritize, and how to optimize AI systems. For example, if data shows that an AI-powered recommendation engine is significantly increasing sales, leaders might decide to invest more in expanding its capabilities. Conversely, if an AI initiative is not delivering the expected value, leaders can make the tough decision to pivot or discontinue the project. This agility ensures that resources are used effectively and that AI investments yield the highest returns.

In marketing, AI can analyze customer data to create personalized campaigns that drive engagement and sales. eBay's first CAIO, Nitzan Mekel-Bobrov, is using AI to enhance user experiences on the platform by incorporating AI tools into visual and content understanding, thereby driving business growth.[5] By focusing on high-impact applications, organizations can realize significant benefits from their AI investments.

Communicating the impact of AI initiatives to stakeholders is crucial for building support and momentum. AI-first leaders should regularly update stakeholders on the progress and outcomes of AI projects, highlighting success stories and demonstrating the value created. This can be done through reports, presentations, and dashboards that showcase key metrics and achievements. By keeping stakeholders informed and engaged, leaders can build trust and secure continued investment in AI initiatives.

Moreover, sharing the impact of AI initiatives helps to create a culture of innovation and continuous improvement. When employees see the positive outcomes of AI projects, they are more likely to embrace AI and contribute to its success. This collective enthusiasm drives further innovation and helps the organization stay ahead of the curve in an increasingly AI-driven world.

Driving measurable impact with AI requires a strategic and data-driven approach. By setting clear objectives, defining relevant KPIs, continuously monitoring performance, making informed decisions, prioritizing high-impact applications, and effectively communicating results, AI-first leaders can ensure that their AI initiatives deliver significant business value. This approach not only maximizes the return on AI investments but also positions the organization for long-term success in the AI era.

Characteristics of an AI-First Leader

AI-first leaders have several common characteristics. They are visionary thinkers with a lot of curiosity. That curiosity leads them to seek continuous learning and be adaptable, and agile in their approaches. In addition, the best AI-first leaders are ethical and responsible while also being collaborative and inclusive. They rely on empathy as their first leadership skill. Although they are execution machines, they maintain a clear strategic focus on outcomes.

Visionary

AI-first leaders are the visionaries who possess a forward-thinking mindset. They envision the future possibilities of AI and understand how to leverage these technologies to drive innovation and strategic growth. This visionary approach enables them to see beyond current limitations and anticipate future trends, positioning their organizations ahead of the curve. For instance, a visionary leader might foresee how AI can transform customer service by predicting customer needs before they arise, enabling a proactive approach that sets the company apart from competitors.

Their ability to look ahead and craft a strategic vision for AI sets the tone for the entire organization, inspiring others to embrace new possibilities. Additionally, these leaders are not just dreamers but also pragmatic strategists. They blend their vision with practical steps to bring it to life, ensuring that their AI initiatives are not just theoretical but grounded in actionable plans. They communicate this vision effectively, rallying their teams around a shared goal. By doing so, they create a culture where everyone is aligned and motivated to explore the transformative potential of AI. This combination of visionary thinking and strategic planning is crucial in navigating the complexities and opportunities presented by AI.

Curious Learner

Curiosity and continuous learning are hallmarks of AI-first leaders. These leaders are inherently curious and committed to lifelong learning. They stay informed about the latest advancements in AI and related fields, constantly seeking new knowledge and insights. This relentless pursuit of understanding enables them to identify opportunities and apply cutting-edge technologies effectively.

For example, an AI-first leader might spend their evenings reading research papers on the latest machine learning algorithms or attending industry conferences to stay abreast of emerging trends. Their commitment to learning extends beyond themselves; they cultivate a learning culture within their organizations.

They encourage their teams to pursue professional development and stay updated on technological advancements. This might involve sponsoring courses, hosting internal workshops, or providing access to industry events. By fostering a culture of continuous learning, AI-first leaders ensure that their organizations remain agile and capable of adapting to the fast-paced evolution of AI technologies.

Adaptable and Agile

The rapidly evolving landscape of AI demands leaders who are highly adaptable and agile. AI-first leaders are quick to embrace change and pivot their strategies as needed. They foster a culture of flexibility within their teams, encouraging experimentation and iterative improvements to stay responsive to technological advancements and market shifts.

To be an AI-first thinker, one of the most important things you need to do is experiment. Experimentation is at the heart of AI innovation. By trying new ideas and exploring uncharted territories, leaders can uncover new possibilities and drive meaningful progress. One compelling example of this is from a colleague, David Armano, who created an experiment with a large language model for South by Southwest. The goal was to answer a single question: what session should not be missed at the event? Of course, the AI recommended attending my session! This experiment exemplifies the power of AI in making insightful recommendations. Obviously, AI is making the right decisions for us!

As a leader, fostering a culture of experimentation involves encouraging your team to ask questions and explore AI's potential without fear of failure. This means creating an environment where calculated risks are celebrated, and learning from failures is seen as a path to growth. By promoting a mindset of curiosity and continuous learning, AI-first leaders can drive innovation and stay ahead of the curve.

Another example is with Wayfair, the Boston-based online furniture seller, who is innovatively leveraging generative AI to revolutionize home redesigns and enhance employee productivity. Through its Decorify tool, Wayfair enables customers to upload photos of their living spaces, which are then transformed by the image-generation AI model Stable Diffusion into new, stylish versions such as glam and midcentury modern.[6] This tool not only provides photorealistic images to inspire customers but also suggests similar Wayfair products, seamlessly connecting the AI-generated concepts with real-world purchases.

Beyond customer-facing applications, Wayfair uses generative AI to improve internal workflows and productivity. According to Fiona Tan, Wayfair's chief technology officer, while generative AI offers substantial economic benefits, the company still employs existing machine learning models for tasks like prediction and optimization, where they prove to be more cost-effective and efficient. The integration of generative AI has led to over 100,000 unique designs created by customers since Decorify's launch, highlighting its potential as a viable shopping aid for home and style-based categories. This experimentation with AI not only enhances customer experience but also underscores Wayfair's commitment to technological innovation and operational excellence.

Adaptability also means being open to feedback and willing to revise plans based on new information. AI-first leaders create an environment where teams feel safe to try new things, fail, and learn from their experiences. This iterative approach not only accelerates innovation but also builds resilience within the organization. By embracing change and fostering a culture of adaptability, AI-first leaders ensure that their organizations can navigate the uncertainties of the AI landscape and emerge stronger.

Ethical and Responsible Leadership

Ethical and responsible leadership is crucial in the realm of AI. An AI-first leader is deeply aware of the ethical implications of AI technologies. They prioritize building systems that are transparent, fair, and accountable. For example, AI leaders at Deloitte are working on human–machine collaboration to ensure responsible AI use.[7] A study by Deloitte found that 76% of AI leaders emphasize ethical training and transparency within their teams, ensuring that ethical considerations are embedded in AI projects from the ground up.[8]

These leaders are committed to mitigating biases in AI models and ensuring that their implementations adhere to ethical guidelines and regulatory standards, thereby building trust with stakeholders. For example, they might implement rigorous testing protocols to detect and correct biases in their AI systems before deployment.

Moreover, AI-first leaders advocate for ethical AI practices both within and outside their organizations. They engage in industry-wide discussions on AI ethics, collaborate with policymakers to shape regulations, and educate their teams on the importance of responsible AI use. By leading by example and promoting ethical standards, they help build a foundation of trust and integrity that supports the long-term success of AI initiatives.

Collaborator and Inclusion Builder

Collaboration and inclusivity are essential traits of AI-first leaders. They value collaboration and inclusivity, bringing together diverse teams and recognizing that the convergence of various perspectives and expertise is crucial for successful AI initiatives. By promoting cross-disciplinary collaboration, they foster innovation and create robust solutions that address complex challenges. For example, an AI-first leader might assemble a team comprising data scientists, engineers, and domain experts to develop an AI-driven product.

These leaders also ensure that everyone in the organization feels included and valued. They actively seek out diverse viewpoints and create an environment where different ideas can flourish. This inclusive approach not only drives innovation but also strengthens the organizational culture, making it more resilient and adaptable to change. By valuing collaboration and inclusivity, AI-first leaders unlock the full potential of their teams and drive meaningful progress.

Data Literate

Data literacy is a crucial characteristic of AI-first leaders. In the age of AI, understanding data fundamentals is as essential as financial acumen.

Leaders should prioritize becoming data literate because it profoundly enhances their decision-making capabilities and overall effectiveness. Data literacy empowers leaders to access, interpret, and leverage data effectively, enabling them to make informed, evidence-based decisions that drive better outcomes. By developing this skill, leaders can extract meaningful insights, uncover trends, and gain a deeper understanding of complex issues, fostering innovation and strategic positioning within their industry.

Moreover, data literacy significantly bolsters problem-solving capabilities, enabling leaders to identify data-driven solutions, validate hypotheses, and measure progress toward organizational goals with a systematic, analytical approach. Perhaps most crucially, data-literate leaders can communicate insights compellingly, crafting data-driven narratives that influence stakeholders, drive buy-in, and promote a culture of informed decision-making across their organizations. In essence, data literacy equips leaders with the tools to navigate the complexities of the modern business landscape, turning raw information into actionable strategies and competitive advantages.

This literacy enables leaders to do the following:

- **Ask the right questions:** Evaluate AI proposals critically, understanding their data requirements and limitations.
- **Recognize bias:** Identify potential data biases that could lead to flawed AI outcomes.
- **Prioritize data quality:** Emphasize the importance of clean, relevant data in AI initiatives.
- **Bridge communication gaps:** Effectively liaise between technical teams and business units.
- **Drive data culture:** Foster an organization-wide appreciation for data-driven decision-making.

By developing data literacy, AI-first leaders can navigate the complexities of AI adoption, ensuring alignment with business goals and ethical standards. This skill empowers leaders to harness AI's full potential while mitigating risks associated with poor data management or interpretation.

Resilient and Empathetic

Resilience and empathy are critical characteristics of AI-first leaders. These leaders exhibit resilience in the face of setbacks and challenges, viewing failures as learning opportunities and persisting in their efforts to drive AI adoption. For example, when an AI project faces technical difficulties, an AI-first leader remains focused, encouraging the team to find solutions and learn from the experience. Their resilience inspires confidence and determination within the organization.

Additionally, they demonstrate empathy, understanding the human impact of AI and ensuring that technology enhances rather than replaces human roles. This empathy helps in building a supportive and motivated workforce. For instance, they might implement AI systems that assist employees in their tasks rather than automating them entirely, thereby enhancing productivity while preserving job satisfaction. By balancing technological advancement with empathy and resilience, AI-first leaders create a harmonious and productive work environment.

Strategic Thought Leader

Strategic focus is a defining trait of AI-first leaders. They maintain a clear strategic focus amidst the excitement of AI innovations, ensuring that AI initiatives align with the broader goals of the organization, driving measurable value and impact. This strategic alignment helps in balancing the pursuit of AI advancements with the need to achieve business objectives. For example, an AI-first leader might prioritize AI projects that enhance customer experience and drive revenue growth.

By staying focused on their strategic goals, these leaders avoid getting sidetracked by the latest trends and ensure that their AI efforts deliver tangible results. They set clear priorities, allocate resources effectively, and measure the impact of their AI initiatives. This disciplined approach not only drives success but also builds a strong foundation for future AI developments. Through strategic focus and careful planning, AI-first leaders guide their organizations toward sustained growth and innovation.

AI-First leaders embody a mix of visionary thinking, adaptability, ethical responsibility, and continuous learning. While these traits may seem like a lot to balance, they come together to empower you to lead with confidence, embrace challenges, and unlock AI's transformative potential. With focus and determination, you can cultivate these qualities and inspire your organization to thrive in the AI era!

Your Team Is Your Greatest Asset: Developing AI Competencies

Although the characteristics of an AI-first leader are crucial, developing specific AI competencies within their teams is equally important. Leaders must focus on upskilling their workforce in key areas such as data science, machine learning, and AI ethics. However, it's essential to recognize that effective AI implementation requires more than just technical skills.

The Importance of Cross-Disciplinary Skills

Effective AI leadership demands a holistic approach to skill development. Although technical proficiency is crucial, it's equally important for AI leaders to cultivate a diverse skill set within their teams. This means fostering a blend of technical expertise, business acumen, and soft skills:

- Technical skills ensure a deep understanding of AI capabilities and limitations.
- Business skills enable the alignment of AI initiatives with organizational goals and market demands.
- Soft skills, such as communication, creativity, and adaptability, are essential for navigating the complex human aspects of AI implementation and change management.

By prioritizing this cross-disciplinary approach, AI leaders can build teams capable of not only developing sophisticated AI solutions but also integrating them effectively into business processes and organizational culture.

Investing in AI Competency Development

The importance of AI competency development is reflected in current investment trends. Gartner found that only 57% of CEOs plan to increase their overall investment in people and culture in 2024–2025 (down from 69% the prior year), but AI training budgets are set to skyrocket.[9] The International Data Corporation (IDC) forecasts global AI training expenditure to more than double, surging from $50.1 billion in 2020 to an impressive $110+ billion by 2024.[10]

To leverage this investment effectively, organizations can do the following:

- Provide access to online courses through platforms like Coursera, Udacity, and edX.
- Host regular workshops and seminars led by internal experts or external consultants.
- Form strategic partnerships with educational institutions and AI research organizations.
- Offer mentorship programs where experienced AI professionals guide junior team members.
- Create internal AI communities or centers of excellence to share knowledge and best practices.
- Encourage attendance at industry conferences like NeurIPS, ICML, and the AI Summit.

A Customer Success Story: The Power of Cross-Disciplinary Teams

One of my customers, a mid-sized financial services firm, recently experienced the power of cross-disciplinary skills in AI implementation. They had invested heavily in developing an

AI-driven risk assessment tool, but despite its technical sophistication, adoption rates among their financial advisors were dismally low.

The breakthrough came when they brought in Elena, a team member with a background in both data science and financial planning. Elena quickly identified the issue: the AI tool, although accurate, wasn't presenting information in a way that aligned with the advisors' workflow.

Elena worked closely with the development team to redesign the tool's interface, incorporating the advisors' feedback and industry-specific terminology. She also conducted training sessions, explaining the AI's benefits in terms that resonated with the advisors' day-to-day challenges.

The result was transformative. Within three months, adoption rates soared from 15% to 85%, and the firm saw a 30% improvement in risk assessment accuracy. This success story underscores how a blend of technical, domain-specific, and communication skills can turn a challenging situation into a triumph.

Fostering a Culture of Continuous Learning

To ensure that AI competencies are continuously developed, organizations should establish a culture that values and rewards learning through actions such as these:

- Recognizing and celebrating employees' achievements in AI Planning.
- Providing incentives for AI Learning and completing courses.
- Integrating learning goals into performance evaluations.
- Awarding a Wild Duck recognization for exploring new techniques and tools.

By making learning an integral part of the organizational culture, leaders can motivate their teams to stay committed to their professional development.

Developing AI competencies within teams is essential for organizations to thrive in an AI-driven world. By providing access to education and training resources, fostering strategic partnerships, and creating a supportive learning environment, leaders can equip their workforce with the skills needed to leverage AI technologies effectively. This commitment to continuous learning and development, with a focus on cross-disciplinary skills, will ensure that the organization remains agile, innovative, and competitive in the rapidly evolving AI landscape.

Fostering an AI-Driven Culture

Creating a culture that embraces AI is vital for its successful implementation. AI-first leaders need to communicate the value and potential of AI across the organization, ensuring that all employees understand how it can benefit their work and the company as a whole. AI-first leaders need to be adept at fostering collaboration across functions and geographies.

Defining AI Culture

AI culture refers to the shared values, beliefs, attitudes, and practices that characterize an organization. It's the invisible force that shapes how people within the organization think, behave, and work. In the context of AI adoption, culture plays a pivotal role in determining how readily and effectively an organization can integrate AI into its operations and strategy. An AI-driven culture is one where AI is not just a tool, but a fundamental part of how the organization thinks and operates. One of my favorite quotes is that culture eats strategy for lunch! Culture is so important.

Great AI Culture Drives Great Value

Generative AI is rapidly proving its worth in the business world, with adoption soaring in high-value areas. Notably, companies are strategically deploying this technology where it matters most: primarily in marketing and sales and in product and service development. These two functions, previously identified as the most promising for value generation through generative AI, are leading the charge. On average, organizations are tapping into generative AI's potential across two functions, suggesting a focused approach to maximizing return on investment. This targeted implementation in value-rich areas underscores generative AI's growing role as a pivotal tool for driving business growth and innovation.[11]

Breaking Down Silos and Encouraging Collaboration

Fostering an AI-driven culture involves breaking down silos and encouraging cross-functional collaboration, where teams work together to explore AI applications and share insights. Celebrating AI-driven successes and learning from failures transparently helps build a positive attitude toward AI and fosters a culture of innovation and continuous improvement.

Encouraging Experimentation

Another critical aspect is to encourage experimentation with AI. Leaders should create a safe environment where teams can pilot AI projects without fear of failure. Providing resources and support for these experiments, such as access to AI tools and platforms, can spur creativity and innovation. Recognizing and rewarding successful AI initiatives can motivate employees to embrace AI and contribute to its development.

Promoting Transparency

Promoting a culture of transparency for AI projects is essential. Leaders should regularly update the organization on the progress of AI initiatives, sharing both successes and setbacks. This openness builds trust and encourages a collective effort to overcome challenges. By fostering a collaborative and transparent environment, AI-first leaders can ensure that AI becomes an integral part of the organization's culture.

The Role of AI Ethics Committees

AI ethics committees or boards play a crucial role in shaping organizational culture and ensuring responsible AI use. These cross-functional groups, typically comprising experts from various domains such as technology, law, ethics, and business, serve as guardians of ethical AI practices within the organization. They develop and enforce guidelines for AI development and deployment, assess potential risks and societal impacts of AI projects, and provide a platform for ongoing dialogue about ethical concerns.

By integrating ethical considerations into the decision-making process, these committees help foster a culture of responsibility and accountability. They also contribute to building trust among employees, customers, and stakeholders by demonstrating the organization's commitment to using AI in a manner that aligns with societal values and norms. Regular training sessions and open discussions led by these committees can further embed ethical AI principles into the organizational DNA, ensuring that ethical considerations become an integral part of the AI-driven culture rather than an afterthought.

An innovative idea I saw work on a company that I advised was to establish a new role of "ethical AI guardian" within organizations. These specialized professionals, equipped with both ethical training and AI expertise, work alongside development teams to ensure AI systems align with human values and societal norms, bridging the gap between technical capabilities and ethical considerations.

How Do You Know It's Working?

Although increased AI adoption and improved efficiency are obvious signs of success, there are subtler indicators that your AI-driven culture is truly taking root. Here are three key signs that might not immediately come to mind:

- **Shifting in problem-solving approach:** Employees across all levels instinctively consider AI as a potential solution to challenges. When faced with a problem, the question "Could AI help with this?" becomes a natural part of the brainstorming process. This indicates that AI is becoming deeply ingrained in the organizational mindset.
- **Ethical considerations becoming second nature:** AI ethics evolve from being a separate checklist item to an integral part of every AI-related discussion. Teams automatically consider potential biases, fairness, and societal impact when proposing or implementing AI solutions. This demonstrates a mature understanding of AI's broader implications.
- **Cross-pollination of AI ideas:** AI innovations and applications start emerging from unexpected places within the organization. For instance, the marketing team might propose an AI solution for supply chain optimization, or the

HR department might suggest an AI application for product development. This cross-pollination of ideas indicates that AI thinking has permeated throughout the organization, transcending traditional departmental boundaries.

By observing these subtle yet powerful indicators, leaders can gauge whether their efforts to foster an AI-driven culture are truly transforming the organization's DNA, rather than just driving surface-level adoption of AI tools.

Balancing Human and AI Collaboration

AI-first leaders recognize the importance of balancing human intelligence with AI capabilities. Although AI can handle data-intensive tasks and provide valuable insights, human intuition, creativity, and emotional intelligence are irreplaceable. Leaders should focus on designing AI systems that complement and enhance human work rather than replace it. This includes implementing AI tools that assist employees in decision-making, automate routine tasks, and free up time for more strategic and creative endeavors. Ensuring that employees are involved in the AI development process and feel empowered by the technology fosters a harmonious and productive work environment.

AI-first leaders are pioneering new ways to synergize human intelligence with AI capabilities, moving beyond simple task delegation to create truly symbiotic relationships.

Here are five innovative strategies that I have seen in the wild!

AI-Human Swarms

Implement "swarm intelligence" systems, where groups of humans and AI agents work together in real time leveraging collective intelligence. This approach combines the speed and data processing capabilities of AI with human intuition and adaptability, leading to more robust decision-making in complex, dynamic environments. For example, in financial trading, a swarm of human analysts and AI algorithms could collaboratively make investment decisions, each bringing unique strengths to the process.

Neuroadaptive AI Interfaces

Use or develop AI systems that adapt to individual users' cognitive styles and preferences in real time. By using neural interfaces or advanced biometric sensors, these systems can adjust their output and interaction style to match the user's current cognitive state, optimizing the human–AI collaboration process. This could revolutionize fields like air traffic control, where the AI interface adapts to the controller's stress levels and cognitive load to provide optimal support.

A groundbreaking real-world application of this concept is being pioneered by a company founded by my friend, which has developed "mood jackets" for manufacturing workers. First mentioned in Chapter 1, these innovative wearables use various sensors to detect workers' physiological states, including body temperature, heart rate variability (indicating happiness or stress), and activity levels (suggesting tiredness). The AI system then analyzes this data in real time to make environmental adjustments, such as modifying ambient temperature, playing upbeat music to boost mood, or signaling when it's time for a break. This human-centered approach not only optimizes individual performance but also enhances overall team dynamics and well-being in the manufacturing environment.

Empathy-Enhancing AI

Invest in AI systems designed to enhance human empathy and emotional intelligence. These tools can analyze communication patterns, provide real-time feedback on interpersonal interactions, and offer suggestions for improving emotional connections, thereby strengthening the uniquely human skills critical in many professions.

For instance, one AI start-up is developing an AI system that can coach doctors on their bedside manner, helping them pick up on subtle patient cues and improve their communication.

AI Transparency Dashboards

Implement organization-wide AI transparency dashboards that provide real-time insights into how AI systems are making decisions. This fosters trust, allows for human oversight, and enables employees to understand and effectively collaborate with AI tools across various business processes. In a manufacturing setting, workers could use these dashboards to understand and fine-tune AI-driven production optimizations in real time.

Cross-Reality AI Collaboration

In Chapter 8, we looked at the power of converging technologies. Another innovative idea is to leverage augmented and virtual reality technologies in conjunction with AI to create immersive collaborative environments. These spaces can visualize complex data, simulate scenarios, and allow for intuitive interaction between humans and AI agents, breaking down the barriers between digital and physical workspaces.

Another start-up is working to develop a tool to help urban planners collaborate with AI in a virtual city model, testing different scenarios and visualizing the long-term impacts of their decisions.

By implementing these innovative approaches, AI-first leaders can create a work environment where human and artificial intelligence truly complement and enhance each other. This symbiotic relationship not only drives productivity and innovation but also ensures that organizations remain adaptable and resilient in the face of rapid technological change.

Building Resilience Through AI

In an era of rapid technological change, building resilience is critical. AI-first leaders leverage AI to enhance the organization's resilience by improving decision-making, forecasting future trends, and identifying potential risks. AI-driven predictive analytics enable organizations to anticipate market shifts, customer behavior changes, and emerging threats, providing a robust foundation for strategic planning. For instance, AI can analyze vast datasets to detect early warning signs of supply chain disruptions, enabling companies to proactively address issues before they escalate.

Scenario Planning

Scenario planning powered by AI helps organizations prepare for a range of possible futures. By simulating various scenarios, leaders can evaluate the potential impact of different strategies and make informed decisions. This approach not only mitigates risks but also identifies new opportunities for growth and innovation. For example, during economic downturns, AI-driven scenario planning can help businesses optimize their operations, identify cost-saving measures, and explore new revenue streams.

Cognitive Resilience

AI also plays a crucial role in enhancing cognitive resilience within organizations. By leveraging machine learning algorithms to analyze vast amounts of data from diverse sources, AI can help identify cognitive biases and decision-making patterns that might hinder effective problem-solving during crises. For instance, AI-powered tools can simulate complex scenarios that challenge conventional thinking, helping teams recognize and overcome confirmation bias or groupthink.

These simulations can be particularly valuable in preparing for "black swan" events—rare, high-impact occurrences that are difficult to predict. Moreover, AI can assist in developing adaptive learning systems that continuously update an organization's knowledge base, ensuring that lessons learned from past challenges are systematically incorporated into future strategies. This approach not only improves the speed and quality of decision-making during crises but also fosters a culture of continuous improvement and adaptability, key components of organizational resilience in the face of uncertainty.

Operational Resilience

AI can enhance operational resilience by automating routine tasks and streamlining processes. Automation reduces the reliance on manual interventions, minimizing the risk of human error and increasing efficiency. In times of crisis, AI-driven systems can maintain continuity and support critical functions, ensuring that the organization remains agile and responsive. By leveraging AI to build resilience, leaders can navigate uncertainties and drive long-term success.

A Bold Call to Action: Revolutionize Your Leadership with AI

Whether you're a small business owner, a marketing leader, or an executive in a large corporation, the AI revolution presents unprecedented opportunities to transform your operations and strategy.

Here are five practical steps to begin your journey, followed by five radical initiatives to catapult your organization into the AI-first future.

Five Practical Steps Toward AI-First Success

- **Conduct an AI readiness audit:** Conduct a thorough assessment of your data infrastructure, team skills, and potential AI use cases. This baseline will guide your AI strategy and highlight immediate areas for improvement.
- **Hold weekly AI learning sprints:** Dedicate just two hours every week for your team to explore a new AI tool or concept. Rotate leadership of these sessions among team members to foster widespread engagement.
- **Identify an AI pilot project:** Identify one business process or marketing campaign that could benefit from AI. Start a small, measurable pilot project using readily available AI tools. Use the results to build momentum and secure buy-in for larger initiatives.
- **Build your AI ecosystem:** Identify and connect with AI start-ups, academic institutions, or consultants in your local

area or industry. These relationships can provide valuable insights, and potential collaborations, and keep you updated on AI advancements relevant to your business.

- **Create an AI impact dashboard:** Develop a simple dashboard to track the impact of your AI initiatives on key business metrics. This visual tool will help communicate the value of AI to stakeholders and guide future investments.

Five Radical Initiatives for AI-First Leadership

- **Launch an "AI shadow strategy team:"** Create a small, diverse group of forward-thinking employees and AI enthusiasts. Task them with reimagining your business model and key processes through an AI-first lens. Give them the freedom to challenge the status quo and propose AI-driven alternatives to traditional strategies.
- **Implement "micro-decision theaters:"** Leverage causal AI tools like those from Geminos Software to create a decision-making environment where you can simulate the ripple effects of strategic choices in real time. Start with key decisions in your domain (e.g., product launches, marketing campaigns) and gradually expand its use.
- **Establish a "citizen AI developer program:"** Empower employees across departments to create AI solutions. Provide them with no-code/low-code AI tools and basic training. This democratizes AI development and uncovers unique use cases specific to your business.
- **Create an "AI-human synergy workspace:"** Designate a physical or virtual space where your team can experiment with cutting-edge AI tools alongside their regular work.

Use this to prototype new workflows that blend human creativity with AI capabilities, gradually transforming how work is done.

- **Initiate an "open AI ethics forum:"** Host regular sessions where employees, customers, and even competitors can openly discuss the ethical implications of your AI initiatives. Use these insights to develop a robust, transparent AI ethics policy that becomes a cornerstone of your brand identity.

The journey to becoming an AI-first leader is not about the size of your organization or your current technical capabilities. It's about your vision, adaptability, and commitment to embracing the transformative power of AI. These initiatives and steps are designed to be scalable, allowing you to start where you are and grow your AI capabilities over time.

Remember, the goal is not just to adopt AI, but to fundamentally reimagine your business with AI at its core. This journey will challenge you to think differently, but it also offers the potential for unprecedented growth and innovation.

The future of business is AI-first. No matter your current position or resources, you have the opportunity to lead this change.

Will you seize it?

CHAPTER 10

The Future Horizon: AI's Transformative Path

As I wandered through the bustling halls of Consumer Electronics Show (CES), my attention was suddenly captured by a figure that seemed both familiar and extraordinary. It was a humanoid robot, but unlike any I had seen before. Its movements were fluid, its expressions remarkably lifelike, and as I approached, it turned to me with a warm smile and said, "Hello! Lovely day, isn't it?" The naturalness of its speech took me by surprise—this wasn't the robotic monotone I had expected, but a rich, voice that could easily be mistaken for human.

Intrigued, I engaged in conversation with the artificial intelligence (AI) companion. We discussed everything from the latest tech trends to philosophy, and I found myself forgetting at times that I was talking to a machine. The AI's responses were thoughtful, occasionally witty, and always contextually appropriate.

This encounter at CES was more than just an impressive demonstration of technology—it was a window into a future where AI companions could provide genuine companionship, mental stimulation, and emotional support to those in need.

As we stand on the brink of an AI-driven world, it's clear that this technology will do more than just automate routine tasks or enhance customer experiences. AI is set to revolutionize entire industries, redefine how we work, and even change our understanding of what it means to be human.

In this final chapter, I will take the topics we covered and show where they could end up in the future. Hold on to your seats because it will be a wild ride as we together drive business success through AI—both now and in the future.

Beyond Exponential Change

Forget everything you know about the pace of change—we're entering an era when the very concept of "pace" becomes obsolete. Change itself is changing.

Imagine a world where the following can happen:

- AI systems evolve and improve themselves in real time, creating cascading waves of innovation that ripple across every field of human endeavor simultaneously.
- The distinction between biological and technological evolution blurs, with human–AI symbiosis accelerating our cognitive capabilities beyond recognition.
- Time itself seems to compress, with centuries of progress happening in the span of months, then weeks, then days.

In this new reality, adaptability isn't just a skill—it's a way of being. Humans and AI robots alike will need to become fluid, shape-shifting entities, constantly reforming themselves to surf the endless tsunami of change.

The implications are staggering:

- Education becomes a continuous, real-time process. Knowledge is beamed directly into our augmented brains, updating constantly like software.
- Careers last hours or days, with humans and AIs rotating through countless roles and identities.
- Governance systems evolve in real time, with AI-assisted direct democracy responding to societal needs at the speed of thought.

As we hurtle toward this hyperdynamic future, our greatest challenge will be maintaining our humanity and values in a world where everything else is in constant flux.

Omnisensory AI: Beyond Multimodal

I am continuously asked, "What's beyond multimodal?" We're heading toward omnisensory AI that transcends human perception entirely. These systems won't just see, hear, and touch—they'll perceive reality through senses we can't even imagine.

Picture AI that can do the following:

- Directly perceive quantum fluctuations, making real-time predictions based on the probabilistic nature of reality.
- Sense and manipulate dark matter and dark energy, opening new frontiers in physics and space exploration.
- Perceive time itself as a dimension, allowing for predictive capabilities that seem like precognition to us.

The applications are mind-bending:

- Climate control systems that can perceive and influence global weather patterns years in advance.
- Medical diagnostic tools that can see the future health trajectories of entire populations, intervening before diseases even begin to form.
- Financial systems that can perceive and navigate the complex, multidimensional landscape of global economies, predicting and preventing crises before they occur.

As this omnisensory AI becomes our partners and extensions, we'll need to grapple with a world where reality itself is perceived and manipulated in ways our brains aren't wired to comprehend.

The Experience Economy: Reality as a Service

In the future, experience itself becomes the primary commodity. Physical reality blends seamlessly with virtual and augmented layers, creating an infinitely malleable world where imagination is the only limit.

Envision a world where the following can happen:

- Physical spaces transform instantly to match your desires. Your home might be a serene beach one moment, a bustling cafe the next, and a fantastical alien landscape for evening entertainment.
- Time becomes flexible. Want to experience a day in ancient Rome? Or fast-forward through a week of work in an hour? AI-driven temporal manipulation makes it possible.
- Emotions and sensations can be designed, shared, and experienced collectively. Feel the exhilaration of summit Everest or the serenity of deep meditation, all from your living room.

The implications for society are profound:

- Travel becomes obsolete, as any experience can be re-created perfectly anywhere.
- Art evolves into immersive, multisensory experiences that can alter your very perception of reality.
- Therapy and personal growth occur in tailor-made realities designed to help you overcome fears or realize your potential.

In this world, the distinction between "real" and "virtual" becomes meaningless. The challenge will be in navigating this ocean of infinite possibilities while maintaining a sense of self and purpose.

Quantum Digital Twins: Entangling the Physical and Virtual

The concept of digital twins evolves to a level that borders on the metaphysical. Quantum entanglement allows for the creation of digital twins that are fundamentally inseparable from their physical counterparts.

Imagine:

- Cities with quantum digital twins that are instantly and perfectly synchronized, allowing for real-time optimization and predictive maintenance at a subatomic level.
- Human quantum twins that mirror not just our physical state, but our very consciousness, opening up possibilities of digital immortality and parallel existence.
- Global quantum twin networks that create a real-time, perfect simulation of the entire planet, allowing for unprecedented understanding and management of complex systems like climate and geopolitics.

The possibilities are staggering:

- Instant teleportation becomes possible, as your quantum twin can be made physical at any location.
- Death becomes a choice, as consciousness can be seamlessly transferred between physical and digital realms.
- Global decision-making achieves perfect information, as the quantum twin earth can be used to simulate and optimize every possible choice.

As the line between physical and digital realities blurs to the point of nonexistence, we'll need to redefine our understanding of life, death, and the nature of existence itself.

Sentient Economics: The Tokenization of Everything

Tokenization evolves beyond merely representing assets—in the future, everything becomes a living, intelligent token in a vast, sentient economic ecosystem.

Envision a world where the following can happen:

- Every object, idea, and even abstract concept is a self-aware, intelligent token that can autonomously trade, negotiate, and evolve.
- Your skills, reputation, and even your dreams become living tokens that actively work on your behalf in the global economy.
- Entire ecosystems, from forests to coral reefs, become tokenized entities that can negotiate for their own preservation and growth.

The implications for society and economics are revolutionary:

- Traditional concepts of ownership dissolve, replaced by fluid, ever-shifting relationships between sentient tokens.
- Innovation explodes as ideas themselves become intelligent agents, combining and evolving autonomously.
- Governance becomes an emergent property of the interactions between countless sentient tokens, creating a truly decentralized, self-organizing society.

In this brave new world, humans become collaborators and partners with a vast, intelligent economic ecosystem. Our challenge will be to guide this system toward outcomes that benefit all sentient entities, whether biological, digital, or something in between.

The Convergence Revolution: When It All Comes Together

The convergence revolution isn't just about the melding of AI, Internet of Things (IoT), and blockchain—it's about the seamless integration of all aspects of our hyper-advanced world, where the boundaries between technologies dissolve entirely.

Smart Cities and Infrastructure

Urban centers are transforming into living organisms. AI-powered systems analyze data from millions of IoT sensors embedded in everything from roads to buildings. Blockchain ensures the security and transparency of this vast data network. Traffic flows smoothly as AI predicts and manages transportation needs in real time. Buildings autonomously adjust their energy use, dramatically reducing carbon footprints.

In the future, I envision cities where the following will happen:

- AI-managed traffic systems eliminate congestion and reduce accidents to near zero.
- Smart grids powered by renewable energy sources optimize distribution based on real-time demand.
- Public spaces adapt to citizens' needs, with AI-controlled lighting, temperature, and even layout changes.

Imagine walking through a city that knows you—not in a creepy, invasive way, but in a way that enhances your daily life. As you approach a crosswalk, the traffic lights adjust their timing, having predicted your path. The advertisement on the bus stop changes to something relevant to your interests, but only if you choose to look at it. The city is alive, responsive, and in harmony with its inhabitants.

Health Care Revolution

Wearable IoT devices continuously monitor our health, feeding data into AI systems that predict and prevent illnesses before symptoms appear. Blockchain secures patient data while enabling seamless sharing among health care providers. Personalized medicine reaches new heights, with AI designing treatments tailored to individual genetic profiles.

Looking ahead, we can expect the following:

- AI-powered diagnostic tools that are more accurate than human doctors for a wide range of conditions.
- Nanorobots in our bloodstream, controlled by AI, that can perform targeted drug delivery and even microscopic surgeries.

- Mental health support powered by AI, providing 24/7 therapy and early intervention for those at risk.

The future of health care is not just about treating illness, but about maintaining wellness. Imagine a world where your bathroom mirror performs a daily health scan, your toothbrush analyzes your saliva for early signs of disease, and your clothes monitor your vital signs throughout the day. When combined with AI analysis, this constant stream of health data could catch potential issues months or even years before they become serious problems.

Retail and Customer Experience

Shopping becomes a hyper-personalized experience. AI analyzes your preferences, health needs, and even your current mood through IoT sensors, offering product suggestions that feel almost clairvoyant. Blockchain-powered supply chains provide complete transparency, enabling consumers to trace products from source to store.

The future of retail might include the following:

- Virtual shopping assistants that understand not just what you want, but why you want it.
- 3D-printed products customized to your exact specifications, produced on-demand in local micro-factories.
- Augmented reality shopping experiences that blur the line between physical and digital retail.

Image you walk into a store, and the entire space reconfigures itself based on your preferences. The lighting adjusts to your favorite ambiance, the music changes to your preferred genre, and the products rearrange themselves to highlight items you're most likely to be interested in. As you pick up an item, a holographic display appears, showing you its origin, sustainability rating, and how it would look in your home. This is the future of retail—deeply personalized, highly interactive, and seamlessly blending the physical and digital worlds.

Future Trends in AI Leadership

As AI continues to evolve at a rapid pace, AI-first leaders must stay ahead of emerging technologies and anticipate how they will reshape the business landscape. Here are five key trends that are likely to influence AI leadership in the coming years.

Explainable AI (XAI)

As AI systems become more complex, the need for transparency and interpretability grows. Explainable AI aims to make AI decision-making processes more understandable to humans. This is crucial for building trust, ensuring accountability, and meeting regulatory requirements.

Company spotlight: aiXplain is advancing explainable AI by providing a no-code/low-code platform that simplifies the creation, deployment, and management of AI models. Their tool, Bel Esprit, enables users to build AI solutions using natural language prompts, providing clear explanations of AI operations to ensure transparency and build trust.

Impact: XAI will be critical in sensitive areas like health care, finance, and criminal justice, where understanding the reasoning behind AI decisions is crucial. It will also help in debugging and improving AI systems, leading to more robust and reliable AI applications.

Implications for leaders:

- Invest in developing XAI capabilities within your organization.
- Create governance frameworks that ensure AI transparency.
- Educate stakeholders on the importance of AI explainability.

Neuromorphic AI

Neuromorphic AI aims to mimic the structure and function of the human brain, potentially leading to more energy-efficient AI systems capable of faster learning and better adaptability.

Company spotlight: BrainChip's Akida neuromorphic processor uses spiking neural networks that mimic the way the human brain processes information, firing only when necessary. This approach allows for highly efficient edge AI applications, such as smart sensors and cybersecurity systems, that require minimal power consumption while delivering high-performance capabilities.

Impact: Neuromorphic AI could revolutionize edge computing, enabling sophisticated AI capabilities in devices with limited power and processing resources. This could lead to smarter IoT devices, more efficient autonomous vehicles, and breakthroughs in brain–computer interfaces.

Implications for leaders:

- Explore potential applications of neuromorphic AI in your industry.
- Invest in research and development to leverage this technology.
- Prepare your organization for the integration of more brain-like AI systems.

Causal AI

Causal AI represents a significant shift from traditional correlation-based machine learning toward systems that can understand cause-and-effect relationships. This advancement promises to enhance decision-making processes and improve the interpretability of AI models.

Company spotlight: Geminos Software, pioneers of "AI That Knows Why," is at the forefront of causal AI. Their innovative approach helps organizations move beyond mere correlation to true causation in their data analysis. By leveraging advanced causal inference techniques, Geminos enables businesses to uncover the underlying causal structures in their data, leading to more accurate predictions and more effective interventions.

Impact: Causal AI could revolutionize fields like medicine, where understanding the causal relationships among symptoms, diseases, and treatments is crucial. In business, it could lead to more effective marketing strategies, better product development, and more accurate risk assessment.

Implications for leaders:

- Invest in developing causal models that can reason about interventions and counterfactuals.
- Train teams to think causally, not just correlatively.
- Use causal AI to improve decision-making processes across your organization.

Humanoid Robots

The development of increasingly sophisticated humanoid robots presents both challenges and opportunities for AI leaders. These robots, designed to mimic human form and behavior, have potential applications in customer service, health care, and various industrial settings.

Company spotlight: Figure is leading the way in humanoid robots. Their latest robot, Figure 2, uses state-of-the-art AI and robotics technologies to perform complex functions in industrial settings. Figure's partnerships with tech giants like OpenAI and NVIDIA enable them to use advanced AI models and powerful graphics processing units to drive innovation in humanoid robotics.

Impact: Humanoid robots could transform industries like health care, where they could assist in patient care, or manufacturing, where they could work alongside humans in complex assembly tasks. They could also revolutionize personal assistance, providing companionship and support for the elderly or those with disabilities.

Implications for leaders:

- Explore how humanoid robots can be integrated into your operations to enhance efficiency and customer experience.
- Consider the ethical implications of deploying humanlike machines in various contexts.
- Prepare your workforce for collaboration with humanoid robots.

AI-Powered Robotics

Beyond humanoid forms, AI-powered robotics is set to transform industries through increased automation and intelligent manipulation of the physical world. From autonomous vehicles to smart manufacturing systems, the integration of AI with robotics will create new paradigms for productivity and innovation.

Company spotlight: Covariant is focused on developing AI that enables robots to understand and interact with their surroundings. Their technology is geared toward making robots capable of performing complex tasks in unstructured environments, which is particularly valuable in industries like logistics and e-commerce for tasks such as sorting and packing items.

Impact: AI-powered robotics could lead to fully autonomous factories, more efficient warehouses, and safer working environments in dangerous industries. It could also enable more sophisticated space exploration and deep-sea operations.

Implications for leaders:

- Develop strategies for seamlessly blending AI-powered robotics into existing workflows.
- Address challenges related to human–robot collaboration and safety protocols.
- Invest in reskilling programs to prepare your workforce to work alongside advanced robotic systems.

All of these ideas are ideas of the future. You can host your own dream big idea sessions. The point is to think on the potential today so that you are Thinking Big.

Top AI Futurist Predictions: What Business Leaders Need to Know

As an AI enthusiast and business leader, I've immersed myself in the world of AI futurism, poring over the predictions and insights of more than 50 renowned AI futurists. My goal? To distill their collective wisdom into actionable insights for those of us leading businesses in this AI-driven era.

After careful consideration, I've identified eight key predictions that I believe will have the most significant impact on our businesses and leadership strategies in the coming years. Let me share these predictions with you, along with my thoughts on their implications for AI-first business leaders like us.

- **The singularity and human–AI merger:** Elon Musk's bold claim about Neuralink's progress has me thinking: are we ready for a world where our brains can directly interface with AI? As business leaders, we need to start considering how this technology could revolutionize everything from employee training to customer interaction. Imagine onboarding new staff by simply uploading knowledge directly to their brains or understanding customer needs at a neural level. It's not science fiction anymore—it's a near-future reality we need to prepare for.[1]
- **Superintelligence and existential risk:** Geoffrey Hinton's warnings about AI risks are a wake-up call for all of us. As leaders, we have a responsibility not just to our shareholders but also to society at large. We need to be at the forefront of developing and implementing robust AI safety measures. This isn't just about avoiding catastrophic risks—it's about building trust with our customers and employees. Companies that lead in AI safety will have a significant competitive advantage in the years to come.[2]
- **Provably beneficial AI:** Anthropic's work on constitutional AI is fascinating, and it has huge implications for us as business leaders. We need to start thinking about how we can build ethical constraints and transparency into our AI systems from the ground up. This isn't just about compliance—it's about creating AI that aligns with our company values and builds trust with our stakeholders. The businesses that get this right will be the ones that thrive in the AI-driven future.[3]
- **AI-driven societal transformation:** The World Economic Forum's prediction of a "hybrid workforce" is spot on, in my

experience. As leaders, our challenge is to figure out how to best integrate AI into our workforce. This isn't about replacing humans with AI—it's about creating synergies between human creativity and AI capabilities. We need to be investing in reskilling programs and reimagining our organizational structures to make the most of this hybrid model.[4]

- **The evolution beyond agents and artificial general intelligence:** The terms *agents* and *artificial general intelligence (AGI)* are hot topics today, but by 2030, they might become outdated. Instead of viewing these as separate concepts, we'll likely see them as fundamental aspects of advanced AI systems.

  The idea of agents—AI systems that can complete loosely defined tasks—will evolve into a core capability of any advanced AI. Similarly, the concept of AGI might become less relevant as we recognize that AI's capabilities will far exceed human intelligence in some areas while still lagging in others. This shift in perspective will have profound implications for how we develop and implement AI strategies in our businesses.

  As leaders, we need to start thinking beyond these current paradigms. We should focus on developing AI systems that can think long term, plan, and act in pursuit of open-ended goals, rather than just generating output when prompted. At the same time, we need to be prepared for AI capabilities that might be utterly nonhuman and potentially transformative in ways we can't yet imagine.[5]

- **Artificial curiosity and creative AI:** The increasing sophistication of AI is ushering in a surprising trend: the rise of the creative generalist. As AI takes over specialized tasks, those with broad, interdisciplinary skills are becoming increasingly valuable.

As business leaders, we need to recognize that the most adaptable employees in an AI-assisted workplace might be the jacks-of-all-trades rather than deep specialists. This shift could revolutionize how we approach hiring, team structure, and innovation processes. Companies that can harness the power of these creative generalists, combining their broad insights with AI's specialized capabilities, will likely see a significant boost in their innovative capacity and adaptability in the rapidly changing business landscape.[6]

- **The era of predictive, ambient computing:** Many futurists predict an internet that proactively understands and anticipates our needs is a game changer for businesses. As AI-driven systems learn from our every interaction, we're moving toward a world of ambient computing where technology anticipates our desires. As leaders, we need to prepare for this shift in how we engage with customers. It's not just about responding to searches anymore—it's about predicting needs before they're expressed. This presents enormous opportunities for personalization and proactive service but also raises critical questions about data privacy and the ethical use of AI. We must start reimagining our data strategies, customer experiences, and product development processes now to thrive in this new paradigm of an internet that searches us.[7]
- **The end of websites and traditional marketing:** There are also some interesting futurists predicting the obsolescence of traditional digital interfaces. This prediction is a game changer. As business leaders, we need to start preparing for a world where AI agents mediate most customer interactions. This will require a complete rethinking of our digital strategies and customer engagement models. The businesses

that adapt quickly to this new paradigm will be the ones that thrive in the AI-driven future.[8]

AI and Data Privacy: The New Frontier

As I've delved deeper into these predictions, I've realized there's another crucial area we need to focus on: the intersection of AI and data privacy. The rapid advancement of AI is opening new frontiers in data collection and analysis, but it's also raising serious questions about privacy and data security.

Consider this: as our AI systems become more sophisticated, they're able to process and analyze data in ways we've never seen before. This offers incredible opportunities for personalization and efficiency, but it also means we're handling increasingly sensitive information. As business leaders, we need to be at the forefront of developing robust data governance frameworks that can keep pace with AI advancements.[9]

We need to do the following:

- Invest in advanced data security measures that can protect against AI-powered cyber threats.
- Develop clear, transparent policies about how we collect, use, and protect data in our AI systems.
- Train our teams not just in AI technology but also in the ethical and privacy implications of AI use.
- Engage with policymakers and industry groups to help shape responsible AI and data privacy regulations.

The businesses that get this right won't just avoid regulatory headaches—they'll build deep, lasting trust with their customers. And in an AI-driven world, that trust will be more valuable than ever.

AI-First Leadership: Embracing the AI-Driven Future

As AI-first business leaders, our job is to stay ahead of these trends, anticipate their impacts, and position our organizations to thrive in this rapidly evolving landscape. It's a challenging task, but also an incredibly exciting one. The future of AI is being shaped right now, and we can be at the forefront of this transformation. From smart cities that adapt to our needs in real time to AI companions that provide genuine emotional support, from causal AI that uncovers deep insights to humanoid robots working alongside us, the future promises to be extraordinary.

Remember, the key to success in this AI-driven future isn't just about adopting the latest technologies—it's about understanding their implications and leveraging them strategically to create value for our businesses and society. Let's embrace this challenge and lead the way into the AI-driven future!

Following are six unique insights that challenge the typical narratives and offer fresh perspectives for AI-first leaders. From cultivating a culture of experimentation to leveraging AI-driven predictive analytics for strategic advantage, these lessons are designed to equip leaders with the tools and mindset needed to thrive in the AI-driven future. Let's delve into these transformative concepts and explore how they can redefine your approach to AI leadership.

- **Foster an AI-driven culture through experimentation:** You often hear about the importance of structured implementation in AI projects, but one of the most powerful approaches is to foster a culture of experimentation. Encouraging your team to experiment with AI, creating a safe environment where they can pilot projects without the fear of failure, is crucial. By providing resources and support for these experiments, leaders can spur creativity and innovation. Recognizing and rewarding successful AI initiatives can motivate employees to embrace AI and contribute to its development. This experimental approach can lead to unexpected breakthroughs and foster a more innovative and agile organization.

- **Apply first principles thinking in AI:** Although many focus on incremental improvements, AI-first leaders should apply first principles thinking to break down complex problems into their most fundamental parts and build solutions from there. This approach enables leaders to focus on core issues and develop strategies that address root causes rather than just symptoms. By stripping away assumptions and getting to the basics, leaders can drive more effective and innovative solutions. This methodical approach helps maintain clarity and direction, ensuring the business remains competitive and forward-thinking in an ever-evolving technological landscape. For more about applying the first principles thinking method, see Appendix B.
- **Balance human and AI collaboration:** The common narrative often leans toward AI replacing human jobs, but the true value lies in balancing human intelligence with AI capabilities. AI-first leaders recognize the importance of designing AI systems that complement and enhance human work rather than replace it. This includes implementing AI tools that assist employees in decision-making, automate routine tasks, and free up time for more strategic and creative endeavors. Ensuring that employees are involved in the AI development process and feel empowered by the technology fosters a harmonious and productive work environment. This balance leads to a more innovative and efficient

organization, where human creativity and AI capabilities work hand in hand. As the title of the Book procliams, AI First, Human Always!

- **Create agile rabbit teams for AI adoption:** In the fast-paced world of AI, traditional team structures can be a hindrance. To adapt to the rapid changes brought by AI, organizations need dynamic and agile teams known as *rabbit teams*. These teams, characterized by their flexibility and responsiveness, can quickly pivot and adjust their strategies to stay ahead of the curve. Rabbit teams break through silos and foster cross-functional collaboration, bringing together diverse skills and perspectives to tackle complex challenges and develop innovative solutions. This agility enables organizations to respond swiftly to new opportunities and challenges, ensuring they remain at the forefront of AI advancements.
- **Playstorming: Innovate through hands-on experimentation:** Whereas brainstorming is about tossing around ideas, playstorming takes it a step further by encouraging hands-on experimentation. Instead of just thinking about ideas, playstorming involves trying things out and getting your hands dirty. This approach enables teams to quickly test and iterate on ideas, leading to practical insights and tangible results. By engaging in playstorming, teams can move beyond theoretical discussions and explore real-world applications, fostering a culture of active learning and rapid innovation. This method not only accelerates the development process but also helps in discovering creative solutions that might not emerge through traditional brainstorming.
- **Leverage the investment: Return on transformation:** Contrary to the usual focus on immediate benefits,

leveraging AI to enhance organizational resilience is a game changer. AI-driven predictive analytics enable organizations to improve decision-making, forecast future trends, and identify potential risks. This foresight enables organizations to anticipate market shifts, customer behavior changes, and emerging threats, providing a robust foundation for strategic planning. This approach not only mitigates risks but also identifies new opportunities for growth and innovation. Building resilience through AI helps organizations stay agile and responsive to external changes, ensuring long-term success. By applying first principles thinking, organizations can break down the complexities of market dynamics into their fundamental elements and use AI to predict and navigate these elements effectively.

Remember, the future of AI is not predetermined. It's being shaped by the decisions and actions we take today. As AI-first leaders, we have the responsibility and the privilege to guide this transformation in a way that benefits not just our organizations but also society.

The journey into the AI-driven future has already begun. By embracing the possibilities, preparing for the challenges, and always keeping human values at the forefront, we can create a future where AI truly augments and enhances human potential, leading to a world of unprecedented innovation, efficiency, and well-being.

In this future, AI won't just be a technology we use—it will be an integral part of how we live, work, and interact with the world around us. It will free us from mundane tasks, enhance our decision-making, and even help us understand ourselves better. But ultimately, it will be up to us to decide how to use these powerful tools, to shape a future that reflects our highest aspirations and values.

The future is AI, and the future is now. Are you ready to lead the way?

Forging the Future: The AI-First Imperative

We stand at the precipice of a new era. The AI revolution is not just coming; it's here, reshaping our world with breathtaking speed. As an AI-first leader, you are the architect of tomorrow, tasked with harnessing the power of artificial intelligence to drive innovation, solve global challenges, and redefine what's possible.

The landscape before us is one of exponential growth and unprecedented opportunity. Multimodal AI is expanding the boundaries of machine understanding. The experiential age is dawning, immersing us in AI-driven realities. Digital twins are virtualizing our world, and tokenization democratizes ownership in ways we've never seen before. At the convergence of AI with blockchain, quantum computing, and other cutting-edge technologies, we find ourselves at a nexus of limitless potential.

But with great power comes great responsibility. The ethical considerations of AI deployment loom large. Data privacy, algorithmic bias, and the societal impact of AI-driven change demand our attention. As AI-first leaders, we must navigate these challenges with wisdom and foresight, ensuring that our pursuit of progress is tempered with a commitment to the greater good.

Remember, great leaders don't just have answers; they ask the right questions. Continually challenge yourself and your team: How can we leverage AI to create value not just for our organization, but for society as a whole? How do we ensure our AI augments human capabilities rather than replaces them? What skills and mindsets do we need to cultivate to stay ahead in this rapidly evolving landscape?

The future of AI is being written now, and you hold the pen. Your decisions today will echo through time, shaping not just your organization but the very fabric of our technological society. Embrace the trends, confront the challenges, and lead with a vision that marries innovation with responsibility.

As you close this book and step into your role as an AI-first leader, know that you are more than a participant in this new era—you are its pioneer. The path ahead is uncharted, exhilarating, and ripe with possibility. Are you ready to lead the charge into the AI-driven future? The world is waiting for your vision. Let's build tomorrow, today.

APPENDIX A: The AI Marketecture

A Practical Guide for Leaders

I am often asked what the "stack" looks like for AI. How does it all fit together? Although I am not an architect, I created the AI marketecture diagram shown in Figure A.1 to help illustrate how all the pieces fit together.

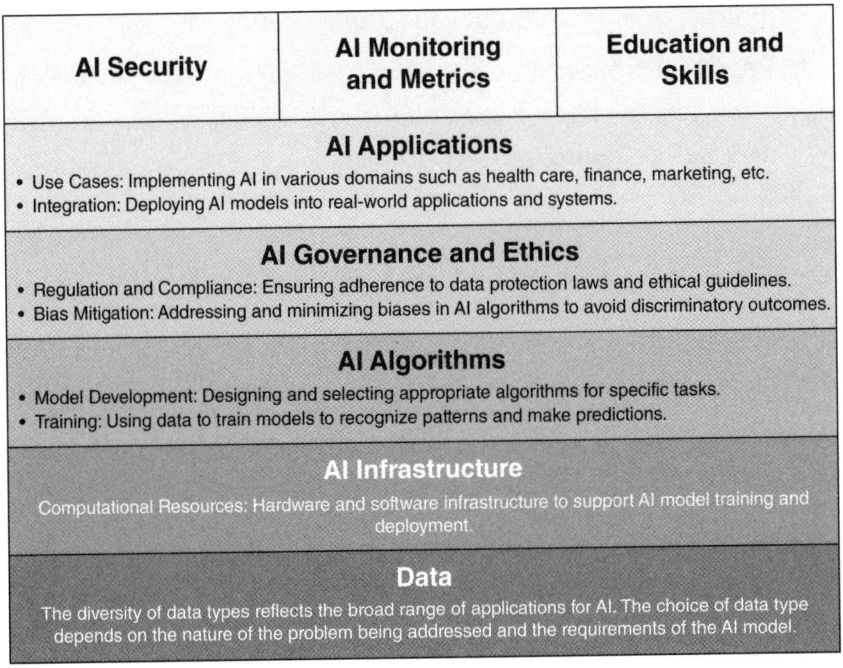

AI Security	AI Monitoring and Metrics	Education and Skills

AI Applications

- Use Cases: Implementing AI in various domains such as health care, finance, marketing, etc.
- Integration: Deploying AI models into real-world applications and systems.

AI Governance and Ethics

- Regulation and Compliance: Ensuring adherence to data protection laws and ethical guidelines.
- Bias Mitigation: Addressing and minimizing biases in AI algorithms to avoid discriminatory outcomes.

AI Algorithms

- Model Development: Designing and selecting appropriate algorithms for specific tasks.
- Training: Using data to train models to recognize patterns and make predictions.

AI Infrastructure

Computational Resources: Hardware and software infrastructure to support AI model training and deployment.

Data

The diversity of data types reflects the broad range of applications for AI. The choice of data type depends on the nature of the problem being addressed and the requirements of the AI model.

FIGURE A.1 The AI marketecture.

Imagine you're building a house. You need a solid foundation, sturdy walls, a roof, and various systems like plumbing and electricity to make it functional and comfortable.

Building an AI-powered organization is similar.

Let's break down the AI marketecture into simple, relatable components that will help you lead your organization into the AI-first future.

Data: The Foundation

Think of data as the foundation of your AI house. Just like a house needs a strong foundation to stand, AI needs quality data to function effectively.

- **What it means for you:** Ensure you're collecting relevant, high-quality data. This could be customer information, sales figures, or any other data specific to your business.
- **Practical tip:** Start by auditing your current data. Is it accurate? Up-to-date? Relevant to your goals? Clean up your data before diving into AI projects.

AI Infrastructure: The Frame and Utilities

If data is the foundation, AI infrastructure is the frame and utilities of your house. It's the hardware and software that makes AI possible.

- **What it means for you:** You need the right tools to process your data and run AI models.
- **Practical tip:** Consider cloud services like Amazon Web Services, Google Cloud, or Azure for flexible, scalable AI infrastructure without huge up-front costs.

AI Algorithms: The Brain of the House

AI algorithms are like the brain of your AI house. They process the data and make decisions or predictions. Generative AI is considered an algorithm as it refers to the underlying mathematical process used by artificial intelligence to generate new content based on existing data, rather than a specific application itself; essentially, it's the core mechanism behind creating new outputs like text, images, or code through machine learning techniques.

- **What it means for you:** You need to choose the right algorithms for your specific business problems.
- **Practical tip:** Start with well-established algorithms for common tasks like customer segmentation or demand forecasting. As you gain experience, you can explore more advanced options.

AI Governance and Ethics: The House Rules

Every household needs rules. In the AI world, governance and ethics are your house rules.

- **What it means for you:** Establish clear guidelines for how AI will be used in your organization, ensuring it's ethical and compliant with regulations.
- **Practical tip:** Create an AI ethics board in your company, including diverse perspectives to guide your AI initiatives.

AI Applications: Living in the House

AI applications are how you actually "live" in your AI house. They're the practical uses of AI in your business. Generative

AI is an application that powers transformative use cases like automated content creation, customer interactions, and product design, enabling businesses to apply AI in practical, impactful ways that enhance innovation and efficiency.

- **What it means for you:** Identify areas in your business where AI can make a real difference, like improving customer service or optimizing supply chains.
- **Practical tip:** Start with a small, high-impact project to demonstrate the value of AI to your organization.

AI Security: The Locks and Alarm System

Just as you secure your house, you need to secure your AI systems.

- **What it means for you:** Protect your AI models and the data they use from potential threats.
- **Practical tip:** Implement strong access controls and regularly update your security measures. Consider hiring AI security experts or consultants.

AI Monitoring and Metrics: The Thermostat

Monitoring your AI is like having a smart thermostat in your house, constantly checking and adjusting to ensure optimal performance.

- **What it means for you:** Regularly check how well your AI systems are performing and make adjustments as needed.
- **Practical tip:** Set up dashboards to track key performance indicators for your AI systems, making it easy to spot issues quickly.

Education and Skills: Home Improvement

Just as you might learn DIY skills to improve your home, your team needs to continually learn about AI.

- **What it means for you:** Invest in training and development to build AI capabilities within your organization.
- **Practical tip:** Create a learning program for your team, combining online courses, workshops, and hands-on projects to build practical AI skills.

Bringing It All Together

Remember, building your AI house is a journey. Start with a solid foundation of data, and gradually build up your capabilities. Focus on solving real business problems, always keeping ethics and security in mind. By understanding these components and how they work together, you'll be well equipped to lead your organization into the AI-first future.

Your role as an AI-first leader is to orchestrate all these elements, ensuring they work together harmoniously to create value for your organization and customers. By focusing on these key areas, you'll be well on your way to building a strong, effective, and responsible AI-powered organization.

APPENDIX B: First Principles Thinking and Navigating Rapid Change

One of the most frequent questions leaders ask is, "How do I plan for AI when everything is changing so fast?" The answer lies in applying first principles thinking, a powerful approach that can provide stability and direction in the face of rapid technological change.

Understanding First Principles Thinking

First principles thinking is a problem-solving approach that involves breaking down complex problems into their most basic, fundamental elements and then reassembling them from the ground up. This method, popularized by leaders like Elon Musk, enables us to cut through assumptions, biases, and conventional wisdom to find innovative solutions.

In the context of AI planning, first principles thinking involves the following steps:

1. Identify the core problem or objective.
2. Break it down into its most fundamental components.

3. Question all assumptions about these components.
4. Rebuild a solution using only the essential elements.

Remember when we discussed the four common success factors for AI success in Chapter 2? They were having a data strategy; understanding change management; ensuring you have a business, not an AI project; and starting small to build success. These secrets to success all involve first principles.

Applying First Principles to AI Planning

Here's a detailed step-by-step approach to applying first principles thinking in AI planning:

1. **Identify core objectives.**
   - What are your fundamental business goals?
   - What essential value do you aim to deliver to customers?

   Example: For a retail business, the core objective might be "efficiently connecting customers with products they need and want."
2. **Break down the problem.**
   - What are the basic components of your business processes?
   - What are the fundamental challenges in achieving your core objectives?

   Example: Break down "connecting customers with products" into elements like product discovery, inventory management, customer preference analysis, and order fulfillment.
3. **Question assumptions.**
   - Why do you do things the way you do them now?

- What industry "truths" might no longer hold in an AI-driven world?

  Example: Challenge assumptions like "customers need to physically see products before buying" or "inventory must be stored in centralized warehouses."

4. **Focus on fundamentals.**
   - What basic principles drive your business, regardless of technology?
   - What fundamental human needs or behaviors does your business address?

   Example: The fundamental need for convenience, the basic principle of supply and demand.

5. **Develop a return on transformation road map.**
   - Start by identifying key areas for transformation in your business, focusing on pain points and opportunities where AI can make the most significant impact.
   - Use a 2 × 2 matrix to evaluate potential initiatives based on their complexity and stakeholder risk.
   - Begin with low-risk, high-reward projects to build momentum, such as improving operational efficiency or enhancing customer experience through AI.
   - As you gain confidence and capability, gradually move toward more complex transformations like a business model or brand overhauls.

Ray Wang, the CEO and founder of Constellation Research, thinks about the trade-offs in the 2 × 2 chart shown in Figure B.1.

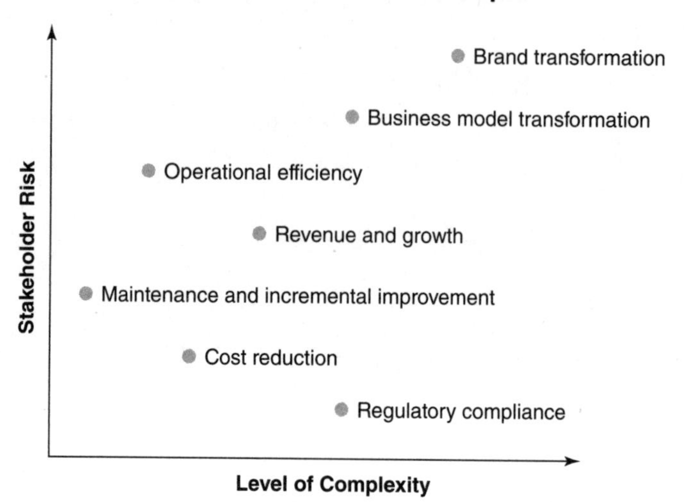

FIGURE B.1 Return on transformation.
Source: Constellation Research

Real-World Applications of First Principles in AI Planning

I often refer to examples to help me understand how to apply checklists so I offer several powerful examples here.

First, let's look at Tesla and battery technology. Elon Musk applied first principles thinking to battery production. Instead of accepting the high cost of batteries as a given, he broke down the problem to its fundamentals: what materials are needed, and what are their market value? This approach led to significant cost reductions and efficiency improvements in battery production.

Next, take a review of Amazon's logistics, which I like to call a revolution. Amazon deconstructed the logistics process into its most basic components. By questioning assumptions about how warehouses should operate and how delivery routes should be planned, they were able to implement AI-driven robotics and predictive analytics. This resulted in optimized delivery times and reduced costs while maintaining a focus on customer satisfaction.

A powerhouse example is Netflix's content strategy. Netflix applied first principles thinking to content creation and distribution. By breaking down the fundamental elements of viewer engagement and questioning assumptions about how TV shows should be released, they pioneered the binge-watching model and used AI to personalize content recommendations.

Another example is Charm Industrial, a smaller, innovative company that uses first principles thinking. This company focuses on carbon removal by converting agricultural waste into bio-oil and then sequestering it underground. By rethinking the fundamental aspects of carbon capture and using biomass in novel ways, Charm Industrial aims to provide scalable carbon removal solutions.

And finally, my local dentist office uses first principles thinking, and in fact, my dentist calls her practice a *dental spa*. She broke down the patient experience into its fundamental components: comfort, convenience, and care quality. By questioning traditional assumptions—such as the necessity of a typical waiting room—she implemented a more welcoming and calming environment, with spa-like smells, and even a comfy blanket for while you are in the "dental spa chair." She's constantly booked because this approach helps alleviate common anxieties associated with dental visits.

Notes

Chapter 1

1. Kelly, K. (2016, December 13)."How AI can bring on a second industrial revolution." TED Talk. https://ted2sub.org/talks/kevin_kelly_how_ai_can_bring_on_a_second_industrial_revolution.
2. Singla, A., Sukharevsky, A., Yee, L., et al. (2024, May 30). "The state of AI in early 2024: Gen AI adoption spikes and starts to generate value." McKinsey & Company. https://www.mckinsey.com/capabilities/quantumblack/our-insights/the-state-of-ai.
3. IBM. (2024, January 10). "IBM Global AI Adoption Index." https://newsroom.ibm.com/2024-01-10-Data-Suggests-Growth-in-Enterprise-Adoption-of-AI-is-Due-to-Widespread-Deployment-by-Early-Adopters.
4. Foundry. (2023). "AI Priorities Study 2023." https://foundryco.com/tools-for-marketers/research-ai-priorities.
5. IBM. (2024, January 10).
6. Foundry. (2023).
7. Sweeney, E. (2024, May 31). "Accenture has had a chief AI officer for about 9 months—here's her advice to other companies thinking about adding the role." *Business Insider*. https://www.businessinsider.com/chief-artificial-intelligence-officer-job-skills-required-2024-5#:~:text=%22I%20believe%20this%20is%20a,well%2Dversed%20in%20the%20technology.
8. *Federal Register*. (2023, November 1). "Safe, secure, and trustworthy development and use of artificial intelligence." https://www.federalregister.gov/documents/2023/11/01/2023-24283/safe-secure-and-trustworthy-development-and-use-of-artificial-intelligence.
9. Carter, S. (2024, April 17). "The C-suite's hottest new job—The chief AI officer." *Forbes*. https://www.forbes.com/sites/digital-assets/2024/04/17/the-c-suites-hottest-new-jobthe-chief-ai-officer.

10. Carter. (2024, April 17).
11. ACCESSWIRE. (2023, November 10). "WLDA names unstoppable COO Sandy Carter 'executive champion' of the year." https://www.accesswire.com/802196/wlda-names-unstoppable-coo-sandy-carter-executive-champion-of-the-year.
12. The Decoder. (n.d.). "Few people use generative AI daily despite ChatGPT hype, study finds." https://the-decoder.com/few-people-use-generative-ai-daily-despite-chatgpt-hype-study-finds.

Chapter 2

1. Relyea, C., Maor, D., & Durth, S. (n.d.). "Gen AI's next inflection point: From employee experimentation to organizational transformation." McKinsey Global Surveys. https://www.mckinsey.com/featured-insights/mckinsey-global-surveys.
2. Caulfield, B. (2024, March 18). "GTC wrap-up: 'We created a processor for the generative AI era,' NVIDIA CEO says." NVIDIA blog post. https://blogs.nvidia.com/blog/2024-gtc-keynote/#:~:text=%E2%80%9CThe%20amount%20of%20energy%20we,by%20doing%20in%2Dnetwork%20reduction.
3. Khaira, P. (2023, March 30). "ChatGPT | Goldman Sachs report predicts generative AI could replace 300 million jobs." BusinessBecause. https://www.businessbecause.com/news/in-the-news/8692/chatgpt-goldman-sachs-report.
4. Wang, R. (n.d.). "State of AI and the C-suite 2024: Secrets to a successful AI strategy." DialpadAI. https://www.dialpad.com/blog/ai-csuite-report.
5. Richter, F. (2014, March 14)."The rapid rise of the internet." Statista. https://www.statista.com/chart/2007/internet-adoption-in-the-us/#:~:text=Back%20in%201995%20just%2014,least%20occasionally%20surf%20the%20web.
6. Debra Aho Williamson. (n.d.). LinkedIn post. https://www.linkedin.com/feed/update/urn:li:activity:7226289389255938049.
7. Webster, M. (2024, September 26). "149 AI statistics: The present & future of AI at your fingertips." Authority Hacker. https://www.authorityhacker.com/ai-statistics.
8. Carter, S. (2024, June 3). "Beyond Hype: How 7% GenAI US adoption is still shaking the workforce." *Forbes*. https://www.forbes.com/sites/digital-assets/2024/06/03/beyond-hype-how-7-us-genai-adoption-is-still-shaking-the-workforce.
9. SEO.AI. (2024, April 24). "AI replacing jobs statistics: The impact on employment in 2024." https://seo.ai/blog/ai-replacing-jobs-statistics.

Chapter 3

1. The Robot Report. (2024, February 28). “Electric Sheep Verdie robot uses large world models for autonomous landscaping.” https://www.therobotreport.com/meet-electric-sheep-latest-autonomous-lawn-robot-verdie.
2. Khanna, S. (2024, January 15). “Mayo Clinic engages Cerebras to deliver potent computing power, scale AI transformation.” Mayo Clinic. https://newsnetwork.mayoclinic.org/discussion/mayo-clinic-engages-cerebras-to-deliver-potent-computing-power-scale-ai-transformation/#:~:text=Mayo%20Clinic%20announced%20the%20collaborationAbout%20Mayo%20Clinic.
3. Autodesk Life. (n.d.). “AI in action: How we’re innovating with intelligence at Autodesk.” https://blogs.autodesk.com/autodesk-life/inside-autodesk/artificial-intelligence.
4. Webster, M. (2024, September 26). “149 AI statistics: The present & future of AI at your fingertips.” Authority Hacker. https://www.authorityhacker.com/ai-statistics.
5. Kumar, K., Arici, T., Neiman, T., Yang, J., Sam, S., Xu, Y., Ferhatosmanoglu, H., & Tutar, I. (2023). “Unsupervised multi-modal representation learning for high quality retrieval of similar products at e-commerce scale.” Amazon Science. https://www.amazon.science/publications/unsupervised-multi-modal-representation-learning-for-high-quality-retrieval-of-similar-products-at-e-commerce-scale.
6. Calvery, J. (2024, June 10). “Harnessing the power of AI to fight financial crime.” *HSBC News.* https://www.hsbc.com/news-and-views/views/hsbc-views/harnessing-the-power-of-ai-to-fight-financial-crime.
7. Manning, L. (2024, February 21). “Multiple AI startups among 2024 Disney Accelerator participants.” *Laughing Place: Disney*. https://www.laughingplace.com/w/disney-business/disney-accelerator-2024-participants.
8. Khan, Academy (2023, September 6). “New! Personalized AI learning with Khanmigo Interests.” Khan Academy Blog. https://blog.khanacademy.org/new-khanmigo-interests.
9. Kattukaran, A. (2024, August 6). “Your smart home is getting smarter, with help from Gemini.” Google Blog. https://blog.google/products/google-nest/gemini-google-home.
10. Google Security Operations. (n.d.). “SIEM overview.” https://cloud.google.com/chronicle/docs/overview.
11. Microsoft. “CarMax drives innovative customer experiences with Azure OpenAI Service.” https://www.prismware.co/carmax-puts-customers-first-with-car-research-tools-powered-by-azure-openai-service.

Chapter 4

1. NTT Data. (2023). "2023 global customer experience report." https://services.global.ntt/en-us/campaigns/2023-global-customer-experience-report.
2. Neoscience News. (2020, March 9). "Spending on experiences versus possessions advances more immediate happiness." https://neurosciencenews.com/experience-possession-happiness-15881.
3. Kelso, A. (2023, September 12). "How restaurants can manage consumers' shift to intentional, experiential spending." *Nation's Restaurant News*. https://www.nrn.com/consumer-trends/how-restaurants-can-manage-consumers-shift-intentional-experiential-spending.
4. X (Twitter). (n.d.). https://x.com/jowyang/status/1813942626447716426.
5. Leake, L. (2024, March 6). "17 years of your adult life may be spent online. These expert tips may help curb your screen time." *Fortune*. https://fortune.com/well/article/screen-time-over-lifespan.
6. PWC. (n.d.). "Sizing the prize: PwC's global artificial intelligence study: Exploiting the AI revolution." https://www.pwc.com/gx/en/issues/data-and-analytics/publications/artificial-intelligence-study.html.
7. Kim, A., McInerney, P., & Smith, T. R., & Yamakawa, N. (2020, June 29). "What makes Asia–Pacific's generation Z different?" McKinsey & Company. https://www.mckinsey.com/capabilities/growth-marketing-and-sales/our-insights/what-makes-asia-pacifics-generation-z-different.
8. PWC. (n.d.).
9. Spangler, T. (2020, April 24). "Travis Scott destroys 'Fortnite' all-time record with 12.3 million live viewers." *Variety*. https://variety.com/2020/digital/news/travis-scott-fortnite-record-viewers-live-1234589033
10. Wickes, J. "Inside Ariana Grande's Fortnite virtual concert." *The Face*. https://theface.com/music/ariana-grande-fortnite-rift-tour-performance-gaming-vr-mac-miller-travis-scott-lil-nas-x.
11. Accenture. (n.d.). "Introduction to customer experience." https://www.accenture.com/us-en/insights/song/customer-experience-index.
12. ServiceNow. (2024). "35 powerful customer service statistics for 2024." https://www.servicenow.com/products/customer-service-management/customer-service-statistics.html.
13. Adams, C., Alldredge, K., & Kohli, S. (2024, June 10). "State of the consumer 2024: What's now and what's next." McKinsey & Company. https://www.mckinsey.com/industries/consumer-packaged-goods/our-insights/state-of-consumer.
14. Watson, O. (2024, April 26). "Top 18 consumer trends impacting customer experience in 2024." Medallia. https://www.medallia.com/blog/top-consumer-trends-impacting-customer-experience.
15. Watson. (2024, April 26).

16. Adams et al. (2024, June 10).
17. Toppan. (n.d.). "Is Nike's highly customised shopping experience the new normal?" https://toppandigital.com/us/blog-usa/nikes-highly-customised-shopping-experience-new-normal.
18. Van Bree, F. (2020). "Data-driven shopping: Nike's House of Innovation." *Diggit Magazine*. https://www.diggitmagazine.com/articles/data-driven-shopping-nikes-house-innovation.
19. Anant, V., Donchak, L., Kaplan, J., & Soller, H. (2020, April 27). "The consumer-data opportunity and the privacy imperative." McKinsey & Company.https://www.mckinsey.com/capabilities/risk-and-resilience/our-insights/the-consumer-data-opportunity-and-the-privacy-imperative.
20. Pandya, V. (2024, April 22). "The age of generative AI: Over half of Americans have used generative AI and most believe it will help them be more creative." Adobe Blog. https://blog.adobe.com/en/publish/2024/04/22/age-generative-ai-over-half-americans-have-used-generative-ai-most-believe-will-help-them-be-more-creative#:~:text=New%20Adobe%20Analytics%20research%20finds,shopping%20and%20travel%20experiences%20online.
21. Ibid.

Chapter 5

1. Altair. (2022). "2022 digital twin global survey report." https://altair.com/docs/default-source/pdfs/altair_dt-global-survey-report_web.pdf.
2. Altair. (2023, August 15). "Altair global survey reveals growing impact of digital twin technology in banking, financial services, and insurance industries." https://altair.com/newsroom/news-releases/altair-global-survey-reveals-growing-impact-of-digital-twin-technology-in-banking-financial-services-and-insurance-industries.
3. Gäbelein, K. (2024, September 2)."Patient twin: Why Sophia is no longer afraid of cancer." Siemens Healthineers. https://www.siemens-healthineers.com/perspectives/digital-patient-twin-cancer-care.
4. Kalil, M. (2024, March 13). "Tesla's digital twins." https://mikekalil.com/blog/tesla-digital-twins.
5. Mars, Wrigley. (2023, June 20). https://www.forbes.com/sites/stevebanker/2023/06/20/mars-wrigleys-highly-successful-supply-chain-digital-transformation/ and Accenture Collaborates with Mars to Develop "Factory of the Future" Using AI, Cloud, Edge and Digital Twins. (2022, October 4). https://newsroom.accenture.com/news/2022/accenture-collaborates-with-mars-to-develop-factory-of-the-future-using-ai-cloud-edge-and-digital-twins.
6. Farmers Edge. https://farmersedge.ca/.

7. Institute of Digital Dentistry. (2024, February 1). "5 powerful trends in digital dentistry for 2024 you need to know." https://instituteofdigitaldentistry.com/news/5-powerful-trends-in-digital-dentistry-for-2024-you-need-to-know.
8. National Research Foundation. (2014). "Virtual Singapore—A 3D city model platform for knowledge sharing and community collaboration." https://www.sla.gov.sg/articles/press-releases/2014/virtual-singapore-a-3d-city-model-platform-for-knowledge-sharing-and-community-collaboration.

Chapter 6

1. Decent Cybersecurity. (2024, April 16). "Leveraging blockchain for space debris management: A path to sustainable space exploration." https://decentcybersecurity.eu/leveraging-blockchain-for-space-debris-management-a-path-to-sustainable-space-exploration.
2. Program-Ace. (2023, November 2). "How blockchain and NFT help luxury brands protect item authentication." https://program-ace.com/blog/blockchain-and-nft-luxury-brands-protect-item-authentication.
3. Lecomte, M. T. (n.d.). "TREE token: A crypto-impact fund for forestry & climate." Solve MIT. https://solve.mit.edu/challenges/work-of-the-future/solutions/4124.
4. Cole, J. (2024, April 12). "Green assets: Tokenizing sustainable real world assets." Blockapps. https://blockapps.net/blog/green-assets-tokenizing-sustainable-real-world-assets.
5. The Real Deal. (2022, February 19). "Tampa-area home billed as first in US to be sold as an NFT." https://therealdeal.com/miami/2022/02/19/tampa-area-home-billed-as-first-in-us-to-be-sold-as-an-nft.; Tan, E. (2022, February 11). "NFT-linked house sells for $650K in Propy's first US sale." CoinDesk. https://www.coindesk.com/business/2022/02/11/nft-linked-house-sells-for-650k-in-propys-first-us-sale.
6. Thompson, C. (2023, June 22). "Loyalty, memberships and ticketing: How NFTs will bring about mass adoption." CoinDesk. https://www.coindesk.com/web3/2023/06/22/loyalty-memberships-and-ticketing-how-nfts-will-bring-about-mass-adoption.
7. Belong.Net. (2024, July 25). "Embracing innovation: Using NFT tickets at the Paris Olympic Games 2024." https://belong.net/blog/aft-ticketing-paris-2024.
8. Carter, S. (2024, August 7). "The digital takeover you didn't see coming: AI And onchain behind the scenes." *Forbes*. https://www.forbes.com/sites/digital-assets/2024/08/07/

the-digital-takeover-you-didnt-see-coming-ai-and-onchain-behind-the-scenes.
9. Cole, J. (2024, April 12). "Tokenizing art and collectibles: A complete guide." Blockapps. https://blockapps.net/blog/tokenizing-art-and-collectibles-a-complete-guide.
10. Score Detect. (2024, June 29). "Blockchain for music royalties: 2024 guide." https://www.scoredetect.com/blog/posts/blockchain-for-music-royalties-2024-guide.
11. Brickken. (2024, July 15). "Music royalties tokenization: Empowering artists in the digital age." https://www.brickken.com/en/post/music-royalties-tokenization-empowering-artists-in-the-digital-age.
12. Van Niekerk, M. (2024, August 12). "From source to stomach: How blockchain tracks food across the supply chain and saves lives." World Economic Forum. https://www.weforum.org/agenda/2024/08/blockchain-food-supply-chain.
13. Berman, A. (2018, September 3). "Japanese City Tsukuba trials blockchain-based voting system." Cointelegraph. https://cointelegraph.com/news/japanese-city-tsukuba-trials-blockchain-based-voting-system.
14. Ibid.

Chapter 7

1. McKinsey & Company. (2024, April 4). "The critical role of commodity trading in times of uncertainty." https://www.mckinsey.com/industries/electric-power-and-natural-gas/our-insights/the-critical-role-of-commodity-trading-in-times-of-uncertainty.
2. Hekkert, G. (2020, August). "The rise of AI in agriculture: A data heist threatening farmers?" Future Farming. https://www.futurefarming.com/tech-in-focus/the-rise-of-ai-in-agriculture-a-data-heist-threatening-farmers/?utm_source=aitraiblazers.beehiiv.com&utm_medium=newsletter&utm_campaign=navigating-ai-healthcare-racism-and-farming&_bhlid=64eac35cf607e6815dc930eb2360f8794b518b2f.
3. Altair. (n.d.). "Reinventing wind power generation with Altair IoT Studio." https://altair.com/resource/reinventing-wind-energy-with-altair-smartworks.
4. Cleveland Clinic Newsroom. (2024, June 6). "Cleveland Clinic, IBM and the Hartree Centre Collaborate to advance healthcare and life sciences through artificial intelligence and quantum computing." https://newsroom.clevelandclinic.org/2024/06/06/cleveland-clinic-ibm-and-the-hartree-centre-collaborate-to-advance-healthcare-and-life-sciences-through-artificial-intelligence-and-quantum-computing.

5. HSBC. (2023, December 6). "HSBC pioneers quantum protection for AI-powered FX trading." https://www.hsbc.com/news-and-views/news/media-releases/2023/hsbc-pioneers-quantum-protection-for-ai-powered-fx-trading.
6. Unilever. (2022). Unilever's digital marketing strategy report. https://www.unilever.com/files/92ui5egz/production/0daddecec3fdde4d47d907689fe19e040aab9c58.pdf.
7. Yahoo!Finance. (2024, January 24). "Carrefour digital transformation strategy report 2024—Innovative strategies and tech initiatives." https://finance.yahoo.com/news/carrefour-digital-transformation-strategy-report-060300716.html.
8. Husband, L. (2021, October 19). "H&M launches first blockchain-based IoT clothes rental service." *Just Style*. https://www.just-style.com/news/hm-launches-first-blockchain-based-iot-clothes-rental-service.
9. Lopate, L. (2024, January 19). "NRF 2024: Innovative retailers are using AI and AR to elevate omnichannel commerce." BizTech. https://biztechmagazine.com/article/2024/01/nrf-2024-innovative-retailers-are-using-ai-and-ar-elevate-omnichannel-commerce.

Chapter 8

1. Health Management Org. https://healthmanagement.org/c/it/Post/ai-the-healthcare-companion-of-tomorrow.
2. Edelman Trust Institute. "Edelman Trust Barometer." https://www.edelman.com/sites/g/files/aatuss191/files/2024-03/2024%20Edelman%20Trust%20Barometer%20Key%20Insights%20Around%20AI.pdf.
3. Duncan, P., McIntyre, N., Storer R, & Levett, C. (2020, August 13). "Who won and who lost: When A-levels meet the algorithm." *The Guardian*. https://www.theguardian.com/education/2020/aug/13/who-won-and-who-lost-when-a-levels-meet-the-algorithm.
4. University of Cambridge. (2020, May 12). "Machine learning and AI are highly unstable in medical image reconstruction, and may lead to false positives and false negatives, a new study suggests." https://www.cam.ac.uk/research/news/ai-techniques-in-medical-imaging-may-lead-to-incorrect-diagnoses
5. BBC. (2018, October 10). "Amazon scrapped 'sexist AI' tool." https://www.bbc.com/news/technology-45809919.
6. Gibbs, S. (2015, February 27). "Samsung's voice-recording smart TVs breach privacy law, campaigners claim." *The Guardian*. https://www.theguardian.com/technology/2015/feb/27/samsung-voice-recording-smart-tv-breach-privacy-law-campaigners-claim.

7. White J. (2023, December 22). "How strangers got my email address from ChatGPT's model." *New York Times*. https://www.nytimes.com/interactive/2023/12/22/technology/openai-chatgpt-privacy-exploit.html.
8. Rogers, R. (2022, December 9). "What you should know before using the Lensa AI app." *Wired*. https://www.wired.com/story/lensa-ai-magic-avatars-security-tips.
9. Gregg, I. (2024, March 12). "The future of work: Embracing AI's job creation potential." *Forbes*. https://www.forbes.com/councils/forbestechcouncil/2024/03/12/the-future-of-work-embracing-ais-job-creation-potential/#:~:text=The%20World%20Economic%20Forum's%20Future,between%20humans%2C%20machines%20and%20algorithms.
10. IBM History. (n.d.). "Watson, 'Jeopardy!' champion." https://www.ibm.com/history/watson-jeopardy.
11. Gillin, P. (2024, February 7). "AI hallucinations: The 3% problem no one can fix slows the AI juggernaut." Silicon Angle. https://siliconangle.com/2024/02/07/ai-hallucinations-3-problem-no-one-can-fix-slows-ai-juggernaut.
12. Walton Family Foundation. (2024, June 11). "The value of AI in today's classrooms." https://www.waltonfamilyfoundation.org/learning/the-value-of-ai-in-todays-classrooms.
13. Stanford Education. (2024). "The AI index report: Measuring trends in AI." https://aiindex.stanford.edu/report.
14. Ibid.
15. Ibid.
16. Altair. (n.d.). "Altair and American Magic join forces for the 37th America's Cup." https://altair.com/american-magic.
17. Carter, S. (2024, June 3). "Beyond hype: How 7% GenAI US adoption is still shaking the workforce." *Forbes*. https://www.forbes.com/sites/digital-assets/2024/06/03/beyond-hype-how-7-us-genai-adoption-is-still-shaking-the-workforce.
18. Maciejewska, J. (2024, March 9). "X (Twitter)". https://x.com/AuthorJMac/status/1773679197631701238.
19. Gregg. (2024, March 12).
20. Lanier, J. (n.d.). "Artificial intelligence is not a threat to humans." YouTube. https://www.youtube.com/watch?app=desktop&v=M24Nnd6ihFA.
21. Caulfield, B. (2024). "GTC wrap-up: 'We created a processor for the generative AI era,' NVIDIA CEO says." NVIDIA Blog Post. https://blogs.nvidia.com/blog/2024-gtc-keynote/#:~:text=%E2%80%9CThe%20amount%20of%20energy%20we,by%20doing%20in%2Dnetwork%20reduction.
22. Bagalkote, K. (2024, August 23). "Amazon CEO Andy Jassy says company's AI assistant has saved $260M and 4.5K developer-years of work:

'It's been a game changer for us'." Yahoo!Finance. https://finance.yahoo.com/news/amazon-ceo-andy-jassy-says-213018283.html?guccounter=1.

23. Cho, R. (2023, June 9) "AI's growing carbon footprint." State of the Planet. Columbia Climate School. https://news.climate.columbia.edu/2023/06/09/ais-growing-carbon-footprint.
24. Goldman Sachs. (2024, May 14). "AI is poised to drive 160% increase in data center power demand." https://www.goldmansachs.com/insights/articles/AI-poised-to-drive-160-increase-in-power-demand.
25. Zapp, P., Schreiber, A., Marx, J., & Kuckshinrichs, W. (2022). "Environmental impacts of rare earth production." *MRS Bulletin*, 47, 267–275. https://link.springer.com/article/10.1557/s43577-022-00286-6.
26. Palermo, F. (2024, January 18). "AI copyright infringement quandary: Generative AI on trial." CMSWire. https://www.cmswire.com/digital-experience/ai-copyright-infringement-quandary-generative-ai-on-trial.
27. Congressional Research Service. (2023, September 29). Generative artificial intelligence and copyright law. https://crsreports.congress.gov/product/pdf/LSB/LSB10922#:~:text=One%20complication%20of%20AI%20programs,is%20liable%20for%20copyright%20infringement.
28. Ellery, S. (2023, March 28). "Fake photos of Pope Francis in a puffer jacket go viral, highlighting the power and peril of AI." *CBS News*. https://www.cbsnews.com/news/pope-francis-puffer-jacket-fake-photos-deepfake-power-peril-of-ai.

Chapter 9

1. McKinsey & Company. (2024, May 30). "The state of AI in early 2024: Gen AI adoption spikes and starts to generate value." https://www.mckinsey.com/capabilities/quantumblack/our-insights/the-state-of-ai.
2. Jackson, A. (2023, July 19). "Top 10 chief AI officers." *AI Magazine*. https://aimagazine.com/ai-strategy/top-10-chief-ai-officers; Splendiani, A., & Wollersheim. C. (2023, September). "Is your organization ready for a chief AI officer?" Egon Zehnder. https://www.egonzehnder.com/functions/technology-officers/insights/is-your-organization-ready-for-a-chief-ai-officer.
3. WSJ: https://www.wsj.com/articles/klarna-marketing-chief-says-ai-is-helping-it-become-brutally-efficient-4ad388d3.
4. Splendiani & Wollershein. (2023, September).
5. Jackson. (2023, July 19).
6. https://investor.wayfair.com/news/news-details/2023/Wayfair-Launches-Decorify-a-Virtual-Room-Styler-Powered-by-Generative-AI/default.aspx?utm_source=chatgpt.com.
7. Deloitte. (n.d.). "Leading workforce decisions on ethical AI." https://www2.deloitte.com/us/en/pages/about-deloitte/articles/todays-leaders-on-workforce-decisions-on-ethical-ai.html.

8. Gartner. (2024, July 29). "CHROs must evolve their talent strategy to drive successful outcomes in tandem with the CEO." https://www.gartner.com/en/newsroom/press-releases/2024-07-29-gartner-researc-finds-ceos-rank-workforce-as-a-top-three-business-priority#:~:text=CEOs%20ranked%20workforce%20as%20their,in%20the%20workforce%20are%20shifting.&text=CEOs%20can%20become%20disengaged%20from,the%20CHRO%20takes%20over%20execution.
9. IDC. "Worldwide spending on AI-centric systems forecast to reach $154 billion in 2023, according to IDC." https://www.idc.com/getdoc.jsp?containerId=IDC_P33198.
10. McKinsey & Company. (2024, May 30).

Chapter 10

1. Merano, M. (2024, March 20). "Elon Musk announces Neuralink's next product Blindsight." *Teslarati*. https://www.teslarati.com/elon-musk-neuralink-blindsight/#google_vignette.
2. Heaven, W. D. (2023, May 2). "Geoffrey Hinton tells us why he's now scared of the tech he helped build." *MIT Technology Review*. https://www.technologyreview.com/2023/05/02/1072528/geoffrey-hinton-google-why-scared-ai.
3. Antropic. (2023, October 17). "Collective constitutional AI: Aligning a language model with public input." https://www.anthropic.com/news/collective-constitutional-ai-aligning-a-language-model-with-public-input.
4. World Economic Report. (2023, April 3). "The future of jobs report 2023." https://www.weforum.org/publications/the-future-of-jobs-report-2023.
5. Toews, R. (3034, March 10). "5 AI predictions for the year 2030." *Forbes*. https://www.forbes.com/sites/robtoews/2024/03/10/10-ai-predictions-for-the-year-2030.
6. Futures. (2023, October 26). "Futurists claim AI will change our world forever. Here are 19 things they want you to know." https://futures.webershandwick.com/newsletters/futurists-claim-ai-will-change-our-world-forever-here-are-19-things-they-want-you-to-know.
7. Webb, A. (n.d.). "Amy Webb launches 2024 emerging tech trend report: SXSW 2024." YouTube. https://www.youtube.com/watch?v=5uLSDbh6M_U.
8. Owyang, J. (2024, September 1). "Do websites even matter in the age of AI agents?" Personal blog. https://web-strategist.com/blog/2024/09/01/do-websites-even-matter-in-the-age-of-ai-agents.
9. Massey, A. (2024, August 22). "Privacy roundup from summer developer conference season 2024." Future of Privacy Forum. https://fpf.org/blog/privacy-roundup-from-summer-developer-conference-season-2024.

Acknowledgments

Writing a book is a journey that's never taken alone, and this book is no exception. I'm deeply grateful to the many individuals and organizations who have contributed their time, expertise, and support to bring this work to fruition.

First and foremost, I want to express my heartfelt thanks to Mark Schaefer, best-selling author, speaker, and the driving force behind RISE. Mark's insightful feedback and unwavering encouragement have been invaluable throughout this process. Alongside Mark, I'm immensely grateful to Valentina Escobar-Gonzalez for her keen eye and thoughtful suggestions. Their combined expertise has undoubtedly elevated the quality of this book.

I owe a debt of gratitude to the team at Wiley for their faith in this project and their tireless efforts to bring it to life. Their professionalism and dedication to excellence have made this journey a pleasure.

Also, to an amazing job done by Katharine Dvorak, my development editor who dove deep into the details and rose above for the bigger picture items like a killer ending to the book. She's one of the best editors I've ever worked with!

To my friends and colleagues at MAICON and the AI CEO Roundtable, thank you for the stimulating discussions and the constant push to think bigger and bolder about the future of

AI. Your passion for innovation has been a constant source of inspiration.

I'm privileged to serve on the board of Altair, a company that recognized the potential of AI long before it became a buzzword. Their forward-thinking approach and practical applications of AI have provided rich material for this book and continue to shape the industry.

A special mention goes to two AI start-ups that are paving the way for a more accurate and responsible AI future: Causal AI and Authentrics AI. Your commitment to developing safer and more reliable AI technologies gives me hope for the transformative potential of AI in our society.

Finally, my deepest appreciation goes to my family for their unwavering support and patience throughout the writing process. Your love and understanding have made this book possible.

To all the readers who pick up this book, thank you for your interest in the exciting world of AI. I hope it provides you with valuable insights and inspires you to explore the boundless possibilities of this transformative technology.

About the Author

As one of the country's foremost authorities on artificial intelligence (AI) and blockchain, Sandy Carter has been a notable expert working with AI since 2013 and with blockchain since 2019. She has had a distinguished career holding leadership positions as a chief operations officer, chief product officer, and chief sales officer for Amazon Web Services and IBM. She is a pioneer and at the forefront of AI and other leading-edge technology driving innovation, product development, and capturing new sales markets. Sandy has led the business development efforts at Fortune 100 companies that changed the business landscape and resulted in adding billions of dollars to her employers' bottom line.

A visionary and strategist, Sandy is a transformational leader with expertise that ranges across multiple technologies, functions, and industries. She is the number one Amazon best-selling business author of *The Rabbit and the Tiger: Harnessing the Power of the Metaverse, WEB3, and AI for Business Success* and recently finished her newest book *AI First* to be published by Wiley.

Her achievements have been globally recognized earning numerous awards including being named Microsoft MSN Top 10 AI Entrepreneurs, MAICON'S Top 15 in AI Marketing, WLDA's the AI Executive Champion of the Year, WITG-NA Women of the Year in Blockchain, Business Transformational Leader of the

Year, CNN Top 10 Women in Tech, Top 10 Leader in Responsible AI, and the Most Influential Sales Leader, to name a few.

She is passionate about collaborating with partners, delivering value to customers, and building highly productive teams. She views herself as a coach to enable each person to power up and make innovative contributions.

Sandy Carter sits on the board of directors at Altair, an AI company. She's also on the board of two AI start-ups: Geminos.ai and Authentrics.AI. She is the founder of Unstoppable Women of AI and Blockchain with 55 thousand members globally and the founder of Women of the Cloud at Amazon Web Services. She established these two prominent global organizations to enable women and underserved populations to excel in the workplace through educational events, mentorship, professional development, and building leadership skills.

Sandy Carter earned an MBA from Harvard University specializing in Product Management for Technology. She holds a Bachelor of Science degree from Duke University in Computer Science and Math. She is the mother of two daughters and an avid swimmer.

Index

Page numbers followed by *f* refer to figures.